The Goodbye Cookie
A Memoir About Never Giving Up

Marcia Meislin

Plus:

BONUS SELF-HELP SECTION
How to Apply The Goodbye Cookie to Your Life

A collaboration between:
Marcia Meislin
Gestalt Therapist & Certified Coach
and **Dr. Jody Popple**
Licensed Clinical Psychologist

TYLA
PRESS

TYLA Press LLC
New York, New York

D0967808

 TYLA Press LLC
New York, New York

Cover design: Sarah Clarehart
Cover photo: Ben Shaul

Library of Congress Control Number: 2013945370

Excerpt from *The Amateur Gourmet* © 2010, reprinted with permission by Adam Roberts.

Excerpt from *Siddhartha* © 1922 by Hermann Hesse. All rights reserved by and controlled through Suhrkamp Verlag Berlin.

Lyrics from "Sweet Baby James," reprinted with permission.

Diagnostic criteria of Binge-Eating Disorder, Reprinted with permission from the Diagnostic and Statistical Manual of Mental Disorders, Fifth Edition, (Copyright ©2013). American Psychiatric Association. All Rights Reserved.

ISBN 978-0-9892365-0-8
ISBN 978-0-9892365-1-5 (ebook)
ISBN 978-0-9892365-2-2 (audiobook)
ISBN 978-0-9892365-3-9 (workbook)

www.thegoodbyecookie.com

The story contained in this book is real and is based on the author's life. Events, locations, and conversations have been recreated to the best of my memory. However, in order to maintain anonymity, I have changed the names of certain individuals and places as well as some identifying characteristics and details.

This is not a book about how to lose weight—it does not contain information on any kind of miracle diets, nor should it be taken as an endorsement of any specific diet plans, therapies or surgeries. I am not recommending that anyone do what I did. Every individual is different. What worked for me in this book may not be suitable for your particular situation and you should always seek out the advice of a qualified professional if you have any questions, issues or concerns.

11/2014

Dear Marlene,

Congratulations on loosing weight and changing your lifestyle. Keep up the good work - it's an hardes job! never give up,

Theresa

To Steve, Jon, and Adam
with love and gratitude
for the sweetest possible life

CONTENTS

PREFACE

She was pretty, that lady in the window. Curly hair—not frizzy. Radiant smile. Chiseled cheekbones. She was thin, size 8, tank top tucked into her jeans. A bounce in her step as she walked.

It took me a minute to realize that "lady" was me. After so many years of rejecting my reflection in the mirror, this time I could look and not flinch. This time, I could smile back and stare, not avert my eyes.

By habit, I would have expected to see a morbidly obese, although still somewhat attractive woman. I grew up with the line, "You have such a pretty face!" followed by a series of buts: "but... you need to lose weight," "but... you need to go to the gym," "but... you will like yourself more if you lose weight."

At 3, I was already chubby with dimpled cheeks and plump little hands. As an adolescent, I was big-busted and top-heavy at 5'2". In my 20s, I slurped a liquid fast to squeeze down into my size 16 wedding gown. After my wedding, I ballooned into my 30s, munching my way into plus-sizes, setting myself up for two precarious pregnancies.

By 40, I weighed 295 pounds (denying any "water weight" that could hit the fatal "300" mark on the scale), and inched up from a size 16 to a 28, on occasion a 32, the largest plus-size I could find at the time.

I was no longer a candidate for diets that all ultimately seemed to fail: I needed surgery. Despite my first weight-loss surgery at 45, I snuck past the implanted ring and shrunken egg-sized stomach to sip and nibble, all the way back to 230 pounds again...Of course, by this time, I was desperate to put an end to the roller coaster ride.

Speaking of roller coasters, I was kicked off more than one actual roller coaster as the safety bar couldn't lock into place over my enormous gut. I looked at my young children's faces as they (and everyone else on the ride) watched me disembark, head high on the outside, mortified on the inside.

When I whispered to the flight attendant, "My seatbelt won't close," trying to be discreet, and the slim stewardess sashayed down the narrow aisle and asked (as though she couldn't tell), "Who needs the belt extender?" I wanted to press an eject button and parachute out of the plane.

I was a helpless, hopeless food addict: I would dumpster dive in my own kitchen trash; go after half-eaten cookies I had forced myself to discard. No heroin addict could have been more desperate than I—when I went on a carbohydrate binge, I would eat pasta by the potful, not the plateful.

The last stop was when my obstetrician had to knock me out in the delivery room with a gaseous general anesthetic because I was too fat for an epidural ("I'm sorry, we don't have a needle long enough to penetrate your flesh..."). As a morbidly obese woman, I knew I had reached my lowest point—or should I say, "my highest point?" It felt like, "Get thin or die."

How I extricated myself from the unhealthy addictive person I used to be is my story. Through a circuitous path, I was able to save my life, a life in which I bask today. I can run when once I shuffled. I can be introduced to new people without cringing in embarrassment. I run my own business as a motivational speaker—and now audiences can believe me. Though I was successful despite my obvious defect (and often I wonder how? How could I teach motivation when I had no control over my own cravings and body?), inside I always felt like a fraud; I binged after every successful performance.

I want you to know how I transformed; why I leap out of bed every day and can put on the clothes in my closet from the year before—I don't have to buy a larger-sized wardrobe every season. I can look in the mirror as a middle-aged woman and know that I look better today than I ever have in the past. I have so much love in my life now… and self-hate is a thing of the past. The self-hate weighed 150 pounds, the entire weight of another me. Fat Marcia, my leaden alter-ego, is now banished.

PART I

BORN TO BE FAT?

"Essentially, for those who've never had them (and I can't believe such people exist), there are three layers of spongy cake: red, yellow, and green. Sandwiched between the layers is raspberry jam and then the whole thing is coated in chocolate. They're so good, if you dropped dead after finishing one you wouldn't mind so much. It'd be a good way to go."

- Adam Roberts re: Rainbow Cookies
in *The Amateur Gourmet* April 23, 2010

CHAPTER ONE

THE HELLO COOKIE

I hear the other kids laughing and riding their bikes but *my job,* my favorite thing to do every Sunday, is to sit on the stoop and wait. I don't care if it's hot. I am wild with anticipation: Uncle Harry is coming.

Every time I hear a car, I jump up. Our own DeSoto sits parked to the side of the driveway to make room for the blue Chevy convertible with the top down. Debbie Gordon comes over and asks me: "Want to play ball?" I shake my head no. Wendy Hanson waves me over to join three other girls playing hopscotch. I just smile, and she knows. She knows because every Sunday it's the same thing. I'm too excited to leave my post; what if Uncle Harry comes and I'm not there?

I hear Paul Anka crooning, "Put Your Head on My Shoulder," and I know right away. It's him. Uncle Harry drives up close, as close as he can, so he can race out of the car, grab me, and twirl me around higher and higher—as high as a bird. When I'm seven feet tall, I giggle and shriek as I reach my hand down and rub Uncle Harry's bald spot. But even that high up, I'm not scared—I know Mom's oldest brother would never let anything bad happen to me. Uncle Harry is handsome and tall, with pearly-white teeth. And then, with the biggest smile in the world, he says those words, the ones I've been waiting for all week: "I have a surprise for you."

He hands me the rainbow cookies—red, green, yellow. The most delicious rainbow cookies, all the way from Brooklyn to our little town of Ardsley! They were cut just for me—bite-size so I can pop them into my mouth whole. Nothing ever, ever tastes as good as Uncle Harry's rainbow cookies.

And then, as he does every Sunday, he asks me to marry him. I say, "Yes," even though of course I know he's really married to Aunt Anne. He pulls out our special wedding ring, and slips it onto my finger, a chocolate-covered raspberry jelly ring. He gives me a big kiss, the kind of kiss only Uncle Harry can give.

We play for hours. We play ball, bikes, dolls, Candy Land, but mostly we just *are* together. Laughing, eating, talking—I never get off his lap. Every Sunday and every holiday.

Then one Sunday, Uncle Harry doesn't come because he has a bad cough. His cough gets worse and worse and he misses more and more of our Sundays until finally, he doesn't visit at all. Mom takes me to see him in the hospital. In the green room, Uncle Harry has a high, small bed. A bunch of machines and tubes are tied to him. When I walk in, Uncle Harry smiles that huge Uncle Harry smile, but he doesn't race out of bed to grab me and twirl me. He calls me *ketze*, short for *ketzele*, the way he always has, so I know I'm his little kitten and he loves me, but I don't really know what to do. He just lies there. I want to be close to him, but I don't know how. Where is his lap? How do I find his lap?

Later, in my dreams, I climb up and lie down next to him in his bed, but I don't think I really did that. I couldn't figure out how to get up there into that high bed with so many wires and tubes.

In August 1959, when I was four and a half, Uncle Harry died. I heard Mom whisper to her friends that Uncle Harry died of *lung cancer*. My brothers and sister were at sleep-away camp, and my parents waited until the end of summer when they came home to tell them. My brothers and sister were mad that so much time had gone by before they heard the news. They loved Uncle Harry (almost) as much as I did.

Sundays were never the same after that. Even rainbow cookies were never the same. From that time on, I developed an addiction to rainbow cookies and spent my life in pursuit of that one cookie that would produce the high I felt while high up in Uncle Harry's arms. Had I known then what I know now, that Uncle Harry's nicotine addiction killed him, just as my sugar addiction would nearly kill me, I might have been able to separate out Uncle Harry's love from Uncle Harry's sugary treats. But that would take a lifetime to learn, or at least half a century.

In the meantime, I sampled a lot of rainbow cookies throughout my life, but none of them ever tasted as good or looked as pretty as the ones Uncle Harry used to bring me all the way from Brooklyn.

CHAPTER TWO

MEET THE MEISLINS

Based on a photograph of me at three years old with pudgy cheeks and a double chin, I would say that overeating has been with me for a very long time. I'm not sure I was even old enough in that picture to reach the refrigerator, so I can't take total responsibility for managing (or not managing) my own food intake and sweet tooth back then. At an early age, those fat cells were making themselves very comfortable in my body and they had no plans—no plans—to shrink for many years to come.

As an only child, Dad hungered for a large family. After five kids, he was ecstatic and looked forward to more. Tired but still feisty, Mom turned to Dad and said, "If you want more children, *you* have them."

First, there were two miscarriages; then Jay was born, distinctive as the first-born son in a traditional Jewish home. After two and a half years, Allan arrived. Mom hoped for a girl as her third and when two years later Arleen was born, she sported a bow in every picture. Right on schedule, after twenty-five months, Mom gave birth to Bobby. The rhythm was altered when there was another miscarriage two years later. There was a five-year gap between babies before I appeared. When I was born—in typical democratic Meislin fashion— the family took a vote whether my name should be Marcia Carol or Carol Marcia. Bobby was the only one who wanted Carol Marcia and to this day, I wish he had won.

Our house was bustling with five kids, an ill grandfather, his lively caretaker, a weekend uncle, a hyper dog, and a multitude of friends and relatives who dropped in for Mom's cooking or her sage advice.

It was fine with Mom to be the hostess of our own Grand Central Station, as she used to call the kitchen. Our fridge was always packed and the spare freezer in the basement was chock full of Millie's homemade vegetarian concoctions.

Vegetarian? You may wonder. *How can you be a fat vegetarian?* In a house that was a veritable temple of vegetarians.

Here is the history: the Meislins were vegetarian long before most Americans knew what that meant. When my father was 13 years old, still in Russia, his father took him to the local slaughterhouse to pick out meat for the Sabbath. Dad abhorred what he saw and declared that he didn't believe in killing animals for food. All his life, Dad remained a steadfast vegetarian, and the day of their wedding, Mom converted. They raised all five kids as vegetarians and to this day, we have never eaten meat, fish, or chicken.

Eating was a ritual. The dinette table was 8 feet long; pink wrought iron with a glass top. Later the whole set was spray-painted black. On Friday night for *Shabbos* and again on holidays, the glass was always covered with a pure white, embossed linen tablecloth; on weekdays, a washable plastic paisley print. Invariably someone would set something down on the table with a heavy hand and we all learned to chime in, "Be careful, it's glass!"

At the head of the long table was Dad, seated under a painting that one of his psychiatric patients made for him. The painting showed a deep winter snow scene with a splash of red for a rustic cabin. For years, Dad was a psychiatrist and Chief of Staff at the VA Hospital in Montrose, NY. Dad loved his patients and his work, but family always came first. He used to say, "I didn't go into private practice because I didn't want work getting in the way of family." Working at the VA, though long hours, meant he could spend *Shabbos* with the family, except when he was in the Reserves. As a Lieutenant-Colonel, Dad served weeks at a time at Camp Drum in upstate New York. When Dad was away, and even after he died, no one ever sat in Dad's chair.

To Dad's right at the table was Arleen Bernice, named after our great-grandmother, Aydla Bracha. Arleen's name meant "refined blessing" in Yiddish and even her middle name, Bernice, had the word "nice" in it. The name really fit; Arleen was and still is sweet and gentle. She played piano for hours and with her very tuned ear, she was a source of comfort and blessing to my parents, who loved to listen to her sonatas and fugues. Arleen took after Dad: introverted, quiet, a great listener, someone who managed to calm others and keep them centered. Even in her 60s, that continues to be the role Arleen plays in the family: grounded, beloved, with a huge heart and a small ego.

In contrast to my older sister, the blessing, my Yiddish name was *Chaya*, the animal, often nicknamed *Vilda Chaya*, "wild animal." While Arleen, with her subdued nature, calmed people down, I riled them up. Restless and passionate, the only thing better than a little drama was a big one. I asked provocative questions, argued my points, and earned the title from my mother of "women's libber" when I refused to do dishes unless the boys did them, too. My parents used to joke that I'd be the first woman president, but I was more interested in becoming an actress. Little did I know I'd end up a public speaker teaching leaders how to find their voice at the table.

To my right was Jay, with his signature 18-ounce yellow-bubbled tumbler filled with iced coffee at lunch and root beer at dinner. When Jay drank too quickly, he erupted into a coughing spasm and his face turned red. He and I had that in common: I coughed because of asthma; Jay coughed because of cerebral palsy. While everyone at the table had suggestions on how to suppress Jay's coughing, I was the only one who knew to leave Jay alone and let him cough.

According to Mom, on November 10, 1942, one day before what was then Armistice Day, she was in protracted labor with Jay, and the doctor was impatient to leave on vacation for the holiday. He pulled out Jay with forceps, resulting in cerebral palsy and legal blindness from birth. From the time he was an infant, Mom established an exercise regimen for Jay that was her own version of physical, occupational, and speech therapy. She worked with him to develop muscle tone, dexterity, swallowing skills, social etiquette, and a positive sense of pride in himself.

In the 1940s, Jay's unique condition defied conventional labels of "physically handicapped" or "mentally retarded," and Mom and Dad struggled to find a program that would meet his intellectual level while catering to his special needs. At Spring Valley Junior High School, Jay found a supportive and encouraging teacher and other companions who understood him and related to him with humor and ease. Upon completion, Jay landed a job as part-time janitor at the East Ramapo school district, where he is now entering his 48th year of employment.

Next to Jay, at the kitchen side of the table, "sat" Mom, the *balabusta*, a woman who manages home and family with aplomb. Rarely in her seat, she was always organizing the next course, transferring food from pot to table, cleaning, doling out seconds, thirds, and giving each person an exclusive "just for you" favorite food. Tireless, Mom gathered us all to the table, served elaborate, gourmet meals, and prepared ritual foods for every holiday. Dad, Bob, and Jay liked their vegetarian chopped liver with nuts but Arleen preferred hers without, which meant two versions of vegetarian chopped liver. My salad had no tomatoes; Dad's teemed with vine-ripe Jerseys. Half of us ate noodle *kugel* with cheese and the other half with raisins and nuts. We were served in birth order: first Dad, then Jay, Allan, Arleen, Bobby, then me, and at last, Mom served herself. I salivated as the parade of plates passed in front of my nose, waiting for Mom to sit down so we could start.

After dinner, after dessert, after the cleanup, Mom would disappear and search for her own stash of chocolate, and I imagine she savored every melt-in-your-mouth morsel, alone.

On Mom's right sat Allan, 10 years my senior. Everything Allan did looked glamorous; he was my first greaser, beatnik, hippie, Soho artist, and the first to own a home in Woodstock. Allan lived the fast life: girls, cars, and motorcycles. Even today, as he nears 70, Allan still drives his Austin-Healey, his Coot—an amphibious four-wheel-drive ATV road warrior—and 14 motorcycles. Allan's drama was never at the dinner table; it was on the road or in the air. Years later, Allan directed and produced corporate training and product videos. For thrills, he shot NASCAR races from inside the car, hot air balloons from the air, and motorcycle rallies from his own bike.

On Allan's right, without a seat between them, was Bobby. Sitting next to Dad, both at the table and temple, gave Bobby an advantage that none of us had. It's no surprise that Bob followed most in Dad's footsteps and became a psychotherapist. On Saturday mornings, Dad and Bobby walked the four blocks to pray at *shul* together, wrapped themselves in their white-and-black prayer shawls, *taleisim*, and sat together on the old wooden bench. The *shul* was a small, converted Cape Cod house, but Dad and Bobby had prime seats, right next to the raised *bima* where the rabbi stood, and they caught all the inside jokes.

Speaking of jokes, Bobby was the prince of puns and he made me laugh so hard, I would start wheezing. Our repartee would begin with an innocent remark:

Anyone: The bread is really good.
Bobby: Yeah, must have cost a lot of dough.
Marcia: You don't really knead all that.
Bobby: Rye not?
Pause.
Marcia: You're on a roll...
Maybe Mom, maybe even Dad: You butter stop while you're ahead.
All (laughing): Ohhh...
But it's still Bobby's turn and he's thinking.
 Bobby: That line was really cheesy.
Marcia: You're spreading it on thick now!
Bobby: That was a pat answer.
Silence... then groans as people start to get it.
Sometimes he'll help them:
Bobby: Pat of butter? Get it? Pat answer.

Everyone else laughs and moves on with their lives but Bobby and I are in it for the long haul. Hours later, he would pop into my room with a comeback and I'd have to drop what I was doing and think of a one-up. Nowadays, we Skype or text, always in search of fresh material to toss, "Tag, you're it!"

When Uncle Jack visited, there were eight of us around the crowded table but the rest of the time it was seven of us eating, laughing, arguing, eating more, making our points, trying to get heard, eating some more. In my case, I also sneaked in food as I would get up to transfer leftovers or dish something out and grab an extra piece of burnt crust from the corner of the pan. Or I'd grab a serving spoon and lick it clean, having then to wash it again so Mom could use it. I officially had one slice of bread at the table, but then stole an extra slice as I was putting the leftovers back into the bakery bag.

Did we pack on pounds? Yes. Other than Allan, we were all big eaters. And our vegetarianism included so much starch and even fat, it was not surprising that we became, for the most part, a heavy vegetarian family. We typically ate more than one portion of the main course along with bread, appetizers, salad, and dessert. Beginning with Dad, we all battled our weight. Photographs of Dad as a boy show he was of average build. In his early 20s, the black-and-white scalloped photos from Europe and Africa portray Dad with dark hair and an average weight and physique, but by his early 30s, Dad's thick hair turned a distinguished white and his entire body had thickened also—thickset shoulders, chest, and a wider waist. Gray and heavy, Dad appeared older than his years.

Photographs of Dad's parents and grandparents present a solid portrait of a very stout family. In a photo from 1923, before the family left for America, Dad's grandmother looks obese. In those days, weight was a sign of prosperity; Dad's family was upper middle class, they owned a lumber mill in town. Clearly none of the original Russian Meislins lacked in sustenance or substance.

As we all did, Dad would eat a substantial dinner. Several hours later, after reading or watching TV in bed, he would descend for his "midnight snack," usually around 9 or 10 at night. He would visit his consecrated "diet" cabinet in a remote corner of the kitchen filled with Metrecal, Special K, or any new lo-cal food that appeared on the market. Dad would create a medley of Metrecal pudding, cereal, raisins. When he felt like a splurge, he mixed in ice milk, Mom's approved ice cream substitute. Several times a week, Dad worked off his calories by swimming laps with his own version of the doggy paddle at Jack LaLanne.

During the ten days between the high holidays—Rosh Hashanah and Yom Kippur—Dad cleaned out his system with a fruit and juice fast. He began this practice in 1936, when he was a 29-year-old medical student in Lausanne, Switzerland. As the U.S. had a quota for Jews attending medical school, Dad went abroad to complete his medical training. His thesis in French was a study of patients who went on juice fasts to detox. The young doctor monitored their vital signs and weight and became convinced that this practice was healthy—not only physically, but also emotionally. For 11 months out of the year, Dad ate large hearty meals, worked out, keeping stress levels down, and then for the entire Jewish month of *Elul,* he cleansed his system with this stringent protocol between the Days of Awe.

Mom's diet varied. If she were "watching," (meaning attending and getting weighed at her weekly diet watchers program), she would eat fewer carbs and more salad, with her low-calorie dressing of saccharin instead of sugar. In later years, she put saccharin in the salad dressing for everyone, not just the dieters. But Mom couldn't resist her seeded Jewish corn bread along with the fresh braided *challahs* she picked up at Pakula's bakery on Friday afternoons.

Mom came from a large family, in every sense. Pictures of her mother show a substantial woman with an ample torso. Mom was the youngest of six and her oldest sister, my favorite Aunt Bea, was the heaviest, standing 4'10" and weighing well over 200 pounds. Sisters Millie (Mom), Bea, and Elsie, loved to dunk mandelbread, the Jewish version of biscotti, or rugelach into their strong coffee, giggle uncontrollably, and argue about everything, but mostly about the relatives. The more they talked, the more they dunked. These were sisters who loved to eat, talk, and laugh.

The men in her family, although they liked their food, didn't seem to have chronic weight or food issues, perhaps because they smoked more than they chewed. They were heavy smokers, with heavy results starting with Mom's father, who died when she was 16. Uncles Harry and Joe had lungs removed because of lung cancer and emphysema, and Uncle Sam, who at 99 was only an occasional pipe smoker, outlived them all. Mom had been a chain smoker but she gave that up after losing her closest brother, Harry. She was 42 when she quit and yet she, too, died of lung cancer at 73. One wonders whether bad pulmonary karma followed my family or was it addiction to nicotine and food?

When Mom stopped smoking, she ballooned up four sizes. Throughout life, food demons haunted her—though she won a huge triumph at age 18 by losing 30 pounds, dating two suitors, Jack and Mac, and securing a new life in which she became desirable to men. I heard this story over and over, like a mantra: "Lose weight and you will get a good man (maybe two)," "Lose weight and your whole outlook on life will change," "Lose weight and you will love yourself." Unfortunately, it was the negative messages that I heard louder: "Fat girls don't get boyfriends." "You can't like yourself if you're fat." "You'll never be happy unless you're thin."

Despite Mom's generous and bubbly personality, happy marriage, loving family and friends, beautiful home, and comfortable lifestyle, Mom judged herself day-to-day on whether she was a good girl or bad girl, depending on what she ate. I would watch her pack her suitcases with cruise wear to safari wear. When she was a size 12, she was ebullient. At size 18, her self-disgust ballooned in proportion.

"Uch, I hate myself!" she would say, tsking at her profile in the mirror. She would turn this way and that, giving herself the evil eye and declaring, "I'm starting Monday." Then Monday she would put herself on a strict diet and the rest of us would have to suffer, too. Mom insisted I join her on every diet in the book (and there were shelves and shelves of such books): Dr. Stillman's diet, Dr. Atkins' diet, the Scarsdale Diet Doctor, the grapefruit diet, Diet Watchers, Weight Watchers calories, Weight Watchers points, Weight Watchers Quick Start, and Mom's own portion modification diet. I usually quit any diet after the first few days. For Mom, sometimes her diets lasted and she lost weight; other times, she was off the diet and munching by Wednesday.

While Jay outgrew his baby fat, and Bobby managed his weight through sports, Mom's greatest disappointment was having two daughters who were fat. She so much wanted to shield us from the pain of yo-yo dieting, hating our bodies, or having trouble finding nice clothes and boyfriends. But Mom didn't have a clue how to stop the vicious cycle that began way before her and may be some part of a genetic disposition for a long time to come.

I remember when I was pregnant, and I found out my children were boys, I was so relieved. While many of my friends wanted girls, I was terrified that I would really mess up a girl: "do to her what my mother did to me." If my daughter were thin, I would be in a constant state of panic that she'd become fat. If she were fat, I'd want her to be thin, but not in the judgmental and critical way Mom was with me. I would do my best to be positive, to let her know that I loved her as she was, that I didn't need for her to lose weight for my approval, while privately I would have been heartbroken. I'd be so scared that an overweight daughter would be doomed to repeat my mistakes that I would stare at her, watch her every bite, and eye her in the department store mirror. I might have said the right words but underneath I'd be killing myself, trying to think up yet another strategy to get her to do what I needed her to do—lose weight and be "normal."

Mom tried all those tactics: love, fear, bribes, begging, withholding, anything and everything she could think of, only I didn't lose weight until much later ...well, that story is the "meat" of this vegetarian's book. My boys had their phases of weight gain but I wasn't as rattled. Don't get me wrong—it bothered me and sent me into a dizzying spin of forward projections: they would be fat or outcasts, they'll have a poor body image, they won't get the right girls, they'll get picked last for teams. None of that happened and none of that obsessive fear took on the proportion of my own childhood when my mother looked at her own little girls and we broke her heart.

For years, Arleen and I rationalized that if Mom didn't nag us so much about being heavy, we'd have stopped eating and lost weight. Nevertheless, long after Mom died, we remained carbohydrate junkies: obese, with co-morbidities. The "blame it on Mom" card ran out; long after she was dead, we were still bingeing. Not that either of us ever stopped thinking about how to get thin, how to stay thin. I remember Arleen telling me one day that if you stopped her at any minute of the day, "dollars to donuts" she would be thinking about food or fat.

CHAPTER THREE

BODY IMAGE #1:
EARLY CHILDHOOD

There are very few pictures of me growing up; many photos of Jay, Allan, oodles of Arleen (first girl), some of Bobby, and very few of me. But there are two sepia-toned close-ups of me at age three; a straight-on view and a side angle. I may have been cute if you looked at my banana curls and deep eyes, but I was definitely fat with chubby cheeks and a big double chin.

I don't remember feeling fat as a young child or having anyone call me fat. My first incident was in first grade when one of my classmates had a birthday party. Her father was taking a picture of the group, and he said, in front of all the other girls, "Marcia, you stand at the end of the line because you're the fattest one." I am? I thought to myself. Before that moment, I didn't know I was fat, let alone the *fattest* one. I knew that relatives pinched my cheeks and called me "Shirley Temple" but I didn't associate Shirley Temple with fat. During those early childhood years, my weight simply never came up as an issue in my house.

After the birthday party incident, it was as though my eyes were open and I began to notice that I was the fattest girl pretty much wherever I went. There was a short period when an obese girl joined my school, and the boys teased her mercilessly. She left, and I was once again the heaviest. For some reason, the other kids didn't make fun of me, at least not to my face. It wasn't until I was a preteen, when boys ignored me that I began to feel shame. I often wonder what would have happened if they teased me: I almost think that would have been more of an advantage than feeling invisible.

When I was 11, the school doctor examined us and weighed us in front of our peers, yelling out each weight. I was a full 40 pounds heavier than Becky, the thinnest girl. That night I looked in the mirror and those early words—"she's the fattest one"—came back to me. I looked at myself and tried to figure out what I was seeing: *What does it mean to be fat? And where is this "fat"? In my arms? Stomach? Chest? I don't really see where I am 40 pounds fatter than Becky.*

People say that the mirror never lies, but my mirror never told me the truth, either. Sometimes I got a glimpse of it: Oh, I see, I'm really flabby on my thighs. I really do have a bigger stomach than other people; mine pops out, other people's stomachs are flat. Other days, I thought I looked beautiful and normal, and couldn't see the difference. Then there was stick-thin, size-zero supermodel Twiggy posted all over the magazines. When I looked at pictures of Twiggy, I could definitely see how she and I were different. I didn't see it with most other people but with her skin and bones, it was clear that someone could be very thin and someone else could be very fat. With Twiggy's popularity, I realized that skinny meant good, and not-skinny was the opposite. I was still puzzled over how people could eat so differently and have such different body sizes. I grew up eating the way I did, and I assumed everyone else ate that way. For the most part, the Meislins were overweight (which was the norm to me) and always at one stage or another of a diet. Yet I didn't quite connect how our way of eating was such a major contributor to our size.

Part of my confusion was that I was small-boned, so I had thin arms, wrists, and legs. I had a small frame, I was short, and the pounds were mostly in my chest, torso, and thighs. I could see my backside only in department store three-way mirrors. Looking sideways through that lens, I didn't think it looked all that big. Even when Mom dragged us to a special store called Robert Hall to buy chubby sizes (chubbette for girls), I still didn't grasp that I was that fat.

Then, as a teenager, everything changed. The outside messages from the media changed. Magazine covers and Hollywood starlets changed. Movies that used to feature shapely size-14 Marilyn Monroe now turned their infatuation to Twiggy. A new ominous message was being sent: There is one way to view beauty: the Madison Avenue way. The media bought in, clothing stores bought in, and Mom bought in. I began to hate myself; this was the first time I felt ashamed of my weight, and therefore—of myself. I saw that the popular girls in school were skinny and flat-chested, and the boys had their eyes on them. As I approached adolescence, and Mom began her warning, "Fat girls don't get boyfriends," and her back-handed compliment, "You have such a pretty face, but..." I took Mom's words literally. Instead of motivating me to lose weight, they motivated me to launch a long-term campaign to prove her wrong. Had I expended as many calories exercising as I had battling with Mom, I might actually have become thin. But I was determined to prove that the inside counts; looks are superficial. Yet below my strong and stubborn exterior, a vulnerable and deeply fragile part of me always wondered if Mom was right.

CHAPTER FOUR

THE OUTSIDERS

When I was four, shortly after Uncle Harry died in early August, we moved across the new Tappan Zee Bridge to a big, dark-green house, so that Grandpa could live with us. Grandma had also died just a few months before, but I didn't think about her death as much because I could only think about one person dying at a time.

We moved from a little town in Westchester to a little town in Rockland. Though separated by only 19 miles, the two towns were worlds apart. At that time, there were very few Jews in Ardsley but when we moved to Spring Valley, it seemed everyone was Jewish— seriously Jewish. Though our street had some non-Jews and some reformed Jews, I couldn't believe how many people walked around with skullcaps on Saturday. I had never seen any *yarmulkes* in Ardsley—only in Tallman, where Grandma and Grandpa owned an Orthodox bungalow colony. Mom didn't want to live in the heart of Monsey, a super-religious community where we wouldn't fit in at all, but Grandpa was observant and he needed a *shul* within walking distance. We ended up at 5 Herbert Drive, a house on the border of Spring Valley and Monsey.

Grandpa had his own room down the hall from the kitchen in the dark-green house. He was old, and my parents had another old man, Mr. Hagel, taking care of him. Mr. Hagel didn't live with us, but he was there almost all the time. My grandpa didn't laugh that much because he was very sick, but Mr. Hagel used to tell stories, laughing and singing and moving his hands all around; stories about, "*Ven-a I vas in the army-a.*" Mr. Hagel liked to talk a lot, and he always added *a*'s to the end of his words.

Grandpa and Mr. Hagel prayed three times a day, every day, and other men came to pray with them. The men would wrap themselves up in white shawls and strap tiny square black boxes on their heads and on their left hands. Once, I asked what the boxes were, but "*tefillin*" was all they said. Mom was busy making food for the men and taking care of Grandpa and unpacking all the giant moving cartons and getting my brothers and sister ready for school. I spent a little bit of time with Grandpa, but he didn't know how to make me laugh the way Uncle Harry had, and he never picked me up to hug me. Most upsetting of all, he didn't know about the rainbow cookies or the jelly rings. Sometimes I just sat alone and pretended I was waiting for Uncle Harry.

Our new community was so different—most of our neighbors were Modern Orthodox Jews. Except for Grandpa, our family was made up of Conservative Jews. We didn't follow all the strict laws the way that Orthodox people did. All around us were people who were *kosher* and kept two sets of dishes, but we were vegetarian, so we only had one set because we didn't need to separate meat and dairy. We never had to face the question: What if we did eat meat? Would we have been kosher, very kosher ("*mehadrin min hamihadrin*"), or just plain "kosher style?"

My grandmother used to worry that her only son, Yasha, wouldn't be strong enough without meat or fish; she created healthy recipes to look like meat, taste like meat, and feel like meat. She cooked mock salmon cutlet without salmon, chopped liver without liver, and gefilte fish without fish. When Dad married Mom in 1938, Mom took lessons from her mother-in-law on how to cook these original dishes plus she invented a number of her own, with more of an international flair. Mom hunted down the only health food store in Rockland County at the time and ordered foods like vegetarian hot dogs and protose, a meat substitute. Most of these products were manufactured by Seventh Day Adventists, a Christian sect which also abstained from meat products and observed the Sabbath.

Mom worked hard to figure out what to feed a family of lacto-ovo vegetarians in the 1950s and '60s. She became an Italian food devotee because she thought pasta and cheese would be an excellent way to get protein. Her children could feel full, enjoy their meals, and live in the world without being too much of an outsider.

As lacto-ovo vegetarians, we ate dairy and eggs, but no meat, fish, poultry, or seafood. In those days, most people had never met a vegetarian so they kind of gawked at us and wondered if we were weird. Sometimes I felt weird when I accompanied my mother to the health food store three towns over to special-order our vegetarian products. My friends did a double take when I would bring fake hot dogs to school and combine them with milk, seeming to violate segregation of milk and meat. Or they ogled my chicken-on-a-stick that I ate raw, enjoying the novel tastes of soy and gluten.

We appeared odd to the people around us—eating strange food and mixing "meat" with milk in the same meal. But my mother was very conscious of not wanting us to feel too different and she pushed back when Dad suggested that we eat whole-wheat bread. Mom wanted us to feel welcome at other people's houses and insisted that we eat regular spaghetti, white bread, and chocolate pudding.

Being vegetarian was one way in which we were set apart—there were many others. The other girls and boys on the block had a lot of grandparents and sometimes even great-grandparents living with them, but we had only Grandpa. Mom gave birth to me when she was 38 and Dad was 48. With his prematurely white hair, sometimes people thought my father was my grandfather.

About a year after we moved in, Mom disappeared for what seemed like a very long time. She just went away and no one explained where she went. Different people took care of us but I don't remember whom because I blocked out that part of my life. It was too much to handle with Uncle Harry gone, Grandma gone, a new dark house, almost a whole different religion, and then Mom gone. When she came home, she had a big, plastic flesh-colored patch on her eye with pinholes in it. It was ugly and I hated the fact that I was the only child whose mom had a patch on her eye. Eventually the eye patch came off, but Mom looked a little different. It would be a long time before I understood what happened to Mom when she went away.

There were more things that were unusual about us. Many of the people in our neighborhood voted Republican while we remained Liberal Democrats. That put us at odds because most of the people in my elementary school voted for a candidate based on where they stood on Israel. My parents were not single-issue voters but the sentiment was so strong among many in our community that we steered away from talking about politics.

There were five children in my family, starting with Jay, ending with me, and most families had only two or three children. Later, our community became mostly Hasidic and they had as many as 15 kids each but when I was growing up, we were the largest family around. Because we were a pack of seven, we didn't get invited to most events as a family. Once in a while, invitations would come for Mom and Dad and one child, and being the youngest, I was never the "plus one." I never attended a wedding until I was 20. And nobody we knew had bad asthma like me or cerebral palsy like Jay so we were distinctive in that regard, as well.

For me, it was a big change moving to Spring Valley. I missed my old friends and my dead-end street where I always felt comfortable and I never felt like an outsider. Within that first year, my old neighborhood began to fade from my memory, and I started to make new friends. The girl next door, Rivkie, was very religious, and I had to learn a new set of rules, which applied when I went to her house. From Friday night through Saturday night, we weren't allowed to turn on lights, write anything down, or watch TV. We couldn't carry a game over from my house to hers because you aren't allowed to carry on *Shabbos*. Her family even had special pre-torn toilet paper to avoid ripping anything on the Sabbath. A lot of these rules didn't make sense to me because I was told that you weren't allowed to "work" on *Shabbos* and I couldn't see how tearing toilet paper was work.

Two houses up my street, there was another girl one year older than me. Sharon went to public school and though her family was Jewish, she didn't go to temple or follow the religious laws. When Sharon, Rivkie, and I played together, Sharon and I had to remember what we were allowed to do and what we weren't, out of respect for Rivkie.

Eating in other people's houses was hard. At the beginning, my friends' mothers would ask me, "What do vegetarians eat?" The only thing they could think of feeding me was spaghetti because they were eating meat, and spaghetti was *pareve* (neither meat nor milk), so it was permitted with meat. Spaghetti was my favorite dinner food, so I didn't mind except when they made it with ketchup. I preferred my spaghetti with tomato sauce and cheese but they never offered me cheese because the rest of their meal was *"flaishik"* (meat). At lunchtime, they served *"milchik"* (milk) and I ate a grilled cheese sandwich made with *kosher* cheese. It wasn't as good as Mom's because Mom used Velveeta (non-kosher cheese) and when Velveeta melted, it was just the right degree of creamy and smooth. I tried to be polite and thank my friends' moms for cooking something special for me. I knew I was unlike the other girls and their parents tried hard to make me feel accepted.

Later, after Grandpa died, on Sundays, we would eat Mario's pizza with mushrooms. As pizza wasn't allowed in observant homes, we would sneak it in the back door. It was important that the rabbis who lived nearby didn't catch us doing things we weren't supposed to do because we would get in trouble. One Halloween I went trick-or-treating and was punished in school the next day because I still had lipstick left on my lips, and I wasn't supposed to celebrate a pagan holiday.

Dad had another motive for doing things undercover. As a sign of respect, he didn't want us doing anything in front of the neighbors that might embarrass them or make them uncomfortable. Living in this community, we learned as a family the difference between what we could do outside and what we could do inside, in private. I continued to grow in my sense of being very different from our neighbors. As Ardsley became a distant memory, I never really said to myself, *we don't belong here,* because Spring Valley was all I knew. But for the rest of my life, that feeling of being an outsider stayed with me. In more ways than one.

CHAPTER FIVE

SABBATH AND HOLIDAYS

Grandpa died when I was in third grade, and Mom covered the mirrors for a week. We sat *shiva*, and the men came to our house three times a day to pray with Dad. The women brought food and talked in the kitchen with Mom. When the seven days of official mourning ended, Dad went to the synagogue every day for a year to say *kaddish* for his father. The old men with beards and prayer shawls stopped coming to our house. My brother Allan moved into Grandpa's room and filled it with pictures of motorcycles and sports cars.

Every Friday night, Mom made a big *Shabbos* feast. Before we ate, she covered her head with a napkin. Then she circled her hands over the two candles three times and whispered a prayer. If you stood close to her, you could hear her. She always said it the same way, blessing the candles with a faraway look on her face. She would then say "Good *Shabbos*" to whoever was around and kiss us with love, and Dad would lift up his engraved silver *becher* from Russia, and say the *kiddush*. Mom lifted up the white covering on the two *challah* breads and Dad said the *motzi* very fast. He would cut the bread and take a bite, being careful not to talk between the blessing and the bite. Then he put a long bread knife through the soft twisted *challah* and cut us each a piece. Everyone glowed in the candlelight.

There were usually seven Meislins around the *Shabbos* table, plus our "bachelor uncle." Grandma's brother, Uncle Jack, had lived with my grandparents in Tallman, a small hamlet nestled between Monsey and Suffern. Though Uncle Jack was busy taking care of Grandma, Grandpa, and their property, he always found time for us kids. On Sundays, he loaded us into his little blue car and drove us to our favorite pizza parlor in Stony Point for the best pizza in the world. Then he took us to the Rockland Drive-In Movie Theatre where he worked as a ticket collector while we watched double-headers in his car and made frequent trips to the snack bar.

Although there was an occasional Sabbath guest or two above our eight, Mom still cooked enough for 30 people. Our meal began with a piece of *challah*, maybe two, or the crusty heel of the Jewish corn bread with caraway seeds (we called them "rye" seeds). Then Mom served the first course, her celebrated "Friday night soup": vegetarian split pea soup so thick that you could only have a little, though I always managed to eat a big bowl. Second course was Mom's famous salad. I ate a lot of salad because Mom's diet programs said vegetables were good for you. What they didn't say is that all the sugar in Mom's salad dressing probably transformed the salad from a health food to (practically) a dessert.

On *Shabbos*, the main course was always Italian food: meatless lasagna, eggplant Parmesan, or stuffed shells. Sometimes we had both pasta and eggplant parm accompanied by a buttered green vegetable. Mom was an expert cook, and not only the pasta, but all seven courses, were mouth-watering. It was my job to help Mom dish out the food to everyone. One for the plate, one for me. Often I had two or three portions of the carbs because I didn't know how to stop eating them even after I was stuffed.

Dessert was scrumptious on Friday nights and holidays, not only because we lived near the two best bakeries in the Northeast— Ramapo Bakery and Pakula's—but because Mom really knew how to pick desserts. During the week, we'd have canned peaches or fruit salad in dietetic syrup, but on *Shabbos*, we enjoyed an assortment of cakes, cookies, and ice cream.

After dinner, the "girls" had to clean up. Arleen and I were responsible for transferring leftovers into Tupperware-like containers. I made an art of picking a container that was too small, so I could eat the scraps right from the pan. No sense wasting the rest.

While Dad played chess with the boys in the living room, Arleen and I would sneak back into the refrigerator for leftovers. When we'd devoured those, we'd go on a treasure hunt to find Mom's special treats—chocolates or other goodies—her own stash that she'd hidden from us. We always found the loot. Mom must have been disappointed every time she had a craving and discovered empty bags. Once or twice, she accused us of eating her snacks and switched the hiding place. But mostly she didn't say anything. She was mad at us for eating so much and having weight problems, but I think she felt bad because she herself was always trying to lose weight. Maybe she was just hiding the goodies from herself?

On Sunday mornings, Mom or Dad would run out to Bubba's Bagels and buy a dozen assorted bagels, with Jay's fragrant onion and garlic bagels in a separate bag. Occasionally, Mom would treat us to pancakes, waffles, or French toast. My favorite was her combination grilled cheese/French toast, with the two outer pieces of bread dipped in egg and the cheese melted in between. To everyone's horror, I poured Aunt Jemima syrup on my grilled cheese/French toast.

Shabbos and Sundays came every week, but Jewish holidays were seasonal. Each holiday brought its own special foods—apples and honey on Rosh Hashanah, potato pancakes on Hanukkah, cheesecake on *Shavuos*. On *Purim*, Mom's friends would bake *hamantaschen* and deliver trays of the three-cornered cookies as well as other pastries to our house. When they rang the bell, I would take their plate and then hand them one we'd made, with a variety of snacks and kosher wine. Some of Mom's friends were really good bakers. I skipped the prune and poppy-seed *hamantaschen* and went right for the other decadent treats. Even though I was highly allergic to chocolate and nuts, I couldn't resist Gerty's nut brownies or Evelyn's marble squares. I would worry about asthma after the fact.

There was good food on every holiday, but Passover was challenging. We couldn't eat bread or pasta for eight days and anything even remotely resembling wheat was taboo. I usually got through the ban by eating sweets. My favorites were the brightly colored candy "fruit" slices dipped in sugar (with no fruit in them whatsoever), Barton's almond kisses covered with chocolate, and a poor facsimile of rainbow cookies, made with potato starch, not flour.

Passover for me wasn't about the food. It was about the *Seders*. In the Meislin household, the ritual story-telling of the Israelites' Exodus from Egypt lasted seven hours. With each hour, I was more and more enthralled. As a preteen, the first time I was allowed to have Mogen David wine to commemorate our liberation from slavery, I got particularly giddy and started dancing around the dining room singing at the top of my lungs, *L'Shana Ha'ba-a B'yerushalayim,* "Next Year in Jerusalem!" My tone-deaf singing and original choreography were a spectacle; not only was I drunk on wine, but I was drunk on the *Seders*.

Before every *Pesach Seder*, my parents worried that I had a fever because I was so flushed. I wasn't sick: I was just in ecstatic overdrive. For seven hours, we read, told stories, argued about different rabbinical interpretations, sang off-key, laughed, and followed the unusual dipping rituals. My father told the same stories every year—of life in Kremenchuk, in Ukraine, of being held at gunpoint by the Bolsheviks, of the drunken farmer who would slur his words and sing songs mixing up the Hebrew letters *B* and *K*. We never tired of these tales; we especially relished the *niggunim*, the tunes taught to my father 45 years before by the *yeshiva* boys who were guests at his parents' table.

My two favorite tunes were the spirited *Dayenu*, followed by "Bim Bom." I never understood *Dayenu*, which translated to "it would have been enough" because I never knew what "enough" meant. In the historical sense, the meaning of that song is that even if God had *only* taken us out of Egypt and not given us food in the desert, it would have been enough ("No it wouldn't!" I argued, "We would have died of starvation!"), or even if God had given us the *Torah* and not brought us into the land of Israel, it would have been enough ("No," I argued, "We could still be roaming the desert!"). Nevertheless, I understand now that *Dayenu* teaches us to be grateful for the blessings we have and not to always crave more, but there was no way I understood that concept then. More, more, more was my personal theme song.

Despite my philosophical discord with the words, I still had fun singing *Dayenu* with everyone. Even Jay sang the chorus, *"die-die-aye-nu, die-die-aye-nu, dayenu, dayenu."* It was all a prelude to the best part: the "Bim Bom." Dad, a bit of a ham himself on *Seder* night, would start mimicking the old world rabbis with their Yiddish accents and full-body swaying. Instead of the Israeli dialect we were taught in school, he would use the Yiddish dialect and sing *"Al Achas comma v'comma..."* Then he would get to the funny part and I'd get goosebumps on my arms and my heart would race. As though in the Old Country, he would elongate the syllables, creating agony in the wait: *"Sheh ...... hoy ...... tzi ...... aaaaaaa ...... nuuu ...... Sheh ... .hoy ...... tzi ..... aaaaaa ...... nuuu ...... mi .... memitzrayim...."* (we were already laughing out loud). Then the gibberish began: "tai lai lai lai lai lail lai lai, bim bom boom bom, tra la la la la la la la, bim bom boom."

Every year Dad made up new words for the tune. It wasn't even that the words were so funny, though they were. It was the look on Dad's face. His eyes grew really big, his eyebrows went up, and he beamed with a smile from ear to ear. His index finger pointed at us with each thunderous note and his normally quiet voice boomed louder and louder at each "bom bom boom." Dad ended up laughing in the middle of the song, so clearly enjoying every second of the drama. He repeated it again, this time we all jumped in, and we each threw different sounds into the mix. No one in the Meislin household won honors for carrying a tune. Arleen came closest; her voice (naturally) was sweet.

After dinner came the rest of the group songs and the treasure hunt for the *afikoman,* the little piece of matzoh representing the paschal lamb. Early on in the *Seder,* the kids "stole" the *afikoman* when Dad and the men went to wash their hands. Dad made a big deal about pretending to leave the room ("I'm leaving to wash my hands, I'm leaving now...") and suddenly whirled around to catch us in the act of stealing the *afikoman* in its blue velvet pouch with the gold inscriptions. Caught red-handed, we had to concede and return it to the table. Dad would leave again, this time stepping completely out of the room, only to rush back and accuse us of stealing. We were all laughing, and Dad was getting the most pleasure out of this game that his father and grandfather played with him back in Russia before the pogroms. Finally, Dad actually went to the bathroom to wash his hands and we knew precisely how many minutes we had to execute the "crime" and we handed it to the fastest child in the bunch. When Dad returned, he feigned shock that the coveted pouch had mysteriously disappeared.

All during dinner, we discussed what kind of ransom we would demand in exchange for the *afikoman*, knowing that the *Seder* couldn't officially end without consuming the hidden *matzoh*. Bobby never wavered from the basketball court he wanted, which he finally built outside his own house on Long Island. Each year, I fantasized about a new this or a new that. The "negotiation" between Dad and his five children—and later their spouses— ended when Mom said, "It's getting late. One of you: bring back the *afikoman!*" And the guilty party would retrieve what was now *matzah farfel* (all crumbs) and announce, "Even if you looked, Dad, you'd never have found it!" to which we all proclaimed what a brilliant hiding place they had found. The *afikoman*, that token piece of ritual *matzoh*, was supposed to be the last food anyone ate that evening. I always promised myself that I wouldn't grab leftovers or dip into the candy box after the *Seder* in deference to the *afikoman*, but every year, I felt guilty that I couldn't live up to my commitment. I always had to sneak something after the celebration, no matter how stuffed I felt.

After Dad died, we tried to recreate the Meislin *Seder* just as it was. Mom still cooked enough for an army, she smiled at us from her seat at the head of the table, but we were all profoundly sad and empty. It took a while to muster the same energy for the *Seder*, knowing that we were one more generation removed from the *Seders* of the Old Country, knowing that the number of people now grumbling at the table that the *Seder* was too long or dinner was too late, were now the majority, not the minority. But we persevered and Bobby, Arleen's husband, Mel, or I took turns leading the *Seder*, with input from everyone according to his or her special song or favorite ritual. Arleen had her Hallelujah song, Mel sang *"Arbah Imahot,"* Mom led us in *Dayenu*, and Jay had the three obligatory Passover words he said and we all repeated.

When Mom died, the holiday felt impossible. No one wanted to have the *Seder* at their own house as it had never been anywhere but Herbert Drive. I volunteered and somehow managed to get through the saddest holiday of my life. Despite the grief, we had a good time and with a lot of boosting from my therapist, Liz, we learned to create "new traditions," some of which we continue years later. Now we rotate houses and leaders. When the festival is at my house, I insist on using Grandma's *Pesach* dishes, the Daisy design amber Depression glass from the 1930s and the rusted *Seder* plate from Mom and Dad's wedding in 1938. We augment with modern, multi-colored enamel trays from Jerusalem, a Miriam Cup to complement Elijah's Cup, and Melmac Seder plates with original drawings that my children made in Hebrew school nursery.

Over the years, on Friday nights and on holidays, I would inadvertently substitute heaping portions of carbohydrates for loving family memories; a smorgasbord of sweets for rich Jewish tradition, mounds of comfort food for nostalgic holiday memories. For decades, every Friday night signaled a time to overeat, binge, or numb myself with food to make up for the closeness, liveliness, and love in the Meislin home that I missed and craved.

CHAPTER SIX

SARAH BERNHARDT

Dinners at our house consisted of a gaggle of people yelling to each other to be heard. I was the youngest but had the biggest mouth, and the biggest emotions, always angling to get heard. My mother dubbed me "Sarah Bernhardt," after the dramatic 20th-century film and stage actress.

I loved the passion and energy of my big, tumultuous family. But with all the fun, laughter, and chaos, it was hard for a little one to get noticed. I was there. I was present, amid the loud conversations, the political talk, analysis of the rabbi's sermon, the jokes, the "pass the cream cheese," the spiritual candlelight, Mom asking, "Uncle Jack, do you want more?"

"Whatever you want, Millie."

"I'm not asking if *I* want more, I'm asking if *you* want more."

"OK, so I'll have a little more."

My voice—even as loud and histrionic as it was—would sometimes get drowned out. Not necessarily the words, but the emotions, the hurt, the need to be special. So I had no alternative but to throw a tantrum. I didn't necessarily like what followed, but at least all eyes were focused on me—and that part felt good.

All of a sudden, I was back in familiar territory: Marcia's crying, threatening to go to her room, nobody's stopping me, three brothers are laughing, and I hear above the crowd, "Here goes the siren." I wail even louder.

Dad wants to get upset, but ends up laughing. Mom's busy organizing and serving, Arleen's characteristically quiet, and I have no choice. I have to follow through. I retreat upstairs to my room, waiting for someone to rescue me. I wait and wait. Sometimes Mom would yell upstairs, "Marcia, come on down," but her voice traversing a whole flight of stairs is not a strong enough magnet to lure me away from the sanctity of my room. All mine for now, though I know eventually Arleen will come up to go to sleep and I'm sure she'll be kind and loving—later. In the meantime, I can dwell on how lonely it is to be the youngest in a mad, loving, wild household, and I can feel sorry for myself. I need Mom's touch. The hand on my shoulder that doesn't come. So I cry and I stew, reveling in self-pity, while listening intently for footsteps on the stairs.

Another night at the busy Meislin household; full of love, full of laughter, full of loneliness. And food.

✳

I realize in retrospect that my parents interpreted my melodramatic exit as a need to have my own space, a cooling-off period. After calling to me once or twice, they made the decision to leave me alone. What they didn't know at the time is that the decision to let me "do it myself" might have been the right strategy for someone else, for someone who just required some private time. But with my temperament and oversensitivity, I needed an awful lot of nurturing and handholding, something that was easy to miss because I walked around acting so independent the rest of the time. Yes, I craved attention, but the mixed signals I gave off made it hard for me to get what I ultimately needed: intimacy and one-on-one time, not just attention.

My periodic tantrums at the dinner table didn't last too many years, but my emotional roller-coaster responses were with me for the long haul. When I was 7, the Meislins planned a cross-country camping trip to California. Dad arranged to take six weeks off work, and all seven of us were going to crowd into the family car, a green

Rambler station wagon hitched to a pop-up Nimrod trailer. Dad and Mom carefully crafted plans for the vacation, and we went over them every chance we got, down to the smallest details—the water canteens and the Coleman stove for Mom to cook vegetarian food.

For an entire year, almost all our conversations revolved around plans for this once-in-a-lifetime holiday—the whole family off on an adventure across the vast United States. My head filled with visions of canyons and cornfields, billboards and buffalo, geysers and golden gates. We started packing a week ahead of our scheduled departure. By the day before, everything was ready. We were waiting for Dad to come home with the trailer hitch so we could attach the car. My excitement was unsurpassable; if I could've jumped up and down without getting an asthma attack, I would have. I would have skipped around the block and done cartwheels if not for my wheezing and coughing.

And then it happened: a commotion downstairs, with everyone talking at once. I couldn't make out the words, but the tone felt like a knife through my heart. My worst fears were being realized. I knew I shouldn't have let myself get so excited. I crept down to find out what was up, and it hit me like a lightning bolt: "We're not going!" Tears just poured down my cheeks out of control. Over and over, I kept saying, "I knew we weren't gonna go. I knew it!" My sister, brothers, mother, and father all tried to knock sense into my head, but it didn't work. They assured me it was only a one-day delay; the trailer hitch wasn't working and had to be replaced.

I was beyond consolation, utter despair. All the pent-up disappointments of seven years of life coursed through me. I could barely breathe. I'm sure my family was very sympathetic, but in my memory of that day there was no one around for that little girl, no one to placate her. I remember Mom saying, "Honey, I promise we're going to leave tomorrow. I promise!" And that was that. I was supposed to accept it and understand. No one in my family, even me, knew then that disappointment was my undoing. If anything could break me or cause me to binge, it was having my hopes up for something only to have them foiled. Though sadness, anger, and jealousy were emotions I had trouble controlling, they were miniscule compared to disappointment. That particular emotion was more than I could handle. (Nearly half a century later, it dawned on me that right before the trip, my parents had given me a loading dose of asthma medication to prevent an attack on the road. Between intense mood swings on prednisone, and agitating side effects on theophylline, I may have been suffering from the chemical reaction of Sarah Bernhardt on steroids.)

We did leave the very next day, and the anxiety turned back to excitement. Every night, Mom, Dad, Bobby, and Allan slept in the Nimrod pop-up tent, Arleen and I slept in the reclining front seats of the Rambler, and Jay in the way back with the rear seat pulled down. During the day, heart-stopping sights such as the Grand Canyon, Mount Rushmore, Old Faithful, Las Vegas, and Hollywood more than compensated for having to sit backwards in the back of a station wagon for 42 days as seven Meislins sang, "California, here we come..."—each in a different key. This was the best time of my life.

After that summer, all I wanted to do was share my exuberant travelogue with my third-grade classmates, who quickly tired of my cross-country tales. I picked up the cues as their eyes glazed over, and despite the rebuff, I couldn't stop obsessing about the sights and sounds of these faraway places. I thought it was a failing on my part that I didn't fit in and that I had a larger appetite. At 8 years old, I wish I had understood that there was nothing wrong with me for wanting a bigger stage, for craving more than the narrowness of Spring Valley. The struggle between "dying to fit in" and "dying to get out" was officially sprung.

CHAPTER SEVEN

THE VAPORIZER

I don't remember when I had my first asthma attack, but asthma seems to have been with me forever. I was up all night with these attacks, wheezing, coughing, laboring to breathe. This was bad, but the worst part of chronic asthma wasn't even the vile-tasting yellow liquid medicine; it was the smell, the sound, and the feel of the vaporizer spitting out wet mist at me. All night, I would lie awake propped up on pillows gasping for breath and trying to stop my coughing fits while the machine hissed and rattled in the middle of the room, filling the air with a foul smell and pea-soup-like humidity.

Every time my father took the fat, clunky glass pot out of its well-worn blue-and-black box I would beg, "Daddy, please don't put on the vaporizer!"

My father looked sad, even sadder than I did. He reminded me that the pediatrician said I had to have the vaporizer. In those days, you didn't disobey a doctor—even if you were a doctor yourself, as Dad was. I couldn't stand that I was feeling so sick, but I couldn't stand it more that Dad looked so vulnerable. Arleen, seven years older than me, watched the interaction unfold from her bed on the other side of the room. She felt so badly about my ordeal and told me later that I cried every time Mom or Dad turned on the vaporizer because I hated everything about the machine.

My favorite TV show at the time was *Dr. Kildare*, and the dashing Richard Chamberlain was able to cure all his patients' ills. I was particularly moved by the episode in which the beautiful Yvette Mimieux, an epileptic, kept insisting she was fine when she wasn't, and the young and handsome doctor rescued her from an attack and saved her life. I waited every night for my personal Dr. Kildare to rescue me from my asthma attacks and my problems. My white knight materialized many years later in the form of a husband who cured my asthma and saved my life. But that's a story for a later time.

Asthma characterized my youth as much as weight, and it augmented the problem. While other girls my age skipped and jumped rope, I watched. When our class went to Bear Mountain or Warwick Game Farm, I waited on a bench with the class mother while the rest of the kids toured the park. When my brother Bob organized punch-ball games in our backyard, I could slug the rubbery Spalding out of the park but couldn't rally enough air to run to first base.

Every July and August, my asthma peaked. At Camp Hillman, where I spent many summers, I excelled at the stationary activities, such as archery, riflery, even baton twirling (the irony of developing a cheerleader-type skill never escaped me). When it came to games like dodgeball or relay racing, I had to sit them out. I mastered "Spit," a sedentary card game during which it was socially acceptable to sit in the same spot for hours. I was surprisingly fast at it, despite the fact that my medication, a blend of theophylline, ephedrine, and phenobarbital, made my hands shake and caused me to shift from lethargic to irritable to speedy, without warning.

Some days were manageable, but my asthma was so bad at night that even the medicines, the vaporizer, and the mountain of foam-rubber pillows didn't help. I had to sweat it out and teach myself how to stop the hacking cough and find my next breath. The coughing spells, which lasted about 20 minutes, reverberated throughout the house. It was bad enough that I couldn't sleep, but it bothered me even more that I was waking everyone else up, too. When the coughing wore off, somehow I found the stamina to catch my breath and get a moment of relief before the struggle started again.

Mom and Dad would monitor my meds, adjust the vaporizer, and check on me before they went to sleep. They would ask me if I "took something," code for "did you take your medicine?" In my house in the '50s and '60s, we didn't use certain words, like *medication, wheezing, inhaler.* To save me discomfort, my parents never told me I had asthma; it was one of those taboo words left unsaid or whispered, like the word *cancer.* Maybe if you didn't say the word, it wasn't true. Or maybe you didn't want to remind the evil spirits you were sick. Or maybe you didn't want to tempt fate. More likely, if you didn't say the word or came up with a less-direct word, the pain wouldn't be so bad. I never knew what my condition was, nor did I know the names of my medicines. The first time I went to camp—when I was six and a half—as I huffed and puffed my way to the first activity, my counselor asked me, "Are you the girl with asthma?" "No," I said confidently, because I had never heard the word before.

Middle of the night was hardest, the in-between when the old dose wore off and the new one didn't yet take effect. Though I had devoured every book in the *Bobbsey Twin, Cherry Ames,* and *Nancy Drew* series, on those nights, they brought me no consolation. My head was pounding and all I could do was wait out the long night by myself, trying in vain to catch a breath. Years later, a therapist asked me why I didn't knock on my parents' door and ask for help. It simply had never occurred to me.

I was aware not only of my own pain—the pain in my chest, back, and head from the constant coughing—but also of the pain on my parents' faces as they watched me suffer and couldn't do anything to help; despite their love, they couldn't make my asthma disappear.

In the summer after eighth grade, my next-door neighbor Rivkie and her family moved to Israel. I went to see her off at the dock. Family friends had driven me to the boat, but I was barely able to say goodbye. I had no breath and no voice. Between asthma, sadness, and the long walk back to the car, I nearly passed out. When we arrived home, I had to be walked into the house. I went into my room and stayed in bed for days.

My summer activity that year was a drama workshop at the local community college. I had high hopes to be a star in the summer stock productions. That summer, my asthma was so active I could barely read lines. On one of our field trips to Broadway's *Little Foxes,* a stranger turned around in his seat and told me I was breathing too loud and he couldn't hear the actors.

Shortly after the Broadway experience, my father gave me an inhaler that had recently hit the market. This "puffer" was the first thing that had ever brought me relief—instant relief. I was finally able to carry on a somewhat normal schedule and feel like a normal kid. The caveat was that you were supposed to wait six hours between doses. I couldn't wait. I couldn't control my use of the rescue inhaler because for the first time in my life, I was able to take a deep breath.

At 13 years old, I overdosed on medication and landed in the hospital for several days, detoxing from the puffer. As I came off the inhaler, I was put on heavy doses of adrenaline and steroids, which curbed my asthma for a week or so. The doctors treated my asthma and weaned me off the potent drugs, but no one thought to treat my addictive personality.

Shortly after, my breathing worsened and the rest of the summer I watched from the audience as other kids my age got the cream parts. I was given a small bit role; it was all I could handle with limited breath.

PART II

ADOLESCENCE

"To be nobody-but-yourself—in a world which is doing its best, night and day, to make you everybody else—means to fight the hardest battle which any human being can fight; and never stop fighting."

- e.e. cummings,
"A Poet's Advice to Students"

CHAPTER EIGHT

THE COLD WAR

Sixth grade was a turning point in my life. That was the year Mom and I began bickering about everything from my weight to whether I was allowed to shave my legs. Yet, what occurred outside my house was even more troublesome than inside. Suddenly, there seemed to be two fronts: the home front in which I was at war with my mother, and the school front, where I was at war with my classmates.

I was 11 years old. Judy Wasserman, who had been my best friend since kindergarten, began to drift away. In late June of fifth grade, I felt our friendship start to unravel right after the new girl, Allison Miller, moved to town. That summer Judy and I went to day camp together as we always did, but something was not right. I knew it was because of Allison. I could feel in my gut that Allison was stealing Judy away from me, and I hated her for that. To make matters worse, Judy's and Allison's mothers became close friends, and both families spent a lot of time together. I was hung out to dry.

After spending an awful summer watching my best friend disappear from me, I turned inward and didn't even tell my mother. She and I were always fighting. I wanted to wear stockings; she wouldn't let me. I wanted to shave my legs; she said no (I did it anyway and she was mad!). I wanted to have my ears pierced; she said that was bohemian.

One warm autumn day at the beginning of sixth grade, it was right before recess when I felt in my bones that something was wrong. Judy and Allison had spent the entire day before whispering to each other. All morning they giggled and passed notes and it was unbearable watching them. I should have been the one whispering and giggling with Judy! When we went outside for recess, the two of them disappeared with two other girls and the four most popular boys. I looked around for all of them and then went over to the other three girls in the class who were milling about. "Do you know where Judy and Allison are?"

They looked down at the sidewalk, at each other, everywhere but at me. No one wanted to tell me. Finally Esther spilled the beans: "They went into the woods with the boys. They're starting a private club."

A private club?! I couldn't believe it; this was the ultimate betrayal. The four girls had been planning this for days. And why wasn't I invited? Why wasn't I joining them in the woods with the boys? The three girls left at the playground wouldn't have expected an invitation, but they knew I would. They didn't confess anything; either that, or they had been sworn to secrecy.

The landscape was changing, and the feelings of rejection and hurt that had been welling up inside me all summer were now compounded by shame. I could barely hold back my tears. Even at 11, I knew that crying would make me weak, and I needed to stay strong. I assessed the situation and came up with a plan to quickly transform my hurt into anger, allowing me to stay in the driver's seat. I went to the three girls, the other outsiders, and I said defiantly, in words that would forever change my life, "Let's start a fight."

In those days "fights" were fairly common among the girls in my class. In our parochial Jewish school, a fight was more intellectual than physical, more passive-aggressive than aggressive. It typically consisted of a group of girls making snide comments about another group for several hours, snubbing the others at lunch, and in view of everyone, telling secrets only to each other.

The girls who had been left behind went along with my idea. I spent the rest of recess laying out a plan for the fight: we would start our own club with our own password, and we would meet at lunch to map out strategy. The girls promised to go along with whatever I said. By the time we got back to the classroom, I was feeling empowered, having built a coalition of outsiders.

Within minutes, I observed a shift in dynamics. Notes were being sent back and forth among the three girls who were supposed to be on my side and the four girls in the club. It became crystal clear to me that it was now seven against one. My new "friends" had defected to the other side.

That morning marked the beginning of a long and torturous standstill. Most fights lasted only a few hours, at most a day. This became a cold war, lasting for months. The boys were engaged in it, too, as it spilled over from recess to the classroom to the lunchroom and to weekend activities. Nobody in my small class said a word to me—for months.

One day, I walked into the girls' bathroom to find my name written on the wall inside a heart with the name of a boy I had a crush on—Sam. No one in the world knew about Sam except Judy; I had revealed that to her when we were best friends. I made her swear she would never tell my secret. Looking at the wall, I felt violated. How could I ever walk back into the classroom? How could I ever face the girls—or the boys? How could I ever face Sam? This was all-out war. And I was without allies or ammunition.

The silence at home was deafening. The phone, which used to ring all the time because I was the social planner, was quiet. I never went out, never got a phone call, never got invited to a party. Food became my only friend and the candy wrappers accumulated under my bed as my readily-available source of Novocain.

I spent recess standing alone and lunchtime at my own table. The teachers noticed and asked me what was wrong. "Nothing," I said. Despite the anguish going on inside, I was determined to hold my head high, not to cry, and not to crumble under the pressure. I became inventive and spent my time creating revenge fantasies. The most comforting fantasy was that I would become a famous actress and everybody would fawn over me. These girls would be sorry they had treated me so badly. Ultimately, I'd forgive them, but not without first putting them through the ringer.

A week or two after the fight began, I knew I didn't have the stamina to keep up my façade forever; I needed a new support system. I had the two friends on my block, but we went to different schools and I hardly ever saw them. Because my own class consisted of only eight girls and eleven boys, there wasn't much wiggle room to find a new group of friends. Had anyone spoken even one word to me, I might have asked for forgiveness or confessed I wanted to start over, but the freeze was on. I had no interactions with anyone. I didn't tell my mother because I felt deep down it was my fault that I wasn't popular enough to be in the inner circle. It was my fault because I was fat and unlovable.

I developed a Plan B: I gradually became friendly with the girls in the grade above me. They didn't appear to be judgmental, and when I took tentative steps toward them, they welcomed me. The older girls included me in their circle and were kind and compassionate. This didn't totally alleviate my problem at school because we didn't share the same recess or lunch period. I still had to endure public isolation at least three times a day every day: one lunch, two recesses, but at least I didn't feel so alone.

Plan B wasn't perfect but it did reinforce for me that I could manage independently, that I could work things out for myself. If I kept a stiff upper lip and didn't show fragility, I could get through the day and pretend to myself and everyone else that I was fine. If I showed too much weakness or neediness, I would crumble, so I made sure never to let my guard down. I was not going to be one of those people to beg for acceptance or tag along where I wasn't wanted. Better to act strong, like you're in control, than to be vulnerable and show your anguish.

After several months, I received a phone call that broke the silence. The mother of one of the original left-out girls asked me if I wanted to get together with her daughter, Helen, who wanted to play with me. I said yes. Helen and I went bowling. Little by little, beginning with Helen, I worked my way back into the social system.

The next weekend, I went to the movies with her and Esther, and slowly I was reincorporated into the girls' group of eight.

For the next two years, the last my classmates and I spent together, there were periods when I was in the middle of things: spin-the-bottle games, boy-girl parties, bar-mitzvah dances. In eighth grade, I was nicknamed "The Queen" because I was strong and people listened to me. I was proud to have that title after being so powerless just two years before. Yet, a part of me was still angry that while I was Queen, the more important moniker, Princess, clearly belonged to Allison Miller, and that title would never be mine. At least I no longer had to spend every waking minute dreaming of ways to kill the hurt, the isolation, and the shame. I was glad that I never had to stand alone at recess again.

CHAPTER NINE

DRAMA QUEEN
EXIT STRATEGY

I had the lead in almost every class play until seventh grade, when we started with musicals. I was tone-deaf and my career as a main character came to a grinding halt. Until then, I was selected for big roles because I had a loud voice that projected, but more importantly, because I had access to a wide range of emotions that could make my audience laugh, cry, or sit at the edge of their seats.

In my 30s, I met a caseworker as I was trying to help Jay secure a grant for an adaptive piece of equipment. As I was vehemently arguing on Jay's behalf, the woman sat back, then let out a screech, "Now I know where I met you! I was in the audience when you played the mother of a slain soldier looking for her son in a war zone. I'll never forget your performance! Your chilling screams—I had goosebumps. Those emotions stayed with me for a long time. How did you do that—go so deep into those feelings?"

I remember being puzzled by her question because that was just me; I had a wide spectrum of emotions that came out, often beyond my control. I learned quickly that my emotionality worked well on stage but not so well offstage with family, where I was teased for my "dramatic outbursts." I often alienated friends when I expressed intense anger, hurt, or neediness. On the flip side, when I was enthusiastic and bubbly, effervescent and glowing, people found me inspiring, and they loved my optimism and passion. Problem was, it was hard to know which "Marcia" would emerge, and how potent my feelings would be at any given moment.

As I zigzagged through adolescence and became more adept at reading people's reactions, I garnered that it wasn't a likeable trait to express prodigious emotions anywhere, anytime. I needed a coping strategy that would allow me to control my over-the-top feelings and not scare people away.

Here was the formula I created to help me survive:

1. Goal: keep my emotions at bay
2. Solution: binge 'til numb
3. In a semi-comatose, carbohydrate stupor, either take to bed or feel sorry for myself—in either case, withdraw
4. Become subdued rather than loud

This system seemed to do the trick. After years of exploding at the dinner table, I was now quieted by carbs. After confronting profound loneliness and sadness, I was mellowed by my personal form of self-mutilation. After a binge, I was one-tenth the drama queen I was before I started. I didn't rage so loud, love so deep, or hurt so much. Food worked its magic.

CHAPTER TEN

GYPSY

It came to me early on that I was never going to be a supermodel. President of the United States? Maybe. Miss America? Never. I had to create a niche for myself that boosted my self-esteem at an age when looks and body size were everything. From sixth grade through high school, I struggled to find an identity. Our combined elementary/middle school ended after eighth grade. I had been with the same twenty kids for nine years. In ninth grade, the start of high school, I began commuting into New York City to a private Jewish school where I imagined my world would expand. It did, though not by much. There were three times more students, sixty in all, with the grade broken up into two groups of thirty each. During all four years of high school, I attended classes with more or less the same thirty kids. For a long time, my social circle stayed narrow and restricted.

My peers fell into the usual cliques: nerds, jocks, political activists, artists, and JAPs (Jewish American Princesses). Although I was in the Honor Society, I wasn't academically driven enough to make it to top of my class. I preferred the anti-war activists and "improv-drama" crowd to the academics and the JAPs. A part of me envied the JAPs, whose job was to look beautiful, shop, and get all the guys. Even when I did spend a little time with their group, I knew I didn't fit in and would never belong.

My life became a vicious cycle: I was fat so I was "fringe." I was fringe so I may as well eat. When I ate, I gained more weight. I couldn't lose the weight so I had to figure out ways to succeed on the fringe. No matter what, I needed to see myself as a winner. I made sure I could win at almost everything I did, and if I thought I wouldn't win, I didn't try. No matter how much my mother and others tried to convince me that I was pretty, I knew by this time that the rest of the world didn't see me that way. And as boys weren't paying attention to me, I didn't even try to act the "femme fatale" or go after the cutest guys.

I decided, "If you can't join 'em, beat 'em," and took on with a vengeance the lessons I learned during my personal cold war and my reign as Queen: I was a force of one. If I couldn't be the most desirable member of a group, I would be its leader. The attraction to leadership was that I didn't have to be one of the crowd; I only had to be looked up to by them. I liked helping people, so the combination worked. I became my eighth-grade yearbook co-editor, then high school chair of the Social Action committee, and founding member of the city-wide Jewish High School Student Alliance.

Even though having influence and feeling powerful was usually enough to bolster my ego, there were moments when I'd still get blindsided, when I knew that it would take me all of a nanosecond to trade places with a skinny princess. While I was working so hard to establish my presence and secure my identity, these girls' detachment, their way of acting "cool," enabled them to get a different kind of attention that appeared easy and effortless. They seemed to get whatever they wanted, and boys (and other girls) ate out of their hands. Which was good, of course, because they themselves didn't eat.

When I would tire of being the responsible leader, the mature "mini-adult," and even Queen, I carved out a new role for myself: Gypsy. This category opened up possibilities for me that were infinitely more fun and less inhibiting. I was a natural. People told me all the time that I looked like a gypsy: dark curly hair, dark brown eyes, olive skin, big hoop earrings (Mom finally let me pierce my ears), and bright peasant dresses. In my mind, gypsies were beautiful, exotic, and wild. What seduced me most about being gypsy-like was that they were seen as sexy and alluring without having to be thin; even being fat was OK for a gypsy. The gypsy persona worked well with my dramatic, flamboyant, spicy, and unconventional personality; I didn't have to compete with ordinary girls. I never had to feel like a second-class citizen. I was bohemian and proud of it, and no skinny Dick-and-Jane type could compete with that. Plus, I was smart and sassy; the combination worked well—most of the time.

When it stopped working, I'd eat until I couldn't move. I hated eating myself sick, but I also hated discipline and deprivation. I was hungry to be thin, but not hungry enough. I preferred applying my talents to accomplishing things—in school and in my community.

The good news was that being Leader, Gypsy, and Queen provided me with a huge host of skills that I probably wouldn't have developed so early in life. I learned to be assertive, witty, clever, and entertaining. I learned how to lead a team and take charge. I also knew better than most of my peers how to set challenging goals and achieve them. I received kudos for being a "mover and shaker" and collected awards, recognition, and feathers in my cap, which helped me feel good about myself.

As co-editor of the eighth-grade yearbook, I remember assembling the page called "Best in Class"—Best Dancer, Best Dresser, etc., in which each classmate won a distinction for something. The yearbook committee said they needed to meet privately to discuss what my co-editor and I would win. They came back with a dilemma; they couldn't decide for me whether I was Best Leader or Best Personality. They suggested I choose, and I picked Best Personality, as that felt like the bigger honor.

That night, I went home and stuffed myself until I couldn't move. I didn't even think about it then but in retrospect, it was strange that I had finally achieved a level of recognition among my peers and, boom, just like that, I ate myself into oblivion. I didn't just eat when I felt bad—I ate when I felt good. It seems that I ate over pretty much every powerful emotion.

This act was repeated over and over. Despite all the accolades I received that day and throughout my life, on every birthday I blew out the candles wishing to be thin. And then proceeded to eat the leftover Carvel ice cream cake just as it was melting.

CHAPTER ELEVEN

LICENSE TO EAT

There wasn't much to do in my remote Orthodox neighborhood so I jumped at the chance to attend a prestigious high school in Manhattan. I passed the eight-hour exam and interview, and my parents made carpooling arrangements with Mr. Franklin, a New York City schoolteacher who lived in our town.

Every day, we took the FDR Drive to the Upper East Side. As soon as we crossed the George Washington Bridge, my body came alive, even at 7 in the morning. Shortly after the first semester started, I began exploring the city with my new friends. I loved the diversity of people, the street theater, the nonstop vibration. More than that, I loved being able to have any food I wanted. I was in heaven. Independent and hungry, I lapped up Manhattan like a thirsty puppy.

There were pizza parlors on every corner. There were bodegas selling a new brand of ice cream called Häagen-Dazs. There were bakeries with rainbow cookies, and jelly rings in big pink boxes next to the register at the deli. When my friends and I got bored with the upper-crust East Side, we took the subway to the West Village and hung out at cafés on MacDougal eating pastry and flirting with passers-by. During the week when I had after-school activities, I stayed over at friends' apartments in the city and on weekends, my friends would come up and stay in the suburbs with me.

At the beginning of my junior year, Shira Gilman, an Israeli, came into my life. Shira's father had accepted a diplomatic post in New York City for four years and Shira joined Ramaz, as a junior. We didn't have any classes together but when I passed "the new girl" in the hallway, I introduced myself. We cracked jokes about being late to class and within a few minutes, we acted like we had been friends for years. When I heard Shira's infectious laugh ripple through the corridor, I started giggling and the two of us couldn't stop laughing; we were out of control. We became fast friends and spent a lot of time in each other's homes.

We were so alike that our parents treated us like twin sisters. Not only did Shira and I share a birthday, but we both loved to talk, laugh, and binge. My downfall was sweets; hers was salt. Between the two of us, there was never a lack of food. Shira loved to eat as much as I did though with her additional three inches of height, she carried her weight better. Our bodies were inverted; I was top-heavy, she bottom-heavy, allowing us to exchange all clothes except for pants. We shared jewelry, hair bands, and long, crocheted shawls. With Shira's dark eyes, long dark hair, and gorgeous, exotic face, my "twin" was always a head-turner. There were times when I was jealous that men always noticed her first and were intrigued by her accent and happy-go-lucky spirit, but we didn't have the same taste in men. She liked the macho, rough-exterior types, and I preferred the soft, emotional guys.

One of the most important principles I learned from Shira was how to be direct. The first time she came to my house for the weekend, we took the Red and Tan bus from the Port Authority as Mr. Franklin didn't have room in his car for extra passengers. During the long trip through every tiny town on Kinderkamack Road in New Jersey, Shira and I jabbered back and forth about things to do, people to meet, foods to taste. I told her that I had just bought a new robe and it was really sexy. I couldn't wait for her to see my purchase.

When we got to my house, I held up the bathrobe for my new best friend, waiting for her *ooh*'s and *ah*'s. She took one look at it and said, "You think that's sexy? That looks like something my grandmother would wear!" I was shocked and hurt. No one I knew was ever that blunt. Though I was offended, it was hard to stay angry with her for long; Shira lived in the moment and didn't allow herself or her friends to take anything too seriously. I soon came to appreciate my friend's honesty and outspokenness. I knew Shira wouldn't lie and I could count on her to be frank. After spending so much time with Shira and her Israeli friends, I became more outspoken, also. I dispensed with the polite rhetoric and told people how I really felt, though I was a bit more diplomatic than the Israelis. There were times when I got in trouble for my forthrightness, but most people knew they could trust what I said because I didn't play games.

The day I turned 16, I became liberated: I got my driver's license. My first solo trip was to Pakula's Bakery, where I filled up on rainbow cookies and black-and-whites. I ordered brownies and cheesecake squares to go. The smashed white box, the red and white string, and the parchment paper in which the white-haired lady behind the counter had carefully folded the individual pastries, were scrunched into a ball and concealed under my bed so Mom wouldn't throw a fit.

Once I had my license, I couldn't wait for Shira to come for the weekend. Mom picked us up at the bus station and gave Shira a big kiss. Then we dropped Mom off at home and revved the motor for our Thelma and Louise fast-food getaway: Carvel (for both of us), the bakery (my favorite), and the Bagel Joint (Shira's favorite). It didn't feel as lonely in the suburbs when friends visited and I had an accomplice in crime. Shira was the most enjoyable eating companion because she would close her eyes and relish every bite, as she commented, "Mmmm, this is sooooooo good." While she ate and savored her food, I'd scarf mine down, in preparation for the next "fix" on the list. To me, the act of eating, pushing the food down, was automatic, almost mechanical; taking in the food was more significant than the taste.

When I wasn't sleeping over in Manhattan or didn't have friends staying at my house, I had a routine. By day I'd borrow Mom's car and stock up at the bakery. By night, I'd write and chomp. My parents had bought me a new typewriter because I loved to write stories, plays, and poetry. Most of the writings were escape fantasies—what it would be like in my new life outside this little town, when I was famous, successful, beautiful, and thin. Between strokes on the keyboard, I ate my pastries, and the dreams got bigger and bigger. And so did I.

For two years, Shira and I had a great time together in high school. When I left for out-of-town college, Shira stayed in New York City, and we visited each other as often as we could. Between my freshman and sophomore years of college, in her last summer before Shira left the U.S. to serve in the Israeli army, she and I traveled cross-country together using the Greyhound Ameripass. This open ticket allowed us to go to any destination where there was a Greyhound bus station for a period of a month. Shira and I had mapped out a tentative journey and we stayed with friends, distant relatives, youth hostels, or *Chavurot*, Jewish communal houses across the country. As two naïve and gregarious 18-year-olds, everything we did turned into an adventure. We stopped to chat with strangers in bus station restrooms at three o'clock in the morning; got off the bus to follow two cowboys to the Grand Canyon; pretended to meditate while laughing hysterically at The House of Love and Prayer in San Francisco.

Every place we went, we sampled the local foods: grits in Tennessee, salsa and chips in New Mexico, Ghirardelli chocolate in San Francisco. Though Shira was not a vegetarian, we always found a place to eat that satisfied both of us. Our diet consisted of French fries from greasy pit stops, grilled cheese sandwiches from dilapidated 24-hour diners, and a bus-snack stash of oversized bags of chips or M&M's to break the ice with fellow travelers and relieve our boredom on the long overnight bus trips. All summer, I had my two best friends with me: Shira and food.

CHAPTER TWELVE

LINK IN A CHAIN

I took the notion of being a link in the Jewish chain very seriously. On Friday nights, I loved to think about how women all over the world were lighting *Shabbos* candles just like Mom. I thought about my grandmother, my great-grandmother, and their mothers, who did the same thing for thousands of years. Then, I dared to think of myself and my own descendants, girls (or boys) who would light the same candles, pray into the same flickers, utter the same prayers. Then, because I believed so deeply in "one big happy family" across the planet, I flashed to other people and other religions around the world, past and present, who lit their own candles—votives, torches, lanterns, or bonfires—to commemorate their special occasions, to whisper their prayers of hope, to see their families' faces reflected in the flames.

That part of Judaism I embraced: the beautiful traditions, symbols, artifacts. I resonated with the notion that this is an ancient religion and we still practice some of the same rituals that Abraham and Sarah practiced. We still open our tents to welcome others to our table, we are still the "people of the book," we are still stubborn and obstinate. When I learned that a synonym for Jewish people in the Bible was *Yisroel*, people who "fight with God," I felt right at home. We Jews are not known for going with the flow or turning the other cheek. We're famous for arguing our point, standing up for what we believe. Our very nickname implies that it's OK to challenge back, to question... even God! All that fit my personality perfectly.

What didn't fit my personality were the millions of rules: everything from how to tie your shoes (right shoe goes on first, but left one gets tied before right) to which restaurants you're not allowed to enter even if you just need the restroom (perchance someone might see you walk into a *non-kosher* restaurant and think that you may be eating *non-kosher* food). There are rules about when boys can get their first haircut and what women can and can't do when they are menstruating because they are "impure." The rules made me feel constricted and oppressed.

This is how I was instructed. Not by my parents, who were more about the "spirit of the law" than the "letter of the law," but by the schools I attended and the neighborhood watchdogs who glanced over their shoulders to see if we were all doing what we were supposed to be doing. Judaism became to me a series of "Don'ts": don't do this; don't do that. Grandpa was comfortable adhering to the doctrines but Dad's version of Judaism didn't include dotting every "i" and crossing every "t," and neither did ours. Arleen, Bobby, and I each had our phase when we came home from *yeshiva* and berated Mom and Dad for not being religious enough, only to find that we ourselves couldn't sustain an Orthodox lifestyle.

We had our traditions: Mom lit Friday night candles at the specified time, Dad attended *shul* on Saturday morning to pray and study Torah, and when he came home, we had our abundant *Shabbos* meal. After lunch, Dad napped, Mom cleaned, and I invented non-electrical, non-writing board games to amuse myself and my friends.

It was hard for me to understand where God fit into the picture. At first, I was a big believer, but the more religious schooling I had, the more trouble I had locating God amidst all the absolutes. On *Rosh Hashanah*, God gave me a score on his giant scoreboard and on *Yom Kippur* my fate was sealed. Whether I lived or died at the hands of fire, water, sword, beast, famine, storm, plague, strangulation or stoning, would depend on my prior year's balance sheet tempered by the rigor of my last-minute pleas and restitution. The image of God as the ultimate micromanager slowly overshadowed my own experience of God as a wise old man (I had no doubt I was living in a "man's world") whose gentle hand was outstretched toward me to support, not to supplant.

One fine day, when I was 16, a new rabbi rode into town. Rabbi Avi Weiss was charismatic and young, only about 10 years older than me. His vision was clear: to create a community of inclusion, to give women more rights, to reach across religions, level of observance, gender, and political spectrums. Avi Weiss's Judaism was one of joy, soul, and song. The emphasis became what "to do," not what "not to do." This man worked tirelessly as a community activist and I was inspired to work right alongside him. Though I didn't always agree with everything Avi Weiss stood for (he was more right wing), I related to his passion, courage, and humanity.

The first time I met Rabbi Weiss, I had *shlepped* to synagogue begrudgingly, sitting in the women's section in the back as I always did, ready to daydream my way through the service and the sermon. Though the bamboo shades were traditionally parted for the Rabbi's speech, sitting behind the partition still made you feel like a second-class citizen, even with a full view. Listening to this new rabbi's animated words for the first time, something stirred in me, a fervor I had never felt before in *shul*. Not only was I excited to be there, I wanted to stand up and yell "Amen, Rabbi, Amen!"

I couldn't believe that I was hearing about the Sabbath as a kind of yoga activity. It was 1971 and yoga was my new fascination. Avi Weiss presented *Shabbos* as an oasis from the busy week, a time for reflection and meditation. It was about reconnecting with your heart, and connecting with God. Rabbi Weiss explained in a way I could latch on to that *not* working and *not* being obsessed with work enabled us to feel the joy of a day at rest, and that's why we refrain from work. It's about rejuvenation (spend quality time with your family, enjoy nature, take a walk), not recrimination (thou shalt not tear toilet paper on the Sabbath, thou shalt not transport an item from one place to another, thou shalt not put pen to paper, nor turn on a light, nor spend money, nor touch money; the list is endless.)

Finally, I found the soul of Judaism. Some congregants were uncomfortable with Rabbi Weiss's brand of Orthodoxy, but I was enthralled. I started going to temple regularly. I couldn't wait for Saturday to come, I joined the newly formed temple youth group, and I started getting involved in social action. I was on fire! At 16, I felt deeply that my life was taking a turn, and that I was being exposed to a new type of Judaism I could believe in, that wasn't oppressive.

I outgrew my dream to be an actress; now I wanted to become a rabbi. As it was inconceivable at that time to be a female rabbi in Orthodox circles, I decided I would become a Reconstructionist rabbi, a more modern branch of Judaism that was progressive and evolving. I remember walking home from *shul* with Mom's friends and they asked me what I wanted to be when I grow up. Unequivocally, I said, "a rabbi." Later Mom admonished me for saying something so fractious to her close-knit circle of Orthodox friends. I suppose I knew deep down that there was a little *chutzpah* involved, but I was also feeling confident and proud that I had found a Jewish identity that fit.

I didn't end up becoming a rabbi, though I have on occasion delivered sermons and led prayers. As a young adult, I realized that I didn't want the pressure of living in a fishbowl where people would judge my every move. I didn't want that level of scrutiny, and that feeling that I had to be a positive role model all the time. I knew that if I undertook that calling, I would set my bar impossibly high.

Over the years, I have met women rabbis from the Reform, Conservative, and Reconstructionist movements. In 2009, I met my first Orthodox woman rabbi. Although many in the mainstream Orthodox council objected, she performed a lot of the same duties as her male counterparts. Which dissident rabbi granted this woman her status? My old friend, Avi Weiss, who is still kicking up dust and igniting sparks wherever he goes.

In middle age, the Jewish spark in me is very strong. As Mom did, I light *Shabbos* candles on Friday night, though not usually at the specified time. I have given up almost all the "rules" and no longer walk around with guilt. I don't make it to synagogue often but I pray many times a day to God, with whom I have a very close bond. The Meislins get together for most Jewish holidays, having traded off Thanksgiving and other secular celebrations in order to give in-law families holiday time.

Regardless of how badly I craved my parents' approval, I found it impossible to be the "nice religious *yeshiva* girl" they sent me to parochial school to become. It was only decades later that the flicker ignited in me at age 16 by this young rabbi became the key to a lifestyle change in which spirituality replaced sugar, gratitude replaced shame, and God replaced the empty holes in my soul. I forged my path as a robust link in that very old and hefty Jewish chain.

CHAPTER THIRTEEN

THE OXYGEN TENT

At 15, I had spent July and August working as a school census taker, which I enjoyed, but socially the summer was boring. My parents saw how unhappy I was, and the following summer reluctantly allowed me to enroll in a Jewish sleep-away camp for teens. They were worried about my asthma, but my doctor gave me the go-ahead and I began to pack while fantasizing about an asthma-free summer, new friends, and maybe even a boyfriend.

We drove to the Poconos and I immediately fell in love with the surroundings. There was a lake, shady trees, and majestic mountains. I found the cabin I would be sharing with other 16-year-old girls and began unpacking my clothes. As I was stuffing my socks into the rickety drawers, I started to feel my lungs constrict. I ignored the symptoms, willing them to disappear. Though it became harder and harder to breathe, I attended the first-night activity with all the other teens. As the night wore on, my breathing grew so labored that I had no choice but to go to the infirmary.

The experience wasn't a total disaster. A gorgeous senior counselor heard my wheezing, saw how sick I was, and offered to walk me under the stars to the camp nurse. With my diminishing breath, I had very little energy and he had to grip my arm the whole way. It was very romantic. A lifelong fantasy of mine was unfolding: While trying to save me, a handsome young Dr. Kildare falls in love with me. This was not only the stuff of romance novels; in my life it was actually happening.

Len wasn't a doctor; he was more like the gutsy Zionist pioneers for whom the camp was established. He reminded me of my hero, Theodore Herzl, whose motto was "If you will it, it is no legend." That prototype was a turn-on for me: an idealistic, strong, kind rescuer who could make miracles happen.

Len walked me, holding me up, as I wheezed my way to the infirmary. I could barely move, barely breathe. The camp nurse took me right away. Looking concerned and protective, Len turned to me and said, "I hate to leave you here, but I have to get back to the kids in my bunk." He gave me a little squeeze and left. He was in charge of the younger boys in a different division, so after that night, I almost never saw him.

The stern nurse gave me a nebulizer treatment and told me I'd have to stay overnight. Then she did the unspeakable: she handed me an inhaler and told me I could use it anytime I needed relief. I told her I had used an inhaler two summers before and had gotten very sick from it, so sick that I landed in the hospital, addicted and dehydrated. She said, "Don't use it a lot, just when you really need it." I wasn't totally convinced because of my previous experience with an inhaler. But I was only 16, and she was the nurse, and I didn't argue. She gave me the inhaler, laid me in the bed with a few pillows to keep my head up, and disappeared. The feather pillows exacerbated my asthma. Time to use the new inhaler.

It was that quick. One puff and my addiction kicked in again. I had been through this already so I thought I could deal with it, especially since the nurse had said it was all right. I had no way of knowing that this time it would bring me to the brink.

After a few days in the infirmary, I was released. I couldn't walk more than 2 feet without having a coughing fit, but camp was in full swing and I was eager to take part. I went out and looked for my bunkmates. They were in drama class, my favorite activity. I walked in to the middle of a rehearsal and it hit me: It was too late for me to be part of the group's play. I was devastated. My nemesis, asthma, had robbed me again of being on stage in a drama production. It was clear I'd have to sit this one out altogether.

I sat in the audience and struck up a conversation with a tall, bearded, good-looking guy. Remarkably, he seemed interested. He asked where I had been, and I didn't lie. I had the sense that he already checked out the other girls. Maybe coming in a few days later than everyone else was an advantage. I had "fresh blood" written all over me. The only problem was I could barely walk or talk. As long as the activity was sedentary, and I didn't have to say much or do much, I was fine.

Dan and I spent the next two weeks together, hanging out, learning how to kiss. I participated in only a few activities, and I had no appetite. Mostly, I sat in the sun, deepened my tan, and hung out, avoiding sports or anything else requiring exertion. When I had to cross the camp to get to meals, I used my inhaler and imagined it was helping. I used it so much that it began to affect me in drastic ways.

One day, a camper my age asked me if I'd been drinking. "What?" I exclaimed. "I don't drink." He insisted, though, that he smelled alcohol on me. Coming from my sheltered hometown, I was pretty naïve and had no idea what he was talking about. Later I discovered that the medicine in the inhaler did contain alcohol. And I was certainly using. I wonder if I might have become an alcoholic if I didn't prefer food so much more?

Life, despite my health, was fun. I had a sort-of boyfriend at home whom I'd just met at a youth group retreat. Even though I'd dated him only twice, he was sending me gifts—a new pillow every few days. Altogether they spelled L-O-V-E. Now I also had a boyfriend at camp to gaze with me at the stars. I excelled at the elective classes because I was smart and because I made sure to sign up for activities that didn't require movement. And the rest of the time, I worked on my tan. I didn't have much of an appetite, so I was getting thinner; and nothing—*nothing*—was better than thin.

Visiting day came quickly that summer. While all the campers were cleaning their cabins and getting ready for the parental onslaught, I did my chore quickly and tried to stay away from the dust. The allergens got to me anyway, and by the time visiting day arrived, all I could do was lie in my bed listless. Thankfully, I didn't have to do anything because for some reason, my parents weren't coming this year. This was strange, as they were devout visitors at all other times, and usually I would have liked to see them. But as the other kids and their parents were swarming over the camp, I was relieved I didn't have to move from my bed.

My parents called that night to see how I was doing. Almost immediately—or so it seemed—they called back. I received a message from the office that they were coming the next day. Really, I wasn't upset about their missing visiting day; what was this special visit all about?

After one look at me, Mom and Dad packed up my clothes to take me home. I was crushed, but didn't have the energy to fight, nor did I have the time to say goodbye to anyone. Not even Dan.

My parents drove me straight to my asthma doctor. Dr. Klein's office was packed as usual but he called me in almost instantly. He glanced at me, and within seconds said, "We're taking you to the hospital." He emptied out his office and jumped into his car. We caravanned to Good Samaritan Hospital where I was immediately put into a bed with a plastic tent filled with oxygen. I needed all the oxygen I could get.

That night, isolated under the tent, I had a hard time hearing people. I was dehydrated from not eating or drinking enough and from sunbathing too much. And I was almost dead from overdosing on the asthma inhaler.

All sorts of people peered in at me during the night—doctors, nurses, respiratory therapists, my parents—but all I saw was a blur of motion and color. Between the plastic, the labored breathing, the dry coughing, and my exhaustion, I pretty much blocked out the whole night. I was in a lot of pain from the needles and the poking, and the doctors had to keep looking for new places to inject me. As an experienced asthmatic, I usually minimized my symptoms, but this night I actually yelled out from the pain.

The next morning, I woke up to a smiling nun. I had never met a nun before. I had also never slept in a bed with a crucifix above my head. The nun was saying something and crossing herself. I couldn't hear her, so she leaned as close as she could to the plastic and said, "Child, thank the Lord you are alive. We didn't think you'd make it through the night." It was quite jarring for me to hear that coming from a home in which people underplayed their problems, or lightened them up with humor, as a way to cope. Though the words hurt, I was touched by Sister Margaret's compassion and candor.

I was in the hospital for a week. The bronze tan I had so carefully cultivated faded and I was pasty from my illness. What a waste. I had worked so hard sitting in the sun all those hours only to have my color disappear in a hospital bed. I had also lost a lot of weight between camp and the hospital, and I was upset that no one would see that either except for the doctors and my parents—because I didn't have contact with anyone else for weeks. Most of my friends assumed I was still in camp for the summer, and I didn't feel like contacting them to say I flunked camp and was flat on my back.

When I was released, all I wanted to do was go back to camp. There was only a week left in the first session, and my parents didn't think it was a good idea. Being 16, I really didn't care if it made sense. I had left a boyfriend in the mountains, and we weren't done yet. My parents hadn't planned on sending me to sleep-away camp for the second session as money was tight after paying for Arleen's wedding, Bobby's college, and my private high school tuition. I understood my parents' financial situation and their concern that it was a health risk to go back so soon but it was hard for me to contain my disappointment.

After several more days of recuperating, my mother called me downstairs to the telephone table, where I glimpsed a letter. I loved getting mail so I rushed down, careful not to trigger my asthma. There, on a small white envelope, was my name, written in Allan's distinctive block writing, no address and no stamp. Inside was a note:

"Dear Marcia, We didn't want you to miss out on camp. Have a great time! Love, Jay, Allan, Bobby." Paper-clipped to the note was enough cash to pay for the second month of camp. I cried and hugged Mom as she stood there beaming. She told me that when my brothers heard my story, they pooled their money and convinced Mom and Dad to let me go back to camp. I packed my bags, inhaler-free, and set out back to camp feeling secure and loved, harboring high expectations for a different kind of love. I knew Dan wouldn't be there during the second session, but he was planning to come back at the end of camp for the national Zionist youth conference. I had much to look forward to.

Second session meant a new bunk, new kids, and new counselors. By the time I got there, the beds had all been taken except an upper bunk. I told my counselor that I couldn't have the upper bunk because I had asthma. She looked at me and said, "I haven't been informed of that. Do you have a note from your doctor?" When I said no, she told me, "The upper bed is yours then." I kept my mouth shut.

The entire month went like that—nothing particularly going my way and me feeling sorry for myself and lonely for Dan. I was in beautiful mountains, there were idyllic settings everywhere, and I was alone while everyone else seemed to have a boyfriend. I was supposed to have one, and we were supposed to be an "item." Then I had landed in the hospital. That was the end of that. How unfair.

I trudged through August spending every waking moment fantasizing about Dan's and my reunion at the conference at the end of camp. Dan would come back, all sad and lonely, missing me so much that he couldn't wait another minute to see me. The story would unfold just like in the movies.

Dan came back. I knew he was there and looked all over for him. But he didn't rush around to find me. He had gotten himself a girlfriend at home, and he didn't seem to be lacking for anything. While he left camp fairly naïve, he returned quite experienced. It was obvious he hadn't been sitting around his house pining away for me.

We spent a little time together—more out of my need than his. Desperation was written all over my face, and although he was happy to indulge my little fantasy reunion, at the end of our fooling around, he said, "I hate girls like that."

"Like what?" I asked.

"I hate girls who are needy."

That line haunted me for a long time to come. Every time I had any kind of sexual encounter with a boy, I kept thinking (and sometimes verbalized), "Do you hate me?" That insecurity, coupled with my mother's warning about fat girls and my own body image, contributed to a decade of neurotic and hurtful relationships.

CHAPTER FOURTEEN

BODY IMAGE #2: THE LESSON

As a teen, better yet—a pre-teen—I could have really benefitted from a benevolent lesson in body image. I had no clue what women's bodies looked like, and that they were so diverse. My mother and sister never undressed in front of me, my elementary school couldn't afford a gym, and in high school, I wore my mandatory blue jumpsuit under my clothes so I rarely went into the locker room. It wasn't until college that I saw other naked bodies and I would have liked to be better prepared. Years before that, I wish someone had tutored me and said, "You're a girl now, soon to grow into a woman. I have lined up five nude women side by side so you can see how different and how beautiful all women are, each one laudable in her own right."

Starting at the top and working her way down, the instructor would point at various features in a nonjudgmental way: "Marcia, some women's faces are round, some are oval, and some are heart-shaped. Yours is round. Some women's skin tones are light, some are dark, and some have your color—an olive complexion—with a goldish green tint to it.

When it comes to hair, women like you have curly hair, while some have straight or wavy hair. Each type has its own charm; some women love having straight hair and some love having your type of pin curls and ringlets.

Moving to breasts, there is a wide array of breast sizes and shapes, which are commonly compared to fruits. There are women whose breasts are small like cherries, a little bigger like plums, maybe grapefruits, and some women have big breasts, like melons. There are round breasts and pointy breasts; some face up, some face down. Some form a cleavage at the top where they come together and some are farther apart.

Moving down the torso, let's talk about waists: There are women with tiny waists, like Scarlett O'Hara in *Gone with the Wind* (my favorite movie in those years). When you put your hands around her waist, the fingers almost meet. Other people have round, thicker waists. Some women's stomachs are flat; others have a little pooch. Some bellies are hard and muscular, others soft and fleshy.

Now let's talk hips and buttocks, nicknamed 'butts'. There are women with narrow hips, not a lot of distance from side to side; others have wide hips. Some women have butts that are shaped high, others low. There are infinite combinations: a woman can have a small waist, big hips, and big buttocks, while another can have a different variation."

The lesson would continue illustrating how every woman and every part of the body is distinctive. My fantasy tutorial culminates with this point: "All these women are beautiful, each in her own way. Feminine allure has as much to do with how a woman feels about herself and the confidence she radiates from within. Marcia, just remember to love and accept your body and who you are, and your special gifts will come through."

Maybe those wouldn't have been the exact words, but I wish someone had explained to me that I was living in a myth generated by Madison Avenue and Hollywood that every woman has to be rail thin with straight hair (preferably blond); and those women who don't fit these images should throw in the towel because they will live a less-than-stellar life. It would have been reassuring to hear that looks count for something but not everything, and our entire self-esteem shouldn't be based around a number on a scale or a size of a dress. That every society has a different view of pretty and none is right or wrong. In certain countries, skinny women are esteemed and in others, voluptuous women are the prize. Classical art typically portrayed beautiful women as curvy (and curly) while modern media favor the opposite.

Under these circumstances, I wonder if I would have been able to hear the other message, that health is important, that being at a healthy weight and eating nutritiously is a way of loving ourselves. I'm not positive I would have embraced the message, but when "fat" was associated with "ugly," swallowing the judgments and enduring the finger pointing propelled me to eat more.

My father was one of those rare people to whom the inside mattered more than the outside. When I was about 10, I had lost a lot of weight on one of my mother's strict diets, and Mom was very excited to take me shopping in a regular store. It was a big milestone as I teetered between Junior sizes 11-13 and Missy 12.

Mom bought me a whole new wardrobe. When Dad came home from work, Mom egged me on, "Honey, why don't you put on a fashion show for Daddy; try on all your new clothes!" One by one, I tried on each outfit, and strutted into the room with dramatic flair. At first, Dad raised his eyebrows and smiled broadly as he exclaimed, "Oh, very nice!" In his effort to support me, he repeated that two more times. When I modeled the fourth ensemble, his smile waned, and he said, just slightly joking, "What, are you becoming... a clothes horse?!"

I had mixed reactions. Part of me was happy that I had a Dad who was an idealist, who felt that the soul, not the clothes, make the person. The other part of me was insulted that Daddy couldn't see how pretty his little girl was, that he didn't appreciate having a little princess. That shouldn't have surprised me because neither Arleen nor I were ever "Daddy's little princess" because Dad wasn't that type. He loved us unconditionally yet barely noticed what we wore or how we looked unless we clearly dressed up for a celebration. I don't recollect Dad ever effusively lifting us off the ground, twirling us around, or telling us how pretty we were. Dad was introverted and serious, and the only comment I ever heard him make about a woman (other than Mom), was when he cooed about the glamorous

French actress Claudette Colbert. When I was in my 20s and had my hair cut in Paris, Dad praised the short bob, telling me I reminded him of Claudette.

Other than those rare moments, Dad clearly wasn't interested in looks, clothes, or material matters. Relieved to have grown up with that value system, I felt safe around Dad even when I looked like a *shlump* with elastic pants and a baggy sweatshirt. The part that I missed was that "wow" look that daddies give their little girls, transmitting to them that they are pretty and irresistible, that they will knock some man off his feet one day. Once Uncle Harry died, I never knew what it was like to be picked up or touched by a father figure, to be adored by a male. For many years, that sense of deprivation added to my shame about my body. I spent many therapy sessions searching for reassurance that there was nothing wrong with me, that I was loveable and huggable, not ugly and untouchable. I spent close to a decade looking for love, acting out in promiscuous ways, and trying to fill that need for tenderness and intimacy. I called it "sowing my wild oats" but I believe it was a yearning for touch, a yearning to feel beautiful and adored as a woman.

Luckily for me, Dad spent a lot of time reinforcing that I was smart, competent, and capable of accomplishing anything. I came to learn that so many women, many of them strikingly beautiful, struggled to accept those parts of themselves that came so naturally to me.

With Dad's acceptance of my insides and indifferent to my outsides, I became more vulnerable to Mom's messages. Dad was a spiritual thinker and if I wanted to learn Esperanto, the universal language, so we could communicate and bond with all of humanity across the planet, he was definitely the right role model. On the other hand, he wasn't very realistic or pragmatic, two traits in which Mom excelled. Mom knew that in our society, you had to look good and dress well. Right or wrong, Mom lived in the real world and she knew—better than anyone—that while certain difficulties were out of our control, man-made challenges could be overcome, regardless of the hard work required.

Mom and I had a battle of wills about my weight all my life and I was determined to win. I didn't realize then that Mom was not the enemy and putting all my efforts into playing tug-of-war with her was not helping my own cause. Yet, I set Mom up as the lightning rod for my eating disorder and held her responsible for my weight and my emotional problems. She blamed the fat and I blamed her.

A small voice in my head tried convincing me I was good enough, but by 15 or 16, even my gut couldn't ignore society's media onslaught. The only fat females on TV or in the movies were either stigmatized ugly ducklings, or middle-aged ladies like Totie Fields or Ethel Merman, who could belt out a song commensurate with their size. The "beautiful" people, the ones with boyfriends, love lives, and sweet, angelic voices, were skinny and feminine. Between my mother's trying to convince me how much better my life would be if I were thin, and the silver screen proving (or so it seemed) that the waifs and the anorexics get the guys, I finally submitted. I allowed the outside forces that were insisting I wasn't OK to overshadow any remnant of an inner voice telling me I was.

Despite the battles and the shame, I didn't hate my life. I had created a lifestyle with a long list of plusses that offset the minuses. Mostly I liked school, family, friends, temple, my poetry and journaling. Because I had an outgoing personality, most people perceived me as vibrant, happy, and charismatic. I wasn't lying. When I was out in the world extroverting, I was typically upbeat and effervescent. It was only later, alone in my room, when the loneliness kicked into gear. That's when I allowed myself to feel depressed, deprived, disappointed. That's when I stuffed myself with candy. The sugar numbed the pain and I didn't feel too bad. By the next morning, when it was time to face the world again, I emerged from my cocoon reinvigorated and revitalized, ready to turn that day's anxiety into accomplishment.

Sometimes I wonder: if no one had informed me (with disgust) that I was fat, and that fat people are pariahs, could I have been a very happy girl? Could I have loved and accepted myself without having to break myself in two: loving one part while disdaining the other?

CHAPTER FIFTEEN

BOYS

My first boyfriend experience at camp put a damper on my self-esteem and sexuality. I took to heart Dan's message that it wasn't OK for a girl to share honest feelings or to have needs (though it's obviously fine for boys). I became phobic about relationships, even though I wanted one badly. I craved a relationship with someone deep, sensitive, and caring, someone who would accept all of me.

I thought I'd found love the summer before senior year in high school when I fell head over heels for Kenneth, an Ivy League "college boy" from another temple youth group function. Not only did Kenneth fit all my criteria, but he was also a psych major obsessed with talking about feelings, dreams, and insights. He would listen intently to everything I said, and then analyze me with Freudian interpretations. I had no idea if what he said was correct but I was wowed by his psychological know-how, which I found out later was called "psychobabble." Between our after-school rendezvous in Central Park and the overwhelming sensation that finally someone understood me, I was sure I was in love. I was so captivated by Kenneth that I neglected to see his emotional instability. Fortunately, Kenneth returned to college and his ex-girlfriend.

I went out with a few other boys over the next year, but none of them interested me. And if they did, I didn't interest them. If a boy liked me, I automatically dubbed him "not my type." If I liked him, it seemed I was not "his type." At the ripe age of 17, I deduced that the common denominator among my failed relationships was that all the boys came from the same circles as I did: Jewish, suburban, well-educated, middle class. Their stories were old hat and our dynamics boring and predictable.

The summer after I graduated high school, I worked at a mental health center and drug treatment program. There I met men with completely different stories from any I had heard before; fascinating men I could listen to for hours. These staff members and ex-addicts spoke of their painful journeys of addiction, trauma, and recovery. I was particularly attracted to the articulate and charismatic men who were passionate about helping others through their struggles.

Meeting these former addicts, I was transfixed. At the time, I didn't equate their addictions and emotional problems with my own addiction to food and instant relief inhalers. What I did know was that I connected on an emotional level more with these men than I ever had with any of the guys in my neighborhood. I felt safe talking with them and the intimacy we developed through revealing our secrets was a turn-on.

I became friendly with Cliff, a recent graduate of the drug program. His foster home was only a few miles from my house so I invited him over to visit me. Cliff and I sat on my front porch all day exchanging stories. My story was short and straightforward—there wasn't much to tell. Mostly I listened, breathless, hypnotized by Cliff's story of abuse, poverty, addiction, recovery, and hope. Periodically, my parents would peek out the dining-room window, curious about this good-looking black mystery man. Later when I told them, my father was nervous because Cliff had been an alcoholic and a drug addict, though I suspect more so because he was black and not Jewish. So much for my father's liberalism.

Cliff moved out of town to live with an aunt and uncle, but our short-lived friendship was a turning point in my life. Getting to know Cliff and men like him opened my world in a way that I could never have imagined. Their stories resonated with me, and more importantly, these men seemed much less judgmental and shallow than most of the males I knew. Weight never came up as an issue, nor did it seem to be the proverbial pink elephant in the room. We were too busy dissecting life, fate, debating whether one actually could change their fate. I was stimulated and free in a way I had never been in my homogenous childhood community. A large part of me had been locked up and untapped, and now the door was open. I had a longing to meet up with more men like Cliff, magnetic men who were less inhibited than the ones I knew.

By this time, the early '70s, the counterculture was in full swing, and I was optimistic that the repressive notions of the past regarding sex, relationships, or what a woman was were all being challenged. I was sad to see that even in hippie circles, Michele Philips seemed a lot more desirable to men than Mama Cass, despite Cass's powerhouse voice and strong stage presence. Sure they wanted Mama Cass to be their friend, or Betty Friedan their intellectual role model. But girlfriend? No thanks. Among the boys I had known, the arm candy, trophy girlfriend was still thin, no curves, long straight hair, with a personality that would fade into the background while her man took center stage.

When I left for Cornell, I had high hopes for my love life. The boys in my dorm found me easy to talk to, engaging, and insightful and I quickly became a friend and confidante to a lot of boys. They would share their innermost feelings with me, then go home to their skinny girlfriends. I went back to my room to binge. I kept fantasizing that one day one of these boys would say "Screw it!" to society and introduce a fat girlfriend to his friends. What I came to realize during those consciousness-raising years is that most groups managed to achieve liberation in one form or other, while fat women continued to be rebuked and marginalized long after the cultural revolution was over.

In spite of my intention in college to branch out and expand my social circles, as if by a magnet pointing north I was lured to the Jewish clubs and Jewish worship services. There I found boys who were familiar: open-minded about politics, close-minded about looks. The coping mechanisms I had developed—Gypsy, Leader, Queen—still worked, but only for making friends, not for finding a boyfriend.

I wondered if I would ever find a boy who would bring to the party a smart, funny, bold, *zaftig* Jew from New York.

At the beginning of freshman year, one of the guys I met at Hillel was Rick, whom I considered "out of the box" enough to appreciate me. He was very intense, almost brooding, and was a staunch activist within the Ithaca community. We weren't all that happy the few times we were together but I didn't know too many other people and I found him interesting, worldly, and a good source of pot. On Columbus Day weekend, my best friend, Shira, came from New York City to visit for the long weekend. We met up with Rick and walked the few blocks from campus into College Town to spend the holiday with friends of Rick's: a mesmerizing retired professor, his European girlfriend, and an exotic crowd of pot-smoking, wine-drinking artists, intellectuals, and graduate students. After partying for a few hours, I dozed to Mahler's Fifth and fell into a deep sleep, despite the cacophonous music.

When I awoke, seemingly hours later, I saw eight bodies strewn across the floor like scarecrows and their eyes radiated a kind of gloss in the twilight-lit room. Among these motionless figures, I was able to make out the two bodies of Rick and Shira, locked into a tight embrace on the zebra-skin shag. Though dressed, they lay coiled together, surrounded by Absurdist books, record albums, and paper plates overflowing with ashes and spit-out sunflower seeds.

Claustrophobia—or was it disgust?—set in immediately, as the suffocating sensation started in my toes, crept up my legs, and surged down my arms. I shot up and darted to the door for a breath of fresh air. Fury raced through my body as I plotted how to get past this betrayal. Still high and hazy, I knew I had to leave the party, get back to my room, and write my Freshman English paper due first period. We could write on any topic we wanted and I knew this paper would serve as my catharsis. I left Shira directions to the dorm, then left the scene, stuffing down the disappointment with two bagels and cream cheese, and a brownie for the road.

I quickly forgave Shira because she swore to me that she and Rick didn't sleep together. I believed her and was able to move on because I didn't really care that much about Rick and I did care a lot about Shira. And, as always, it was hard to stay mad at Shira for long. I was less fazed about what happened than I was about my patterns of relationships. What happened felt familiar: I was the victim, the underdog. No matter what boy was interested in me, if I had a prettier friend or a thinner friend, that boy would opt for her and reject me. That wound was old and painful but somehow I felt I deserved it, that it was inevitable. I tucked it away, ignored Rick, and resumed my best-friend status with Shira.

Sure that I was doomed to fail with Jewish boys, I reached out to non-Jews—blonds, from rural towns. Our conversations were definitely different and as some of them had never met a Jew before, there was a curiosity on both sides. The first time I met a boy who wasn't circumcised, it freaked me out, but I soon began dating boys from all around the country; farm boys who came to the Ag school, and aspiring lawyers from the Midwest who were studying Industrial and Labor Relations. I was dating Catholics, Protestants, Episcopalians; I didn't understand the difference but I loved the freedom of breaking out of Jewish jail.

Eventually, I came to discover that I felt most comfortable with foreign men. Instead of looking at my size-14 body and thinking, "she's so fat," these men seemed to appreciate my size. Rubenesque women were desirable in certain European cultures, and Arab men had been more than willing to trade multiple camels for me when I was in Israel. African men preferred my ample curves to the pinched, size-4 women; "more to squeeze" was a compliment, not a criticism.

With all these new options for dating, I was like a kid in a candy store: I craved familiar candies, but exotic ones gave me a rush. New looks, tastes, sensations were flowing within me: I felt beautiful, sensuous, alluring. In contrast to the stilted kissing and petting I had experienced with boys from home, these men imported new cultures, languages, and romantic styles into our repertoire. Regardless of culture or country, I picked only good-looking men, thin (the irony didn't escape me), with fascinating stories. I know that part of my appeal to them was that I was big-busted and top-heavy but I was also very sensual. And with my bottomless-pit need for touching, I happily traded sex (to a point) for the cuddling that followed.

In an irony that would ultimately change my life, as I was reaching outside my Jewish middle-class experience for love, I happened to befriend a Jewish middle-class freshman. Steve and I met the first week of freshman year. We both lived in Clara Dickson Hall, his room two floors above mine. My triple room was at the end of the hall, near a large window where students congregated. The first time I saw him with his friends at the window, I was taken by his dark features, shoulder-length hair, wire-rimmed glasses, and blue-flannel shirt. I stood watching, listening.

After studying Steve for a few minutes, I realized that I had met him two years earlier when one of my campmates from the Bronx had invited me to her house for the weekend. I accompanied her to a youth group meeting and met her friends, one of whom was a smart, good-looking, wise-guy named Steve, who went to Bronx High School of Science. That night by the window, he and I reminisced about that youth group meeting and quickly bonded. It turned out that despite the feisty spirit and mischievousness that we shared, we were very different. He was pre-med and filled with rational thoughts; I was in human development brimming with unbridled emotions. He seemed stable and focused; I felt unstable and unfocused.

For a few months, we hung out together as friends, while I was busy experimenting with my newfound liberation. That worked well for Steve, too, because he was an introvert and liked to keep his thoughts and feelings private. After months of our friendship, he still hadn't revealed very much about himself. Unlike the riveting, garrulous, worldly men with whom I discussed Kafka, the Buddhist notion of Self, and Moody Blues symbolism in *Searching for the Lost Chord*, Steve was pragmatic and scientific, and for him most issues were fairly black and white. In place of conversation, Steve had many hobbies. His multi-dimensional talents continually intrigued me. One minute he would ace an impossible organic chemistry exam, the next minute he'd hop on his 10-speed bike to buy components for his homemade stereo. Then he'd sit under the Tensor light in his little room crafting silver jewelry or leather belts, followed by a visit to the local supermarket to cook us a gourmet dinner on his one-pot burner. After dinner he retreated to the drafting table to create cartoon illustrations for the school's biology club.

Second semester, as I moved from a triple to a single, my relationship with Steve began to change. We spent a lot of time together studying, attending campus events, walking to classes, hanging out in his room (on red satin sheets he sewed himself). At some point, our relationship escalated, and we became boyfriend and girlfriend. It was fun; we tobogganed down Libe Slope, laughed over silly things, held hands wherever we went, and made love under the phosphorescent stars he painted on the ceiling of his dorm room. With Steve, I didn't feel fat and self-conscious and I was able to be myself. Our sexual relationship was tender and we loved to snuggle, making it tough to get out of bed and go to class.

We also fought a lot—about big things, little things, but mostly about how we fought. When we had a problem with each other, my style was to scream and yell and Steve's was the opposite: he became silent. The quieter he became, the more frustrated I became. I ended up becoming more emotional as I tried shaking him out of his silence into some form of communication. He became more aloof and I felt more abandoned. Though we couldn't have named the problem at the time, we both suffered from fear of intimacy. For both of us, this was our first real relationship and we often got stuck. An entry in my diary from that period read: "I'd move close, he'd move away; he'd move close, I'd move away."

In addition to my problems with Steve, I felt inadequate in my friendships with girls. I could make friends but I couldn't keep them and I didn't understand why. I realized that I was unhappy and that my early childhood and family issues were infiltrating my relationships. After summoning up the courage to ask my parents for money, I started therapy for the first of many times with a local psychologist. Mom and Dad were very supportive and glad I was tackling the tough issues about why I was moody and difficult to be around—and why I was so round.

Like clockwork, every week I would come back from my therapy session, and fill Steve in on everything I learned. He expressed interest but shared very little about his own parents or childhood. I was in achievement overdrive, working without letup to find the cure for my eating disorder, negative body image, and fear of intimacy. The harder I worked, the more distant I felt from Steve, who, by self-admission, wasn't comfortable with introspection and was content to live the status quo.

Sophomore year, Steve and I moved together into The *Chavurah*, a Jewish co-op house off campus with ten other people. We each had our own room but shared a common kitchen, living room, and dining area. There were cliques in the house but since neither Steve nor I were "groupies," we stayed independent and on casual terms with everyone. We did make friends with Marcy, the attractive woman occupying the room next to mine. Though Marcy wasn't from Long Island like so many of the JAPs at Cornell, she was definitely into clothing, looks, and the white convertible with red interior that Daddy bought her for school. Marcy was also intrigued by therapy and she used to join Steve and me in these weekly de-briefs after my sessions. Rotating rooms, the three of us would lie on one of our beds as I shared the newest insights, then Marcy would pipe in with her issues. Steve was quiet but clearly enjoyed the intimate conversation (or maybe just the company) of the two of us. One day our friendship blossomed into a ménage-a-trois which we later repeated once or twice. Although Steve was my boyfriend and Marcy was very pretty (and thin), I encouraged the alliance. I'm not sure why—because of course I became jealous after it happened—but inside I felt magnanimous and happy to have earned my seat in the sexual revolution.

For a year and a half, Steve and I lasted in our roller coaster relationship. Halfway through sophomore year, we broke up. We both knew there was a lot of tension in our relationship but I was the one who took the initiative. I didn't remember what I said back then, but years later Steve repeated my breaking-up words: "I love you, but you're too nice, and I'm not ready for that kind of relationship." At 18, I wasn't ready for a committed relationship with a nice guy; I had too many adventures in me that needed to unfold.

After the breakup, we both stayed in the house and managed to enrage each other and everyone else by being distant at the dinner table. Steve started dating Marcy, and I reciprocated by bringing a series of different men to dinner. We were adept at playing cat and mouse.

Junior year, Steve took an apartment with some friends, and I took an apartment by myself. We were barely in contact for almost a decade.

For years after this, Steve was the bar against which Mom and Dad measured every other boyfriend. I'd bring home accomplished, sophisticated men, well-degreed, well-mannered (very few white or Jewish), and my parents would say, "He's very nice, and I'm sure he's a wonderful person. Whatever happened to that boy from Cornell, Steve Weinstein?"

"Mom, that was eight years ago! I have no idea where he is, and besides, he's not as interesting as these guys."

It took me a very long time to find the right man. I couldn't seem to come to terms with men from my own background, with whom I never felt pretty enough, thin enough, good enough. And when I did, as with Steve, I didn't know what to do with the relationship: Do I succumb to what my parents and their community want for me? Do I end up being a Jewish American (suburban) Princess after all? Or do I defy tradition and continue searching for that unusual man who will rescue me from the narrowness of my past, one who will find me as exotic and exciting as I find him?

PART III

WANDERER

"What could I say to you that would be of value, except that perhaps you seek too much, that as a result of your seeking you cannot find."

- Siddhartha to Govinda in *Siddhartha*,
by Hermann Hesse

CHAPTER SIXTEEN

CABBIE

After three years, I knew it was time to leave Ithaca. In the middle of my junior year, I discovered that I had almost enough credits to graduate a year early, and jumped at the chance to leave "farm country" though I had no idea where to go. The only place I could think of was the Berkshires, a Meislin favorite, adored for its beautiful mountains, abundance of culture, and magical spirit. I loaded up my lemon yellow Dodge Swinger and drove east. I embarked on the four-hour drive without a specific plan, and hoped one would materialize by the time I reached Western Massachusetts.

When I hit Great Barrington, I stopped for lunch at a vegetarian café. Next door was a visitor's center and I went in to inquire about housing. Mitch, a guy about two years older than me with a short ponytail and warm smile, asked me where I wanted to live. "A place near Stockbridge, my favorite town," I replied. Mitch's friend, Sue, lived in Stockbridge directly behind the famous Red Lion Inn, and she was looking for a third roommate. The house, a worn, but charming Dutch colonial, overlooked the Housatonic River and sat across from an old stone bridge. The situation seemed ideal; Sue commuted back and forth to Amherst, and Bonnie, her roommate, was the strolling violinist in the courtyard of the Red Lion Inn. I signed on to be the third roommate.

I had a list of places I wanted to visit, but first needed a job. A few blocks from my house, a quaint restaurant and tourist shop had a "Waitress Wanted" sign in the window. In the past, I wouldn't have considered a waitress job where I had to maneuver trays of food around crowded people and tables. But I had lost 20 pounds at school, and at size 14 (about 140 pounds), I felt more confident that I could navigate small spaces. I interviewed for the position with the owner, Alberta, who was very gregarious and morbidly obese. We hit it off immediately and had a lively conversation. When I asked about the waitress job, she replied, "I'm sorry, honey, there are no waitress jobs. Why don't you talk to my husband, Bill, in the back of the shop? He owns the local taxi service, and he may have a job for you."

I met with Bill and was hired as a hack. Most often, I drove tourists to tourist sites: Tanglewood, Jacob's Pillow, the Norman Rockwell Museum. The rest of the time, my job was taking 92-year-old Claire food shopping, bringing the village dowager to her daughter's mansion, and delivering six-packs to Lou, the town drunk. The summer was enchanting. After driving a cab all day, I would head over to my "Theories of Personality" class, to fulfill my final graduation requirement. The rest of the time, I danced at street fairs, swam in tucked-away swimming holes, and listened to the music of local folk singers.

That summer, my house was a hub of activity. My parents made their bi-annual pilgrimages to Tanglewood and were excited and proud that their daughter lived and worked in the hubbub of their favorite resort. One Sunday, my brother Allan and his longtime girlfriend, Donna, drove up in their vintage Austin-Healey convertible to hang out and drive around the area.

Another weekend in August, my brother Bob arrived with five single male friends to "crash." Friday night, we all stayed in my place with sleeping bags all over the floor and on Saturday, the guys camped out across the street at the state park. We had a great weekend picnicking, drinking, getting high, sunbathing, and sitting on a blanket at the Great Lawn for a Joan Baez concert. There was a lot of sexual tension in the air, with one of Bob's friends latching on to my violinist roommate, and Bob's guitar-playing friend from Holland, Roman, exchanging glances with me for two days. Roman was

Surinamese, born into an aristocratic family that sent him abroad to Holland to receive his education. Roman was a social worker and political activist who shared common interests, so we talked, laughed, and flirted all weekend.

My favorite part of the summer, aside from the myriad of interesting activities, was time spent with Mitch. Though he already had a girlfriend when we met, theirs was an open relationship and he and I spent guilt-free time together. Mitch's secluded house was set on a pond and we jumped off his deck into the water and lay on rubber floats staring up at the tips of the Eastern Hemlocks. As a massage therapist, Mitch was always looking to hone his skills, and we were well matched with his need to touch and my need to be touched. With Mitch, I felt beautiful and desirable.

After two months of this fantasy-like vacation, I began to think about my next move. While at Cornell, I completed an internship at a residential treatment center for adolescents, where I co-led groups, counseled the girls, and ran creative drama programs. I loved the work and considered becoming a social worker. That summer in psych class at Berkshire Community College, I was introduced to Gestalt therapy and was so intrigued, that I resolved instead to become a Gestalt therapist.

To demonstrate Gestalt, Professor Gilbert cut through layers of rhetoric to help us connect with our deepest feelings. I was intrigued by the Empty Chair technique, in which I confronted my mother, furious at her for harping on my weight. I had to switch seats back and forth, until both views became clear. At age 20, though slightly more sympathetic to Mom's outlook, I was far from ready to forgive her for my hurt.

One of our class assignments was to write an epithet for our tombstone. I envisioned that at 95, mine would read: She moved mountains. With my newly acquired "aha" moments, I believed I had the gift to help others discover theirs and now I had the medium. I no longer wanted to be an actress or a rabbi; I wanted to be a Gestalt therapist. I fantasized that in the process, I'd stumble upon my own giant breakthrough—the one that would finally make me thin.

I was having so much fun and learning so much that I made a new plan to live in Western Massachusetts and begin my therapy career. All summer, driving down country roads listening to James Taylor, I was drawn to the lyrics in "Sweet Baby James":

Now the first of December was covered with snow
And so was the turnpike from Stockbridge to Boston
Lord, the Berkshires seemed dream-like on account of that frosting
With ten miles behind me and ten thousand more to go.

Stockbridge seemed as good a place as any and I noticed that Austen Riggs Psychiatric Center was three blocks from my house. I hiked up the long driveway to the majestic white building with its beautifully manicured lawn and submitted a job application at the front desk.

As I waited for a response, Labor Day came and went, and with it, a major change came over my little town. Traffic cleared out, streets emptied, storekeepers looked weary, and I grew despondent. Beyond the elementary school bake sales and church breakfasts, there was almost nothing to do—at least for someone young, single, and itching to start an exciting post-college life. "What happened to the cultural mecca I was living in?" I asked the locals.

"Season's over. Tourists and summer folk gone home."

Disappointed and lost, and not having heard from Riggs, I packed my bags and headed home. I hadn't lived with my parents for three years and though my college town was confining, I knew their suburb would feel oppressive. I had to devise a strategy; there was no way I could stay there long without going stir-crazy. A full year ahead of schedule on my life plan, I hadn't really thought about, much less decided, what I was going to do when I graduated college. Returning home seemed like the only thing that made sense at the moment.

CHAPTER SEVENTEEN

WANDERING JEW

After arriving home, I contacted Shira, newly discharged from her stint in the Israeli army, and asked her if she wanted company for a year. She was jubilant. Just as Shira was an honorary Meislin, I was an honorary Gilman. Although I was going to live with Shira and her parents, they weren't *my* parents and modern Tel Aviv was no Orthodox Spring Valley.

I missed Shira. I had met a lot of girls over the last three years. Yet, after each move, I severed ties with them because I never felt the closeness, ease, or loyalty that I had with my best friend. I was eager to see Shira again but also scared; what if she already had a new best friend, or a boyfriend? Where would that leave me?

I spent the next six weeks in Spring Valley, observing the Jewish holidays with my family and getting ready to leave. Mom noticed that I regained some of the weight I had lost at school and was back to size 16. It was hard to measure an exact size as the big beaded Indian kaftans and colorful peasant blouses came in sizes L and XL—the bigger, the better. Mom dropped a hint about a new diet-pill doctor a few towns away. I jumped at the opportunity for a miracle cure. Armed with an arsenal of multi-colored pills, water pills, and vitamins, I began my diet, even escorting Mom on occasion to Jack LaLanne, where my mother was the Esther Williams of water aerobics. I lost weight fast dropping six pounds in the first week, then four, then stabilizing at about 2 pounds per week.

Mom was only too happy to take me shopping for form-fitting clothes such as polyester pantsuits, knit dresses, bathing suits, and cover-ups. Mom's ultimate thrill was browsing the size-12 rack in the "normal" department of "normal" clothing stores. We spent a fortune, but both of us were very happy with the purchases and with each other. I spent hours in front of three-way mirrors, daring to take in my rear view—I had not owned fitted clothes in years! What a change from my shapeless gypsy costumes, long hippie skirts with bright colorful flowers and paisley prints. I splurged on a beaded see-through cover-up for my bathing suit, imagining myself a bronze goddess sunning on a chaise lounge at the Red Sea in Eilat, while sexy dark Sabras engaged me in conversation.

Because we did so much shopping, Mom and I split the driving. When it was my turn, I was having a hard time controlling my starts and stops; they were jerky and erratic. After screeching to a stop at two different traffic lights, and nearly skidding into the car in front of us at the mall, I allowed Mom to be the chauffeur. I had no idea why I was driving so poorly. As a cab driver, I had gotten many compliments on my driving and now I didn't even trust myself. Weeks later, when I went off the diet pills and my driving stabilized, I realized that being on speed was not conducive to operating a moving vehicle.

Mom bought me so many new clothes that when I arrived at the airport, the ticket agent told me I had to leave one suitcase behind because the baggage weight was excessive. Standing in front of the El Al counter, Mom and I squatted down on the ground switching items from suitcase to suitcase, unraveling underwear, shorts, tops, deodorant, shampoo, and boxes of Tampax. As we held up each item, I had to make an immediate decision whether it went into Suitcase 1 or Suitcase 2, which Mom promised to ship as soon as possible. The pressure was so high, I couldn't contain myself and began sobbing into my new skinny clothes and the two open suitcases while a line of irate passengers grumbled for me to move over and get out of the way.

Mom calmed me down and in a soothing voice told me everything would be fine. I could tell that she and Dad were nervous, too. There was a big question mark about how long I'd be gone and what I'd be doing and why I was even going in the first place. All these submerged tensions funneled themselves into a suitcase calamity, and I couldn't control my emotions. The diet pill amphetamine-withdrawal added to my agitation and separation anxiety.

Weeping, I kissed and hugged Mom and Dad and set out alone for the 11-hour trip. As soon as I found my seat and calmed down, I felt guilty about the distress I had just caused my parents. I had no way of letting them know right away that I was fine and I wasn't crying anymore. I took out my stationary and composed a five-page letter telling Mom and Dad that I was all right and they didn't need to worry about me. I was looking forward to my trip and was sorry I put them through such an emotional roller coaster. I also told them about 10 times how much I loved them.

I landed in Tel Aviv. Shira greeted me at the airport screaming, "Mashinka!" and I yelled back, "Shirala!" as we both ran to each other. The first thing we said after we hugged was, "Wow, you lost so much weight!" Then we went to eat. Within a week after landing on the hot tarmac in Israel, my second suitcase arrived. None of my new clothes fit. Shira and I ended up back in tunics and dashikis; comfortable, loose fitting, no waistline. We spent the first few weeks visiting Shira's favorite eating spots on Diezengoff Street in Tel Aviv, meeting her friends, and people-watching at outdoor cafes. An Israeli guy we met, Coby, told me about a place called Nueba, a hippie beach in the Sinai desert, where people from all over the world came to "tune out of civilization and find themselves." I tucked that information away for future reference.

Shira and I talked and ate as we reminisced about high school and our exploits on the cross-country trip. I liked teasing her about the time she lost her Ameripass in Albuquerque and we had to double back to Phoenix for a new one. She liked joshing me about how I fumed for two days, acting self-righteous and superior.

After our binges went stale and our stories tattered, I was heartbroken to realize that my best friend and I had drifted apart. While Shira had spent the last few years in the army and was hooked on oldies by Elvis Presley and Chuck Berry, I spent those same years loosening up from my traditional background and embracing a hippie lifestyle, listening to The Moody Blues, Ravi Shankar, and Earth, Wind & Fire. While Shira avoided topics of feelings, that was pretty much all I wanted to discuss. While she would get all dressed up, painting on thick eyeliner and eye shadow, I would sport my wash-and-wear frizzy hair and my natural look and engage people in serious exchanges about higher consciousness. Despite the Gilman generosity, Shira's and my values and lifestyle had diverged and we needed space from each other. I took off for Nueba.

When I arrived in the Sinai Peninsula, I felt the strong sun, lighting up miles and miles. I gazed at the vista of the azure-blue sea and fine, golden sand. Then I looked down the horizon and saw a mish-mosh of shapes. I started to hike over the dunes and as I got closer, I noticed that these shapes were living units; some actual tents, some made out of blankets strung together, some created out of pieces of large driftwood and *shmatas,* torn up rags and filthy beach towels.

I had no idea that I needed to bring my own tent so I had nowhere to sleep that first night. Nils, a Swede, was leaving and told me I could have his makeshift tent, a plastic sheet hanging on twisted hangar wire. Apparently he had said the same thing to Rafi, an Israeli fresh out of seven years in the army. Rafi had deep-set blue eyes, his hair somewhere between a crew cut and a mullet, in an attempt to grow it out, after many years of regulation crewcuts. Rafi was thin and bony, wearing just a loincloth. As I looked around, I realized that he wasn't the only one sporting very few clothes. Some people had bathing suits but the majority had underwear, shorts, kaftans, or nothing at all.

I watched Rafi for a minute as he was reinforcing the wiring on Nils's hut and then summoned the courage to say, "Excuse me, Nils said I could stay here." In a clipped voice, Israeli-style, Rafi replied, "So what's the problem? You can stay with me."

I shared the tent. At night, the atmosphere was very quiet except for the waves patting up against the sand. I could see the sky from inside our hut. The stars were amazing; I had never seen so vast a sky in my life (and never have since). Every few seconds Rafi pointed out another shooting star. He showed me the constellations and I was impressed with his English. We talked for a bit, listened to the people in nearby tents making love, and finally moved closer to each other and cuddled. As the night air was chilly, we were both wearing layers of clothing, which were removed little by little. Sometime in the middle of the night, we kissed and lay together, in the Biblical sense, absorbing the ethereal quality of this remote and mysterious piece of the universe.

Though not quite love at first sight, Rafi became my boyfriend for the next six months. His goal in Nueba was to shake off all the rules from the army, do whatever he felt like, and grow his hair to his waist—which he did. He had been there for several weeks and knew the "regulars"; he introduced me to other young travelers and to the locals, whom he knew by name. Without any specific agenda other than to break with the rigidity of our pasts, Rafi and I and the other nomads spent our time playing in the sand dunes, carving driftwood, and drinking tea and nana (mint) with the Bedouins. In this small tent village, these Israelis and these Arabs co-existed in harmony. Occasionally in the evenings, a group of us would sit in someone's elaborate tent—real canvas—drinking wine, smoking hashish, playing *Sheshbesh* (Backgammon), spitting out sunflower seeds, and there would be a lively discussion among Israelis, Americans, Bedouins, Palestinians, and Europeans. We typically didn't discuss politics, and sometimes we didn't talk at all, just staring at the candle in the beer bottle, wax drippings forming pretty colors on the glass.

In the daytime, we would swim, sleep, eat, and walk around the desert. I became less and less self-conscious as the weeks wore on and had no trouble wearing whatever I felt like at the moment, usually just a kaftan. A major event was to walk miles to the kiosk, where we would buy fresh water and limited groceries, like potatoes, canned vegetables, and *glida*, Israeli ice cream, which we ate right away. I liked the snacks at the kiosk but hated the walk. On the way back, the water jugs were heavy and I had to walk very slowly, especially up the dunes. Rafi was in excellent shape and had no problem carrying most of the containers, and others pitched in to share the load. On the way, we liked to fantasize what it must have been like for our ancestors in ancient times to haul their water for miles over sand dunes in excruciating heat. And they had to supply a whole village, and camels, too. Those of us who had grown up with Bible stories would argue over whether they were literal or metaphorical and whether the very sand we were walking on was part of the exodus of the Israelites from Egypt to Palestine.

After a month, tired of the unstructured days and nights in the desert, I left Rafi at the beach and grabbed a ride back to Tel Aviv with some British tourists. It was common for our hippie group to come and go in Nueba, and I was sure I would see Rafi again. I didn't plan to stay with Shira for long, just long enough to plan my next step. When I reunited with Shira, I shared my adventures and it became clear that this was not her cup of tea.

As I began job hunting, I ran into an old friend from Cornell who was taking classes at Tel Aviv University. She was living in Givatayim, an outskirt of the city, with two other Americans. Attached to their house was a vacant mother-in-law apartment. I moved in, and after a month or so, Rafi came up north and moved in with me. Similar to our first "moving in" together in Nueba, Rafi took it as a given, not a big deal. That forced me to let go of my idyllic notion of love and replace it with a more pragmatic live-in relationship minus true romance. I hoped that passion would follow but I was more enamored of the concept of a boyfriend than the boyfriend himself. Rafi and I were still a couple, but we weren't monogamous. He went back and forth to Nueba, and I would probe into his affairs, but he never asked me about mine. Rafi and I both had strong personalities and strong views and we clashed all the time. He said that for him conflict and disagreement was a sport, and arguing was fun. For me, there was nothing fun about his comments. I called them "criticisms" and he called them "teasing." I stuffed down my anger in falafel with a *rugalach* chaser.

What *was* fun was touring Israel on Rafi's motorcycle, with me seated in the mini sidecar. Five years earlier, I had been to Israel and Europe on a teen tour with Rabbi Weiss and we visited the well-known landmarks: the Wailing Wall, Masada, Yad VaShem. This time, Rafi was introducing me to a different side of the country: unknown beaches, edgy art galleries, shady parks. We drove through a poor but charming section of Jaffa where Rafi grew up, and he took me to his mom's house, where she loved feeding me homemade cakes.

Food in Israel was new and interesting. I sampled falafel in each neighborhood, hummus, pizza, fresh breads. My favorite stops were the patisserie-style bakeries that offered sample-size cakes, baklava, pastries made in Israel and Europe. I tasted them all: cream in the middle, no cream in the middle, milk chocolate, dark chocolate. I ate the fruit filled sweets—with nuts, figs, dates, apricots, none as rich or brightly colored as the Jewish bakeries in New York. The dashikis continued stretching to accommodate my lifestyle.

I found a job tutoring English so I was free to enjoy typical Israeli evenings: A member of our *chevra,* our group, would pop by our house with a few friends or cousins. They would call up other people to join us and we ended up with an alchemy of people from around the globe. Plenty of food materialized out of nowhere, and the area was electric with alcohol, tobacco smoke, hashish-laced cigarettes, and loud discussion, often debates. No one asked permission to bring friends or even strangers. No one thought twice about overstaying their visit, and no one stood on ceremony in terms of expressing views—no matter how radical. This was Israel.

Having a job, apartment, and boyfriend wasn't enough to settle my restlessness, but I avoided introspection. My initial plans were to stay in Israel for another few months, work on a kibbutz, and then travel to Amsterdam to meet up with Roman. Years before, he and my brother Bob had bonded "like brothers" while backpacking through Europe. After Roman met me in the Berkshires, he began sending romantic postcards from breathtaking sites in Europe saying he wanted to take me there. I was swept off my feet with Roman's poetry, his persistence, and his dreamy postcard from Marbella. I agreed to meet up with him on my way home from Israel. I didn't plan ahead much because that trip would occur "on my way home" and I wanted to live in the moment.

My parents were less than thrilled. Though they met Roman when he came to New York and liked him very much (as Bob's friend), they couldn't understand why I would need to travel alone with a man I hardly knew, or why I needed to get involved with a Surinamese man when there were so many Jewish boys. My mother was also a firm believer in the saying, "Why buy the cow when you could get the milk for free?" When I argued that Allan and Bobby were living with their girlfriends, Mom would say, "It's different; they're boys."

In mid-March, I received a long-distance call from my parents. Both Mom and Dad were on the line so I knew it was important. They were strongly suggesting that I come back to the States. A letter had arrived at home inviting me to a group interview for a psychodrama internship in Washington, D.C., which I had applied for back in October. Psychodrama and Gestalt were closely related and this was a unique opportunity to train and get paid. My parents convinced me that I needed to go to the interview. "There aren't many jobs here," Dad said. "There's a gas shortage and a severe recession and jobs are scarce." More important, I knew, Passover was coming and they sounded almost tearful when they asked if I would be home for the *Seders*.

I thought about the *Seders*... home... the family gathered. I thought about Rafi, Shira, Nueba, my life. I was having a good time but still had a big inner hole that remained unfilled, no matter how hard I tried living in the moment and no matter how much food I consumed. Deep down, I knew that I wanted to have my place back at the table, the Meislin table.

I had a very small window to close up my affairs and head home. Rafi had gone back to the beach in Nueba, and there was no way to reach him in the Sinai desert to say goodbye. I called his mom to tell her I was leaving and she was brokenhearted that I was leaving so soon and that her son wouldn't be able to say goodbye. She tracked down the little kiosk in Nueba, miles from his tent, and asked that if Rafi came by to get water, would they please tell him Marcia's leaving the country? My friends and I pulled together a last-minute ad-hoc party. I was glad Shira came; even though we weren't close day-to-day, we meant a lot to each other.

The night before the final get-together, Rafi magically appeared on his bike. He had seen his mom's cryptic message posted at the kiosk. He abandoned his driftwood sculptures, bid farewell to the Bedouins, and headed back north to say goodbye. He couldn't understand why I was leaving so soon. It was hard to explain that my restless spirit was still trying to find a home. And like a homing pigeon, I never missed a Meislin *Seder*. Though I wasn't sure what would cure my emotional and spiritual hunger, some part of me knew that coming home would have a palliative effect.

Another strong part of me was determined not to miss my planned rendezvous with Roman. During my stopover in Amsterdam on the way home, Roman and I had only two days together—not quite the months we had planned to spend crossing Europe in his car. We toured the windmills, the red-light district, flower shops. Then I boarded a plane to fly home.

With apprehension, I kept thinking "How will I face my mother?" I was easily 50 pounds heavier than when I left, back when we had gone shopping together and she was deliriously happy that I was thin. How will I reveal the live-in boyfriend? How will I rationalize the time (and some of their money) spent without much to show for it? And how can I explain that even though Shira had been like a twin sister, she and I didn't really click anymore? And forget the beach, the nudity, the hashish, and the sex—that would never be confessed.

Though I had left hungering for a "geographic cure," my experiences halfway across the world hadn't produced the results I had hoped for. I anticipated with panic Mom's nonverbal greeting; she used words when I lost weight, glares when I gained.

At the airport, Mom and Dad were so relieved I was home that Mom's customary ritual of looking me up and down didn't even take place. Our family would be reunited for the Jewish holidays. That is what mattered most to my parents—that and having Marcia back on the same continent.

Shortly after my return, I drove to Washington, D.C., to audition with 30 other people in a group interview for the much-coveted paid internship. After rushing back from abroad, I didn't get the job. This was a huge disappointment for me and I didn't know how to deal with the setback. I used my interrupted travels through Israel and Europe as another lightning rod for all my feelings of anger and resentment at my parents. I had hoped to return home only after I had grown up and settled some of my internal anxiety, after I had sown my wild oats and *was ready* to come home. Instead, I was lying on my twin bed, staring at the black-and-orange wallpaper, having just frittered away what would have been my senior year in college. At 21, I asked myself the familiar question with a new sense of urgency: "What now?"

CHAPTER EIGHTEEN

NEW AGE

Within a few months, I decided to move to Cambridge, Massachusetts. Ads in the hip *New Age Journal* confirmed that the area was a hot spot for many of my interests—yoga, Gestalt therapy, holistic health, creative drama, and Jewish renewal. I borrowed Mom's silver-gray Oldsmobile Cutlass and drove northeast toward the Boston YWCA. Never having driven in Boston before, I was completely baffled by the traffic rotaries. I would circle around and around before I could figure out where to exit. I also had trouble navigating the downtown maze of tiny streets that changed names and direction midstream. I got lost so many times and was so disoriented that I almost turned back to New York. Later I was informed that these streets were horse paths before being paved over for automobiles. I think they were better suited for horses than for cars.

I finally arrived at the Y and spent the night in a pristine room with a shared bathroom down the hall. While I was scared to be in this place by myself, I also felt bold and courageous. I enjoyed the intellectual challenge of exploring new places and ignored the fear. The next morning, I vacated the room, certain I would find a better place to live. I ventured out, ready to embark on my new life. First stop: Boston Gestalt Institute. I held their ad in my hand, stating that I could receive training and become a Gestalt therapist. I met the director upstairs in a charming little house the Institute occupied near Harvard Square. He seemed to be truly sorry when he told me that not only was the class full, but there was a waiting list. Noticing how disappointed I was, he suggested I inquire across the street where there might be a graduate program in education.

The sign on the door across the street read Institute of Open Education/Antioch Graduate Center. I was intrigued by the Antioch reference, as that was one of the nontraditional schools I had researched as a high school senior. Antioch's undergrad college was in Ohio, and I was delighted to stumble upon one of its satellite graduate programs.

Inside this non–institutional-looking building, I was greeted by Ginny, a warm, smiling administrator, who told me that the school was geared for teachers to earn an accredited master's degree during weekends, evenings, and two full-time summer sessions. July's session started in a few weeks, and there were openings.

As Ginny spoke I became very excited. Then she said, "You'll have to get a job right away because the program is based around your job or internship. One of our faculty members will be a mentor for your work." I was unnerved by the thought of finding a job in so short a time but I felt as if somehow my life was falling into place. I asked her if I could take a job in counseling or mental health; would that qualify?

Ginny said that would work as they already had a small percentage of students who were guidance counselors or youth workers. But the existing track was definitely for teachers, so I would have to tailor my own program.

No problem, I thought. That's my specialty: being an outsider.

Ginny handed me the application together with a student loan form. The first question had me stymied. "I'm sorry. I can't fill out the address; I don't have one. I'm staying at the Y and looking for a place to live."

With a broad smile, Ginny replied, "I have a room for rent, a mile or two down the street in Central Square. If you're willing to live with me and my two daughters in a total mess, come have a look. If you come back here at 5:00 this afternoon, I'll bring you over."

My Aunt Bea's favorite Yiddish expression came to me just then: "This is *bashert! It's meant to be!*" Part of me was convinced that kismet was at work and the other part of me thought: Are you crazy? Who is this person? And this program? Is it legit? I listened to my gut and decided to trust what was happening. At 5:00, I followed Ginny to her place, took one look at the room and her two bare-footed young girls and said yes on the spot. The next morning, I completed the paperwork, and called my parents to tell them I would start graduate school in a few weeks. They were stunned but relieved that I had a plan. I drove back to New York, returned Mom's car, and rode the bus back to Boston.

On the first day of school, we were assigned core groups. When I walked into mine, the professor handed me an envelope. It said "Principal." For the next two hours, we were going to simulate a school environment, and I was to be Principal Marcia. I was the youngest in the class with a roomful of experienced teachers, so my first inclination was to panic. But we were on the clock, and my first staff meeting was scheduled in four minutes. In the meantime, there were memos to review, unruly students to address, and an irate parent itching to speak to me. For two hours, I led the school, the teachers, the students, and the board meeting. No grass grew under my feet.

In the de-brief afterwards, I got criticized for trying to do too much, take on too many issues at one time, move too fast. I was told by some old-timers, "You can't be all things to all people." But most of the feedback was very positive, including my professor's. Despite the few naysayers, I loved it. I loved being in charge. I loved tackling a variety of challenges and working through all of them. I loved making decisions, solving problems, building a team, and turning around resistant people. I loved standing in front of a captive audience giving presentations, articulating a vision with passion and persuasiveness. By the end of the two hours, I was hooked on leadership and public speaking.

That night, Ginny asked if I wanted to go to a club. She and her straight friends frequented Boston's gay nightclubs, where the music mix was so stimulating you could dance all night. Pumped up from the day's activities, I dressed in clubbing clothes and with Ginny's guidance, fluffed out my big hair and added the right amount of lip gloss. I expressed doubts that I would fit in, but she assured me that lots of straight people went to these discos and there'd be interesting men from all over the world. "You'll love it," she told me.

She was right. I walked into my first colorful, crowded, cavernous nightclub in the South End. Young, and filled with confidence as a leader, I glittered in a sexy white dress, dark tan, high-heeled shoes tied at the calves, slathered in musk and lavender body essences. It didn't matter that I was fat. It didn't matter that my curly hair was a ball of frizz. For the first time in my life, I noticed a roomful of eyes staring at me when I entered. I felt lit up from within and I knew that I sparkled.

For a girl who could never keep up with a simple *hora* or follow any prescribed steps in jazzercise or aerobics classes, I hustled, discoed, moved my body, and pulsed around the floor taking in the gazes and ignoring any harsh internal critics. As Donna Summer was moaning, "Love to love you, Baby," I danced with gay men, straight men, black men, Latino men, a handful of white men, gay women, straight women, groups, couples. I didn't care. The music was right, my self-assurance was high, and nothing held me back from moving my body and experiencing the euphoria of the evening.

I was so turned on by the experience that the next day I signed up for a disco class at the Joy of Movement Center. The hustle suited me. It was fast-paced, rhythmic, not too complicated, and a dance that I could do for a long time without getting bored because of its infinite variations. I grabbed at the chance to have the instructor as my partner and relaxed into the rubber band–like tension of his pull. He was in charge, but for the first time in my life, I enjoyed following. I also liked practicing with other women in the room (five women to every man). I frequently got to play the lead and call the shots.

Ginny and I went out often, sometimes with a group of people, sometimes with her flame of the week, sometimes just the two of us. I found a vintage store in Boston where I bought a few funky outfits. Dressing up, accessorizing, and dancing became my new hobby.

With an inner glow and a diminishing timeline, I had to find a job. Though I thrived on leading workshops and groups, I still wanted to be a therapist and applied for a mental health worker position at the prestigious McLean Hospital, Harvard's psychiatric teaching center. By midsummer I secured an interview with Mr. Burton in Personnel. The meeting was extraordinary. We had a stimulating dialogue and he told me he was impressed with my background, drive, and creativity. I was sure I'd get the job.

I didn't hear from Mr. Burton for several weeks despite my many phone calls and a gracious follow-up thank-you note. It seems he was always "in a meeting." One day, I dressed in my very best clothes, boarded the #73 bus to the end of Waverly Square in Belmont, crossed Trapelo Road and Pleasant Street, and walked the steep hill to the hospital. I found my way again to the Personnel Office and walked up to the secretary (I was sure she'd remember me) asking to see Mr. Burton.

"He's in a meeting."

"OK, thanks, I'll just wait."

"Do you have an appointment?"

"No, but I haven't been able to get hold of him, and I really need to talk with him."

"Mr. Burton will be in meetings all day. You can leave him a note."

"Oh, that's OK," I said, ignorant of professional protocol, "I'll just wait here until he's free."

The secretary looked at me as if I had two heads. But Mr. Burton's reaction to me during my interview convinced me that there was a job waiting for me, so I would wait for him. For two hours I sat as the secretary popped her head out every 30 minutes to tell me I really should leave. She wasn't angry, just persistent. And I wasn't rude, just determined. So I waited some more. I read every piece of literature I could find about the hospital: annual reports, brochures, newspaper clippings. I had no doubt this was the place to begin my career.

Finally, after realizing that his door never opened, I decided to write Mr. Burton a note. I wrote that I was in his waiting room, that I really wanted an entry-level job at McLean, that he had given me very positive feedback during the interview, and that the job was still posted as vacant. I slipped the note under his door.

Within 30 seconds, the door opened, and there stood Mr. Burton. "Come in," he said, laughing. "You sure have moxie." Though I wasn't quite sure what "moxie" meant, it sounded optimistic. Mr. Burton told me that although he no longer had an opening for a mental health worker, he saw me as a good fit for the Clinical Educator Aide opening in the Psychoeducation Unit, a school within the therapeutic environment. The children in the in-patient unit had individualized curriculum and treatment plans, and I would help with teaching, counseling, workshop design and delivery, creative arts, and interdisciplinary treatment meetings. I accepted at once; this job sounded even better than the original.

Autumn that year became very busy. The daily commute to the hospital via public transportation was long. The job was rewarding but exhausting. Attending school two nights a week and doing homework kept me going at a good clip. On weekends I still went dancing with Ginny, though I was beginning to meet new friends at school and work. My asthma was under control some of the time, but climbing the sharp incline to work usually triggered my wheezing. I tried to stagger my commute, so I didn't end up walking with anyone else because I was embarrassed at how long it took me to get up the hill. For some reason, the dancing didn't set off any attacks.

Much as I loved hanging out with Ginny, I couldn't continue to live in the mess and chaos of her apartment. Though I kept my room clean and tried to pitch in with the rest of the house, there were always stacks of dirty dishes, morsels of food everywhere, wet, dirty towels all over the bathroom floor, and piles of clothes—some clean, some not—that you had to move to find a place to sit. Ginny made jokes about her lack of domesticity and even did a thorough cleaning every now and then, but I needed to live in a place that was less cluttered and sticky.

I scoured ads for apartments right in Harvard Square, in the middle of the action. The roommate interviews were rigorous. Three weeks later, I "matched" and moved into a four-bedroom prototypical Cambridge apartment: tree-lined street, high ceilings, natural-wood built-ins, walking distance to the Square, and a myriad of ethnic restaurants within a four-block radius. I didn't much like the women who lived there but "location, location, location" seemed paramount. My gut said, "These are not nice people. They are snobs and have a superior attitude, and you won't feel comfortable here." I overrode my gut and moved to The Square.

It wasn't long before I realized my mistake. The women in my apartment were bright but snooty. They came and went without even looking over their shoulder at me. I acted as if it didn't matter and tried to find a place for myself. I felt so rejected by this puritanical New England conclave, a place where I thought I could feel at home. Even though my New Age magazines promoted Cambridge, and specifically Harvard Square, as a Mecca of liberalism and openness, the neighborhood didn't feel liberal or open to me. I found it ironic that two miles down the road, I had lived in the land of faux leopard skins and exotic nightclub jaunts and that seemed real. Now I lived among the middle-class Ivy League elite in the land of pure cashmere and natural fibers and that world felt phony and superficial.

One night, a few weeks after I moved to Harvard Square, I started to get short of breath and developed a pounding headache. Although I was used to shortness of breath, this was different; as if my chest were being crushed and my head were in a vise. I needed help and had no idea where to turn. Most of the time when I was sick, I would go off to my room and talk myself through it, but this time felt more severe and I didn't think I could get through it alone. Ginny was away for the weekend, and I didn't have phone numbers for my new work and school acquaintances.

I called one of my roommates at her friend's house and asked if she could take me to the emergency room. I told her I was in a lot of pain and was afraid to go by myself. "We're having a party," she said, "and I can't leave." She hung up. Her dismissive tone threw me. I never asked for help; when I did, it meant that I was in dire need and couldn't manage my way out by myself. She had no way of knowing this, but I still thought it was shocking that someone who had brought me in as a roommate (after layers and weeks of screening) didn't have the courtesy to help me out or offer alternatives.

With no one left to call in Boston or Cambridge, I decided to call Rafi, my Israeli ex-boyfriend, whose extensive army training provided some medical know-how. Rafi had sworn he'd never move to the United States, but he was now living in Manhattan with a former girlfriend. He asked me questions to rule out a heart attack, talked with me for a while, and told me to lie down and try to sleep, which I did. When I woke up at three in the morning, I still had shortness of breath but was stable enough to talk myself through the terror and discomfort. Somehow I endured the long night, and in the morning, I felt better.

That morning, I decided to move out of that apartment. I know I didn't suffer from an asthma attack that night, even though the apartment had mold and mildew from the musty old Oriental rugs. No, I had an anxiety attack and it was time to give up my dreams about fitting in to Harvard Square. Maybe it was time to give up my dreams about fitting in anywhere. I wondered if my early experience of feeling like an outsider was going to follow me throughout my life.

Would I ever stop living in the margins?

CHAPTER NINETEEN

MICE IN MY CHEST

Moving from Harvard Square down Mass. Ave. to Inman Square on Broadway was like traveling to another country, even though both were in Cambridge. Broadway was offbeat, diverse, and unpretentious. A block away from where I lived were jazz clubs, and on our street were working adults, not just college kids. After my prior experience with roommates in Harvard Square, I was attracted to an ad in the local paper that mentioned "building a community," not just sharing a house. The two women who interviewed me, Trisha and Randy, asked nothing about what college I had attended, my GPA, or my future goals. Unlike the interrogations up the street, our meeting was a casual get-to-know-you discussion and free-for-all. We felt instant camaraderie and comfort with each other, and two days later, I moved in with them.

The outside of our pale yellow house with brown shutters was shabby yet inviting. Three rickety steps led to the front porch where a moth-eaten settee looked as if it had been parked in the same spot for decades. On the second floor were Trisha and Randy's rooms and the communal bathroom. I had to climb two sets of stairs leading to my charming attic room with asymmetrical eaves and casement windows.

Trisha and Randy worked long hours in the anti-nuke movement and in women's health centers, and persuaded the entire household to be more conscious of environmental issues. In the 1970s, we each had recycling chores, organic cooking responsibilities, and food co-op duties long before most of the country had ever heard of "going green."

All of this was an adjustment for me. I often made mistakes when it was my turn to shop, or whined when we voted to give up yet another luxury item like Styrofoam takeout containers. Soft, squeezable toilet paper was replaced by rough, enviro-friendly, 100% postconsumer-recycled toilet "cardboard." And we didn't own a TV. When I acted pouty or crabby, Trish and Randy challenged my acting-out behavior with humor. Rather than castigate me and make me feel guilty, they taught me to laugh at my own sense of entitlement, comparing me to those very princesses I had spent my life denigrating.

Despite our differences, I bonded quickly with the two women. I was stirred by their passion for social and political activism. Shortly after I moved in, they were arrested for protesting the Seabrook Nuclear Power Plant in New Hampshire. Within a few days, a political advocacy group negotiated for their release. Our house was often the site of political meetings and strategy sessions with like-minded activists. Although I had dabbled in sit-ins and anti-war moratoriums in high school, I was overwhelmed by Trisha and Randy's level of commitment.

While I was inspired by their dedication and generosity, Trisha and Randy enjoyed my zest for life and willingness to learn. We spent a lot of time talking about life, politics, oppression, nonviolent civil disobedience, our feelings, and ourselves. Both women wanted to understand as much as they could about Judaism and relished their experiences at the Meislin Family Seders. In turn, I soaked up Trish's stories about growing up Quaker and her adult experiences in Unitarian churches. We all studied Eastern religions, tried Eastern medicine, and explored the mind-body connection. We experimented with medicinal teas, homeopathic remedies, hypnosis, and acupressure points. As I discovered a new avenue for weight loss, I tested colonics and intestinal flushing treatments. One acupuncturist sold me metal balls to tape behind my ears and squeeze every time I felt hungry. While our holistic jaunts were eye-opening and avant-garde, so were the prices, and my roommates and I weren't flush enough to cover the long-term commitment required for results.

The best times at home were when Randy pulled out her guitar and played folk songs as we sang along; sometimes she made up songs on the spot. We were quite a threesome: Randy in little hippie sundresses, Trisha in sensible L.L. Bean outdoorsy clothes, and me in my leftover vintage outfits minus the funky accessories.

The lone man moved out and Nick, a self-proclaimed "neurotic," moved into the room next door. Nick and Trisha enrolled in co-counseling, a form of peer counseling, to help them unleash their hidden emotions. When it was Nick or Trisha's night to host, Randy and I would sit on the steps and gawk at the twelve peer counselors who incited each other to scream, sob, cackle, and shake. As the decibel level increased, my own level of anxiety increased. Eventually, Randy and I would sneak into her room and let out our own giggles and jitters with each other. I may have been Sarah Bernhardt in my family, but I couldn't hold a candle to the public display of emotion that went on in our Cambridge house. Though the whole re-evaluation counseling drama made me uncomfortable, I was still relieved to live with people who weren't afraid to examine their feelings, childhoods, and insecurities.

Living in this third location in Cambridge didn't seem to help my asthma. I was a frequent visitor to the hospital two blocks away where doctors would administer epinephrine shots, have me lie down for a while, and then send me home. The shots lasted only a short time, but at least I had a chance to catch my breath before the next attack. Many times, doctors prescribed adrenaline-type drugs and steroids—and I would shuffle home, half an inch at a time, my lungs not yet open, with hormones and speed raging through my body.

Despite my newfound sense of community, I went to emergency rooms alone and coped with my illness alone. When my wheezing was so bad it could be heard by others, I retreated to my room and locked the door in disgrace. Alone, I would calculate how to manage my meds, still my coughing, and find enough oxygen to take another breath. I had nothing to offer other people when I could barely breathe myself, so I withdrew and waited till I felt well enough to pretend I was fine and be of interest to others.

On one of the many afternoons when my coughing and wheezing were at their peak, my housemate Trisha knocked on my door: "Can I come in?"

"I'll talk to you later," I barely could get the words past my labored breathing.

"I'd really like to see you. Can you unlock your door?"

"Later," I wheezed.

"Please, open up. I want to help you."

"There's nothing you can do. I'll be fine."

"I could sit with you."

This was humiliating. How could I let anyone witness my excruciating struggle just to utter a single word? Finally I said, "Trisha, I don't let anyone see me when I'm like this."

She didn't leave my door. I was pit-bullish, but she was worse.

"I want to sit with you. I care about you. I love you. Maybe sitting together would help."

I have no idea why I acquiesced. No one had ever lasted that long, not even Mom or Dad. When my parents ministered to me with that sad sense of helplessness, I would persuade them to leave me, insisting, "I'm fine. Don't worry. I'm fine." And then I was left on my own to catch my breath and nurse myself to sleep.

But that day I actually slid off the bed, walked over to the door, and unlocked it for Trisha. When I let her in, I said, "I can't be much of a friend right now."

"I'm here to be a friend to you, to support you. Maybe I can just sit next to you or rub your back."

"No," I said. "I never let anyone see me this way. I sound like I have mice in my chest."

She laughed, and so did I. That day I let her sit next to me for an hour, rubbing my back. I was amazed that although the wheezing didn't cease, my labored breathing calmed down. I was more relaxed.

I was being taken care of and no longer had to struggle on my own. It was a real turning point: in that one afternoon, I learned to accept help, that I did not have to be perfect in front of others, and that I could let go of the shame I'd felt at being "defective."

Throughout my life, so many "well-meaning" people had opinions: "If you just lose weight, your asthma will get better," or "Asthma is psychosomatic; you can control your symptoms," or "Asthmatics have attacks to get attention." With Trisha's help, I knew that day that it wasn't my fault. I was sick, and I had an illness. Having asthma didn't make me a bad person.

Trish didn't pass judgment or make any of those hurtful comments. All she said was, "I want to be here with you. I'm fine with you just the way you are. You're my friend. I don't need anything from you, and I just want to be a support." For the first time ever, it felt OK to have someone see me battle the mice in my chest. To be comforted and not have to give back. That day, the day I let Trish in the door, was my first true experience with intimacy.

CHAPTER TWENTY

N'ORLINS

I spent two years living on Broadway with Trisha and Randy as I completed my master's, worked at two professional jobs, and learned how to become a responsible member of a household. After my initial hesitation, I embraced the food co-op, the recycling chores, and the pride that came from paying rent with my own paycheck. As busy as I was, and as generous and loving as my roommates were, a familiar sensation began to re-emerge, "I've got to get out of here."

After graduation, I was still working at the hospital when a prominent and authoritarian psychoanalyst took over our unit on an interim basis and tightened the rules, managing with more of an iron fist. I volunteered to represent my co-workers and share our concerns at an upcoming staff meeting. I spent many hours preparing my comments in order to sound professional and composed. As I spoke up in the meeting, I looked around me, expecting to see supportive faces. Instead my peers were stone-faced, happy to have me representing them in the face of an unresponsive management team. By playing "hero" (or maybe "martyr"), I had put my own career on the line.

By the end of the meeting, it was clear that my efforts were in vain and our administration was unmoved. One of my mentors, a staff psychologist, had observed my behavior in the meeting and called me into his office. Off-the-record he told me he thought I was well-spoken and persuasive with strong leadership skills, but I had to learn to pick and choose my battles. He suggested I keep a low profile for now as I was perceived by senior management as a "rebellious child." I thanked him for his honesty. Despite his sound advice, this incident wasn't the last time in my career that I went headlong into battle on my white horse, yelling "Charge!" only to turn around and see that I was alone.

Shortly after, James Robinson, a colleague from graduate school, offered me a job as assistant career education coordinator at a middle school in an inner city Boston neighborhood. It was a start-up grant and I liked the idea of creating something out of nothing. I also liked the idea that funding was for six months and would give me time to test out a school environment, which I hoped was less stifling and depressing than a mental hospital. I jumped to take the job.

James was charged with designing a bilingual career resource center in a corner of the gym where students could poke their heads in to learn about careers and job skills and research local high schools. Since James didn't want to be involved day-to-day, he empowered me to build the center myself. Using partitions, I created a small, inviting room with a hooked rug and two arm chairs lined with English and Spanish books about careers, values, and educational choices. With my Berlitz crash course in Spanish, I was able to converse with a seventh grader, Maria, about her dream to be a nurse, and an eighth grader, DJ, about which Boston high school offered the best courses in journalism.

I loved having autonomy and working with a team of two neighborhood aides who were assigned part-time to the center. Despite their limited English and my limited Spanish, we were able to achieve a comfortable space for the students, teachers, and parents to ask questions, explore options, and interact with state-of-the-art vocational software. The only challenge came when the principal or superintendent dropped in to speak to James, and I had to cover up for my boss who was rarely there. My standard line (per his instruction) was that James was out in the field scouting locations for class trips. Each grade was entitled to one field trip to explore an industry.

James had decided that the eighth grade would visit Provincetown, a Cape Cod beach resort over two hours away, and he would chaperone that trip. The students would travel by bus and their itinerary consisted of a whale watch and lecture by the whaler captain and crew. Carmela, one of the outspoken aides, asked me repeatedly, "What kind of job is that for a child from this community? Who is ever going to be captain of a whale-watching boat?" I shrugged my shoulders and said nothing. On "trip day," I heard a buzz about school before I actually saw for myself: James, a 6-foot-3, good-looking African-American man showed up at school with earrings and a full face of blush, eye shadow, mascara, and lipstick. He had a head wrap and tight-fitting T-shirt emphasizing his six-pack. It was 1977, and no one in Roxbury had ever seen a male faculty member with a do-rag, earrings, and makeup at school.

The buses were waiting and James, head high, escorted the eighth graders to the bus as they drove off to P-town, to learn about careers in whale watching. Two class parents watched the students as they walked around town while James periodically appeared and disappeared.

The story lit up the grapevine for weeks. I refused to engage in the gossip, although a part of me enjoyed the fact that I was the "normal" one for a change. Nevertheless, I kept my nose to the grindstone and organized events and speakers to keep the students busy until school ended. The career fair, which my aides and I organized, attracted the attention of local celebrities and school board members. The two aides threw me a party to thank me for my dedication to their children and the community and I was very moved by their gifts and their gratitude.

As a result of this job and my exposure to key administrators, I was invited to co-author a workbook for the Boston Public Schools titled *Careers: The Path to Your Future,* a curriculum used in all middle and high schools. I worked with two other teachers and a graphic designer on this grant. My parents proudly displayed their copy of the yellow softcover manual telling all their friends, "Marcia wrote her first book!"

After the book was published and the funding ran out, I looked for another job. My professional life had been so compelling that I hadn't time to think about how unhappy I was with my social life. My two roommates, Trisha and Randy, though straight, had become politically active in the gay and lesbian community, and I no longer felt at home in my house. My school friends—teachers—were mostly minorities, at least ten years older than me, and I didn't fit comfortably into their world, either. Colleagues at my various jobs were friends at work, not outside of work, and we didn't keep in touch after I left the job.

An old beau named Pete owned a Mexican import store and every year he traveled to Mexico to stock up for Christmas. I had met Pete while living at home the summer between freshman and sophomore years; I was 18, he was 38. One night, looking for something to do, I found a craft fair at the local college. Surveying the room, I was drawn to an artsy-looking older man standing behind a table of Mexican imports. Pete was explaining different grades of onyx to potential customers and in between, shot lusty glances my way. I meandered over to his booth and it wasn't long after Pete and I flirted and chatted that he asked me to have dinner with him after the show. Pete and I went out for sushi. I had never heard of sushi and scanned the raw fish menu for several minutes before I found a vegetarian entrée. Soused on sake and seduction, Pete and I drifted from the restaurant to his bohemian apartment upstairs. That night began a torrid summer affair that lasted until I went back to college. When I left, Pete extended an open invitation for me to accompany him on any of his annual trips to Mexico. "It's quite an adventure," he promised.

Now I was 22, and hungry for adventure. Without a job and with a dwindling social life, I was eager to leave Boston for a few months. I didn't realize when I said "yes" that Pete's new girlfriend, Maggie, would also be coming. When I found that out, I wanted to back out but we had already begun making arrangements.

My parents were not fans of Pete's at all. Though he was Jewish, they didn't like that he was almost double my age, divorced with three children, with a sinister quality about him. The very traits I liked—his confidence, cockiness, take-charge attitude, his exotic store with interesting artifacts including drug paraphernalia—were exactly the qualities my parents hated. They didn't trust him and they certainly didn't want me to travel to another country with him. I'm not sure if they were relieved to find out that Maggie, a nice Catholic school girl, would be traveling in the bus with us but for me, it wasn't exactly my vision of the trip Pete and I had talked about for the past four years.

We left Rockland for Mexico in a huge hollowed-out yellow school bus: Pete—bald on top with thinning hair on the sides forming into a goatee—in the driver's seat, skinny Maggie, with her plain khaki shorts and tank top, sitting behind the driver, Pete's three young children sharing a seat across from Maggie (they were getting dropped off at Grandma's in Mexico), and me, sitting behind Maggie in the last seat on the bus. The rest of the bus was empty, waiting to be filled with Mexican artifacts.

I liked Maggie, sometimes more than I liked Pete. To save money, we shared a hotel room, with Pete and Maggie in one double bed and me in the other by myself. Though I wasn't attracted to Pete anymore, I did peek when they were making love, hoping they didn't catch me playing "voyeur." I spent those long nights berating myself for agreeing to go with another couple and putting myself through the loneliness and jealousy. I rationalized that it was a small price to pay when the alternative was looking for a new job and staying in Boston. Pete had also suggested that I pick up extra merchandise for myself at the dirt-cheap prices he could negotiate (his ex-wife was Mexican and had many contacts) and sell it at flea markets for extra cash. I scraped up whatever cash I could from friends and relatives to capitalize on this opportunity. Despite Mom and Dad's reluctance about the trip, Mom gave me some money to buy her a turquoise ring. I think it was Mom's excuse to give me pocket money without condoning my actions.

Pete was concerned that he had gotten a late start for Christmas buying, and he pushed the old bus to its limit. Somewhere near Louisiana, the bus sputtered and made dangerous creaking noises, forcing Pete to stop at a gas station. The attendant wiped his brow with his oily rag and in his southern twang, declared that the bus needed two days' repair. I rolled my eyes in exasperation when I heard the news. "No way I'm staying in Picayune, Mississippi, for two days. How far are we from New Orleans?"

"It's N'Orlins, ma'am, and you can get a bus right there on the corner."

It didn't take long for me to pack an overnight bag and bid adieu to Pete and Maggie. "See you in two days!"

The public bus to N'Orlins smelled of cheap wine and piss. But something happened to me when the bus reached its destination and I arrived at The Big Easy. The energy. The buzz. Music blaring from funky jazz outlets. People all over the streets. Catcalls. Very forward men. And Zac.

Zac was part Creole, part African-American. Light skin with freckles and red hair in a short ponytail. His eyes bored into mine the minute my feet hit the sidewalk. Yes, by golly, this place was electric.

Zac offered to show me around. After several stuffy years in Boston, this city was party paradise, and Zac, the ultimate tour guide. His hybrid energy fused with a rush of sultriness and exotica that coursed through me in this pulsating, offbeat town. With a nonstop adrenaline rush, we roamed the streets, gasping at the uninhibited and vibrant sensuality of this town. That night, I became hooked on N'Orlins and hooked on Zac.

After two days, I returned to Picayune and told Pete and Maggie to drop me off in N'Orlins on our way back from Mexico.

"But what will you do there? Where will you live?"

"I'll figure it out when I get there," I said. "This is my kind of town!"

We tooled around Mexico for a month, loading up on silver jewelry, knit sweaters, colorful ponchos, onyx pipes, chess sets, ceramic vases, leather wallets, wood figurines, and turquoise stones at dirt-cheap prices. True to my word, on the way home, I loaded my green army jacket and backpack with as much merchandise as I could and had Pete drop me in New Orleans at the home of a distant friend of my brother Allan. The friend lived in an upscale neighborhood. As we stood outside his plantation-like mansion in a suburb of the city, he took one look at me and said, "You can only stay here one night. Then you have to find your own place."

The next day he drove me in his Ferrari to the French Quarter. I stood on Bourbon Street, calculating my next move. It wasn't the first time I'd said to myself, "What the hell are you doing here?" I was scared, and a little mad at myself for taking such risks, but I reminded myself that I had done this before and survived just fine. I had moved on my own to the Berkshires and Boston, not knowing anyone or having a plan, and I made it through. I told myself, "You'll figure it out this time, too."

In front of me was Dr. Feelgood's Old Tyme Photo Shop, with a sign in the window saying Help Wanted. I went in, and was offered a job dressing tourists in old-fashioned costumes for sepia-tone photos. First thing every morning, they told me, the photographer needed to take test shots—I could model for those if I wanted. There couldn't be a better job for a wannabe actress. I think there was even a Sarah Bernhardt outfit. My scrapbook still has faded shots of me as a saloon girl, a Bible-toting church lady, a princess, a stripper, and my personal favorite—Bonnie—standing next to the owner, who posed as Clyde.

One of the employees was looking for a roommate to sleep in her living room and share her rent. I jumped at the chance to live and work in the French Quarter. Weekdays I was a photographer's assistant, and weekends I worked the flea market with my assorted Mexican novelties. Most of what I brought, I ended up bartering since no one was making much money at the flea markets. One

Sunday I stepped away from my table for three minutes to look at a cloisonné necklace, and my green army jacket was stolen. I felt violated, and never having had anything stolen before, I was devastated. I took it as a sign to quit that moonlighting job.

In between shifts at Dr. Feelgood's, I focused on catching my breath as my asthma was in full gear. N'Orlins is surrounded by the Mississippi River, Lake Ponchartrain, and the Gulf Coast. Between the humidity and the mold, I wheezed and coughed the entire three months I was there. The partying was fun but dealing with my poor health without close friends or family was difficult. Many nights I lay awake, asking myself—why had I run so far from home? Those few months were both the most fun and the loneliest I'd ever experienced. My parents kept calling and asking when I was returning. My roommates in Cambridge wrote to me asking if they should leave my room vacant. I couldn't say; I had no future plans. They finally insisted I send them back-rent money, and I ended up paying for two places. That's when I set the departure date for the Wednesday following Mardi Gras.

With a job smack in the middle of Bourbon Street, I was intoxicated by all the hoopla and forgot about food. We were so busy dealing with hordes of tourists that we often sipped our meals rather than chewed. As I was only an occasional drinker, the pounds flew off even with my sugary "Golden Cadillac," a local concoction of Galliano and crème de cacao. I was young, thin, and audacious, and I flirted with every aspiring Don Juan or Pancho Villa who walked through our door.

In the weeks leading up to Carnival, the Mardi Gras spirit was so alive that everyone in town was swept up in the excitement. The Quarter throbbed with energy. On every street corner and at every crossing, people were consumed with conversations about beads, costumes, doubloons.

When Mardi Gras arrived, I was dazzled by the colors and the spectacle was just my style: dramatic and over-the-top. I hung out with my co-workers, but as many of them were gay, we had different interests. At some point we separated, and I was left to experience the rest of the day on my own. I didn't feel alone, but I was overwhelmed and breathless.

At the end of the day, the sidewalks emptied and the parades moved on, and then I became aware of how isolated I felt. It didn't matter how many people were left on the streets; I was by myself. It had never occurred to me that the anticipation leading up to Fat Tuesday might be more exhilarating than Fat Tuesday itself.

At the stroke of midnight, the cleanup crews came out in their orange sweatshirts and swept away all signs of festivity. Every piece of garbage was collected, every coin, every streamer. Within a few hours, it was as if nothing had occurred in the French Quarter. I was standing in an eerie ghost town. No sound, no clutter, no energy. Dead. And creepy.

Definitely time for me to go home. One small glitch: there was a blizzard in Boston, and all the roads were closed. Wednesday morning, I took the only ride I could get, which was to Florida. I visited Aunt Anne and her new husband, also Harry, for a night. Then, with whatever money I had made at the shop, I hopped a plane and flew home. Mom and Dad were thrilled to see me, but I couldn't really look them in the face. Too many unanswered questions, too many exotic stories, too many derailed dreams. They were trying to understand why I kept moving around and seeking new adventures. I couldn't tell them, because I really didn't know. I had found a plaque for my wall that read: "It's easy to come and go. The hard thing is to remain."

I gave Mom the gift I bought her in Mexico. Pete had insisted that instead of buying my mother a ring, I should buy her several turquoise stones and let her design her own ring. I argued with him but then gave in. I could tell that Mom was not pleased with her stones in the same way that she wasn't pleased with my recent choices or my travel buddies. She didn't say anything, though I was a master at reading Mom's face.

Two days later I left for Boston. The snowstorm had held the city under siege, and there was a pervasive sense of camaraderie among those folks who had survived the blizzard together. My roommates told me stories of how they cross-country skied across Cambridge. They brought food supplies to the elderly and the homebound. Everyone in the neighborhood had shoveled snow together, and restaurant owners gave out free hot chocolate and cookies. Boston and Cambridge had loosened up during this experience, which was nice to see. Only it didn't make me feel more at home. Having missed the crisis, I had unwittingly returned to the familiar chill of being an outsider. Lying in my warm bed, I knew that I had managed to avoid the big Boston blizzard outside. Inside, a raging tempest still swirled.

CHAPTER TWENTY-ONE

HOME AT WORK

Trish and Randy, though glad I had returned, were also hurt that I had disappeared for so long. I told them I was going to Mexico for a month and stayed away for almost five. They took my absence as a personal slight and couldn't quite grasp why I had left. Neither could I. All I knew was that Boston didn't feel like home. New Orleans didn't feel like home. Israel didn't feel like home. My parents' house didn't feel like home.

The only place where I ever felt at home was at work. I probably would have moved away from New England sooner had it not been for great jobs. I was 23 when I returned to Boston. My relationship with my roommates was strained and now I had no job to hide behind, no protective shell to keep my self-esteem from hitting bottom. The sensation of being an outsider, rudderless, became more acute each day. Five months earlier, I had left for Mexico on a high with a published workbook under my belt and a commendable reputation at the Board of Ed. The trip left a gap in my résumé as the only new talent I could boast was taking sepia photos of inebriated tourists.

Each day I felt less and less of a fit in my communal living situation, and I withdrew. When the atmosphere in the house became too radical, I crossed the Charles River and moved from Inman Square in Cambridge to Oak Square in Boston. My new roommate spent most of her time at her boyfriend's house, which allowed me to be alone in a beautiful sprawling Victorian apartment with wood paneling and bay windows. I chose to make the sun porch my bedroom with its floor-to-ceiling windows facing the backyard. The room was cold in the winter but I overlooked the drafts in exchange for the garden view and eccentric beauty. I awoke to light and trees, which lifted my spirits when I felt good and deepened my depression when I felt lonely.

Within a month of my return, I received a call from the executive who funded the book project. She offered me a job as career counselor and workshop leader in a federally funded project sponsored by the Mass Bay Transportation Authority. The objective of the program was to teach skills in architecture, engineering, and graphic design to low-income high-school students and dropouts. Trainees would then intern at the architectural and engineering firms that were building the new train lines through their neighborhoods.

My job was to help the participants with their professional development to insure success in their internships and, ultimately, in their careers. Though my counseling sessions were supposed to be vocational, more often what these teenagers needed were tips on how to navigate the rest of their lives: family, relationships, lifestyle. I became their life coach and worked overtime to help them solve their problems.

My boss and mentor, Lorena, took me under her wing. Time and again, she reminded me to set realistic expectations and hold tight to my boundaries. Some of the kids' stories were heartbreaking. I was sure that if I only pedaled harder, I could help the more troubled kids with their tough issues. It was hard to reconcile my expectations with their realities; most of their problems were beyond my scope. I became a workaholic and my students' concerns kept me up nights as I thought about new strategies or resources to offer them. I took their behaviors personally even though their choices had nothing to do with me, but I was overinvested in their lives and didn't know how to draw the line.

I immersed my whole self in the job and food became the only salve that offered relief. Cookies kept me from feeling overwhelmed; ice cream kept me from feeling guilty I didn't do enough; and spaghetti kept me from looking at my own difficult life. The parallels between my trainees' overt out-of-control lives and my covert one made it that much more imperative that I help them succeed. I was *their* life coach with *my own* life issues I couldn't manage. Food helped me feel that some part of my life was in control. I started individual therapy again with the hope that I could overcome my issues with food. While I had many insights about my early childhood, none were powerful enough to give me that great answer I was looking for; the answer as to what was wrong with me, why I turned to food to solve all my problems.

Beyond the frustrations, there were so many joys. Cal, one of our go-getter students, struggled to pick a college, torn between Boston University and Colorado State. He made pro and con lists for weeks until he wore himself out and begged me to decide for him. I suggested he close his eyes and we did a guided imagery: *"Visualize yourself walking from your dorm across campus to your classes, paying attention to your surroundings. Imagine yourself listening to the sounds around you, taking in the smells."* I guided him through a typical college day step-by-step, general enough to encompass both locations. After a few minutes, I prompted him to open his eyes. *"Where were you?"* I asked. Without hesitation, he said, *"Colorado,"* and that's where he went. For the rest of that day, I walked around with a smile on my face.

I was especially proud of a high school senior named Greg, whose artistic talents were amplified in our graphic design studio. Greg created flyers for our events, and his impressive portfolio netted him a scholarship at a local art school.

In addition to counseling, my role was to design and deliver workshops on leadership, communication, and teamwork. My greatest thrill was facilitating these workshops with 60 high-energy adolescents who were fully immersed in personal discovery as the room echoed with laughter and learning. Though only a few years older than them, I felt like Mother Hen, beaming and clucking as my kids transformed themselves into polished, self-assured young adults.

I earned a reputation as a guru on "success," yet in my own life, I felt like a fraud as food and friend struggles continued to plague me. My career expanded while my social life contracted. I was a fish out of water. After a rich and rewarding work week came Friday night, my lonely time. I didn't have many friends in Boston, having drifted from my Inman Square roommates. There was one interesting and intense man I met at a party. He was married, though he convinced me that he and his wife were about to separate. He worked the night shift at an alcohol treatment program. On Friday nights, on his way to work, he would stop by my apartment for a few hours. We got high and slept together and then he left and I cooked up an entire box of spaghetti.

I would start with a hefty bowl. Then I went to the pot to transfer the leftovers into a container. Instead, I ate forkfuls straight out of the pot. An angry voice inside my head warned me to leave the kitchen. I ignored it, dished out a second helping, and left the room. Never owning a television all the years I lived in Boston, I went to read in the living room. Within a few minutes, I wolfed down the spaghetti in my bowl while the remains in the pot continued to beckon. I ignored their call at the beginning, and allowed hours to pass without giving in to the temptation. By 10, 10:30, my "what-the-hell" attitude took over, and I went back in the kitchen to devour the rest of the pasta. When the strands were gone, I took the wooden spoon and scooped up every droplet of sauce. Then I went into my bedroom to sleep. With no energy to move, my carb coma accomplished its mission—I was anesthetized.

I wasn't oblivious to my eating problems; I just didn't know how to fix them. In 1979, I heard about a new therapy group with a radical philosophy: dieting is jail. The only thought we have is to break out of jail so we can eat. To quit the yo-yo cycle, you can indulge in your favorite foods as long as you eat and chew mindfully. The key was to become so attuned to our bodies that we would eat only when hungry and stop when satisfied. With conscious eating, our bodies would signal to us when they were full and we wouldn't overfeed ourselves nor would we continue to crave unhealthy foods.

My group was made up of anorexics, bulimics, and overweight women. At size 18, I was the fattest, and the anorexics wanted nothing to do with me. I scared them to death, as though I were contagious. I ignored their looks of contempt (and fear), and arrived at class with my homework: a pillowcase of my binge food—M&M's at the time. The social worker led us through a guided eating meditation, encouraging us to experience each bite in a slow, reflective manner. One by one, I tasted each M&M individually, observed how it felt on my tongue, how it slid down my throat, into my gut. During the session, this slow pace worked and I savored each candy, even tried to discern between the reds and yellows in my mouth. On the way home, I perched the pillowcase on the passenger's seat and proceeded to eat a few more handfuls. I was able to stop after a few, still an improvement over the bingeing I had done in days prior.

By the end of the pilot program, half the people in our group lost weight. I was in the half that gained. I prayed that this alternative approach would work for me, but I kept missing the point when my body would tell me to stop. Once I started eating my trigger foods, all alerts had shut down.

Within a few months after the workshop, though I had made progress, I went back to my old habits and spent Friday night, Saturday, and Sunday on one long bender. I sequestered myself on weekends because any attempts to meet new people or change my situation felt futile. I had already tried sailing lessons on the Charles, stage acting with a community theatre, and carrying banners at political rallies. After five years, I pursued the goal that brought me to Boston in the first place, and signed up to train as a therapist at the Boston Gestalt Institute. During my final year in Boston, I spent my weekends studying Gestalt. Though I loved this form of therapy, the principles weren't enough to fill the large void that had grown inside me. The emptiness was so great that even tried-and-true standbys like work and school couldn't fill the abyss.

One Friday night in July, a platonic friend Andy and I decided to go out on a "date." After dinner at a trendy restaurant, we returned to my place for wine. As we were getting cozy, the phone rang. I picked up and Mom was on the line. Almost every time Mom called on a Friday night, I snapped at her or was curt because I was bingeing, smoking pot, or having sex with my married friend. I couldn't believe my luck; this time, I was on a date with a nice Jewish boy, single and professional. In my never-ending cycle of wanting Mom's approval and rebelling against it, I started blabbing about my date. Mom was quiet. I took her silence as disapproval.

"Marcia," she whispered, "Arleen's baby is very sick. He's in the hospital in intensive care."

I know I must have gasped; I was frightened by her tone. What could be wrong with such a tiny baby? Everett was only eight months old. I had seen him just a few months before at the Passover Seder. He was healthy and active, a miniature of his two older brothers.

"We don't know. He started out with an ear infection but it's much worse than that. It's very serious." More silence.

"I'm coming home, Mom. I'll leave in the morning and I'll be home by tomorrow afternoon."

"Good," she said, "That would be great."

The next morning, I drove home in my newly acquired electric-blue Ford Maverick, praying that baby Everett, beautiful dimpled "Evi," was still alive. During the four-hour drive, my hands gripped the wheel and a new truth: it was time to return home for good. I lost my appetite for Boston, the New Age city that never quite felt new age to me. Over the last five years, I had great jobs, a master's degree, a side trip to New Orleans, and a year of Gestalt training, but my most vital needs were still unmet. I could feel myself reaching some frantic acceleration. A message hammered at the back of my brain as I drove out of Boston for the second-to-last time: *You're not happy here—this is not the right place for you. Go back to New York. Go back to your family. Go home!*

PART IV

YOUNG ADULT

"I'm selfish, impatient, and a little insecure. I'm out of control and at times I'm hard to handle. But if you can't handle me at my worst, then you don't deserve me at my best."

- Marilyn Monroe

CHAPTER TWENTY-TWO

SINGLE IN THE CITY

After six years of searching for myself in Boston, I was back in New York living in Marsha Mason's old apartment. Even though my rent-stabilized one-bedroom cost less than $450 per month, I still needed a roommate to help cover expenses. My friend Darlene, another transplanted New Yorker I met in Boston, had moved back and was looking for a place to live. Darlene moved into my living room and the two of us explored the Upper West Side and had pasta parties. My miniscule galley kitchen made it hard to cook fancy meals, but Darlene and I mastered spaghetti and lasagna on two burners and a half oven. The mini fridge held only enough vegetables for a salad. As the supermarket was six flights down, we stocked up one meal at a time.

Darlene had musician friends living in Manhattan and I had my brothers, Allan and Bob, my ex-boyfriend, Rafi, and one high school friend, Cheryl, with whom I was back in touch. Between Darlene and me, our social network grew. Waiting for the elevator, I met three neighbors and we decided to tour each other's apartments. In and out of two studios and two one-bedrooms, I met Karen, a woman my age from #608, who amazed me with how she fit two sets of dishes and two sets of pots into her tiny kitchen. She explained that she was kosher and the two of us started talking and became instant friends. Over the years, we dropped in on each other in bathrobe and slippers to commiserate about work, share boyfriend woes, and watch *Dallas* and *Falcon Crest.*

That year, as an early Chanukah present, Mom and Dad gave each Meislin $2,000 to buy ourselves something special, not to be used toward rent or other necessities. I knew right away what I wanted to do with the money: I joined an upscale New York City health club to meet men and exercise. Though I had joined gyms in the past, after the first few weeks I never went. This time, I was determined to shape up as I swam laps in the luxurious pool and warmed up in the posh yoga studio. I became a "regular" and was very pleased when the attendant recognized me and directed me to my "regular" locker. After my workouts, I walked around Manhattan feeling svelte and beautiful even though I was still a size 14-16.

On December 8, 1980, a few weeks after I moved in, I turned left at my 72nd Street subway exit to head home when I heard a commotion down the street. I made a U-turn and walked the two blocks to the Dakota. All I could hear was that John Lennon had been shot right there. We all stood waiting for more news and when we found out that he died, I cried together with everyone else. I played Beatles albums for a week. Darlene, in her beautiful soprano voice, tried to teach me how to sing "Hey, Jude," but even with infinite patience, she couldn't train me to sing on key. I sang anyway, tone-deaf and oblivious.

The only damper in my life was the tenuous and somber nature of baby Evi's illness. My nephew Evi had been born a healthy bouncy baby. At eight months old, when he took ill, the pediatrician diagnosed an ear infection and prescribed antibiotics. Despite repeated visits and changes in medication, the high fever persisted and my sister and her husband, Mel, rushed Evi to the emergency room. He was quickly placed into intensive care where he was treated for bacterial meningitis. That was when Mom summoned me from Boston.

By this time, Evi had suffered extensive bilateral brain damage. The significant deterioration meant that he could no longer roll over, sit up, crawl, feed himself, talk, or understand language. Because he was so young, doctors admitted Evi to a children's rehabilitation hospital for a year with the outside hope that his damaged brain cells could be retrained. Arleen sat vigil at her son's bedside as a team of neurologists and physical, occupational, and speech therapists ministered to the lethargic baby. Mel made a pact with God that if Evi got better, he would give up cigarettes.

I had never seen Mom cry so much in her life. In spite of her depression at this déjà-vu experience, Mom packed her bags and moved into Arleen's house to take care of 7-year old Elliot and 3-year-old Eric. Dad came when he wasn't working and Bob or I relieved them on occasion by hosting the boys in Manhattan as we toured Central Park, Museum of Natural History, and FAO Schwarz.

To find a job, I answered ads from The New York Times and attended professional meetings for career counselors. One night in mid-December, Rafi invited me to a networking event and holiday dance. As I whirled around, carefree and overjoyed to be back in New York, I danced with a corporate-looking guy with a nametag. Over the loud music, I yelled, "Your name is Tony? And what is NBNA?"

"It's a bank, National Bank of North America."

"I never heard of it. Where is it?"

"We're based in Long Island. What do you do?"

"What? The music is so loud, I can't really hear you… what do I do? I lead workshops on leadership and communication. And I'm a career counselor. Just moved here from Boston. I'm looking for a job."

"I think we may have an opening at the bank in our management training department. Give me a call tomorrow at work if you're interested."

I had never worked in a bank or any corporate-type environment nor had I even considered that a possibility. I didn't know that banks taught soft skills, and I had never been a manager. All that aside, I decided to give it a shot as anything new and different piqued my interest. I called Tony the next morning and he referred me to his colleagues in Human Resources. We set up an interview date. With leftover money from Mom and Dad, I bought a new gray suit and arrived at the exclusive bank office to meet with Joanne, a Vice President from the Corporate Training Department in charge of professional development. Tucked under my arm was a 36" x 24" poster. Before I left Boston, I had asked Greg, the talented art student, to illustrate a large-scale model of a four-step career development process I designed for our workshops. He spent hours with my sketch, manually attaching white press-on letters onto a black background, culminating in an impressive design of the four career stages.

In the interview, Joanne told me that even though I didn't have direct experience in corporate training, she was impressed with my dynamic personality and willingness to learn. She also told me that she never met anyone before who brought a poster to an interview. I made the cut and the next step was to interview with Dimi, Joanne's peer in charge of management training. For my second interview, I bought a purple suit and took the train out to Long Island to meet Dimi. The minute I walked into Dimi's office, I knew I would like her. She had a huge smile and then she gushed, "Wow, I love your purple suit!" My interview anxiety was gone and we relaxed into a warm and lively discussion. Though I liked Joanne a lot, I had an instant rapport with Dimi, who assured me that if I were hired, we'd have ample opportunity to work together.

Within two weeks, I landed a job at the bank to design programs and train managers and professionals in leadership, public speaking, and coaching and counseling. I would report to Joanne and occasionally to Dimi. The learning curve was huge, but so was my level of enthusiasm and ambition. My first project was to co-train presentation skills with Joanne and Dimi's boss, Vice President of the training department. He took a liking to me and we complemented each other in the classroom; he with his balding white hair, thirty years of experience, and formal teaching manner, and me with my curly bob, minimal experience, and creative, lively training style. From there, I branched out into teaching customer service, sales, and product knowledge.

As the youngest person in the classroom with groups of experienced managers, among them decorated marines and army vets, I mustered up enough confidence, humor, and humility to engage people in learning. I believed that people learn best when they're having fun so I paced my classes to be fast, dynamic, and hands-on; a combination of learning and entertainment. Nothing electrified me more than witnessing participants have breakthroughs about their leadership or communication style. The more electrified I was, the more the managers responded.

Within a short time, graduates from my seminars would call me to discuss people problems in their department. They invited me to visit their site and give them feedback. They began to open up to me as I administered personality tests and conducted team-building sessions. Trust grew and soon I was labeled the "resident shrink." I was called to consult on anything from an employee performance issue to a conflict between two supervisors. A top-ranking executive called me for advice on how to transition his elderly father into an assisted living facility.

My favorite projects were those when Dimi and I co-trained. We had so much fun playing off each other that our participants always said the days flew and they were never bored. We were passionate about our mission and passionate about people.

Dimi and I became very close professional and personal friends, and we were dubbed "the dynamic duo." Dimi always attracted a huge following and despite calling ourselves "fristers" (friend/sisters), I never felt special enough because Dimi always had a long list of people on her radar. In addition to being beautiful and talented with a vivacious personality, everyone who met Dimi fell in love with her and I felt like second fiddle in her presence. I perceived Dimi as possessing the Midas touch—everything she touched turned to gold: career, friends, well-decorated house in the suburbs, adoring husband, baby on the way. It wasn't the first time I struggled with the polarity of loving a best friend on one hand, and feeling jealous of her on the other.

My sister-in-law, Donna, tried to console me with her maxim: If you want what someone else has (their body, career, husband, etc.), you have to take their whole package, everything about them. Once you look at it that way, you'll keep what you have. Maybe so, but back then, I coveted Dimi's life. How was I to know that twenty years later, in her early fifties, beautiful Dimi would be widowed by this same adoring husband, whose chain smoking caused him an early death from lung cancer?

My job at the bank came with an unexpected perk: four weeks' vacation. On the first of these vacations, my co-worker Elaine, a single woman my age, and I decided to travel through Europe together. We argued about the itinerary for a long time. Elaine was only interested in Europe if we visited the Black Forest in Germany and I couldn't let go of the boycott from my Jewish childhood of all things German. The trip was on, then off. I ended up compromising and we visited Baden-Baden, the Black Forest, Strasbourg, and Koln. On the way, we made a stop in Utrecht, Holland, to visit Roman, his new wife, and their baby.

In between sightseeing jaunts, I mailed postcards to all my friends. I debated whether to send Steve Weinstein a card. Steve and my parents were in touch now and then, and Mom told me that after staying at Cornell to earn two master's degrees, Steve was living in the Bronx pursuing an M.D.-PhD. at Albert Einstein. She gave me his new address and I decided I would write. The postcard said, "Having a great time traveling around Europe. I hear we're both back in New York. Give me a ring."

CHAPTER TWENTY-THREE

RING IN THE NEW YEAR

Steve called, and we met. Over the last nine years, I had seen him at most three times and didn't recognize him when he stepped out of the elevator. His hair was short; he was clean-shaven, and about 20 pounds trimmer. Steve was no longer the scruffy, flannel-shirted Bronx boy of my college years; he was a professional-looking man with sculpted features and an air of sophistication. When he walked into my apartment, I saw him through different eyes: here was a real nice guy—kind, stable, serious, the type of man you could make a life with, have children. How different he seemed from so many of the men I had met in my wanderings whose mysterious stories appended their Peter Pan syndrome.

Within a few weeks of becoming reacquainted, I asked Steve if he wanted to start over and give our relationship another chance. He hesitated. "I don't know," he said. "There's nothing like a first love, and you were my first love. I'm not sure we can rekindle that." Though he agreed to give it a try, he was right. We were no longer teenagers, and as mature young adults in our late twenties, we had to find a new way to connect after being on our own for almost a decade. Neither of us had been adept at steady relationships, and both of us were still mired in memories of the past.

"Remember when we made spaghetti on a hot plate on the floor right in front of your dorm room?" I asked.

"Yeah, and that Stevie Wonder concert in Bailey Hall. That was amazing!"

"What about the time I came to your parents' summer house at Lake Louise Marie and we took the boat out?"

"And what about the time we slept outside the *Chavurah* in the *sukkah* with just bamboo sticks on the roof, and we were freezing?"

"Remember when I used to come back from therapy, and you and Marcy would hang out on my bed while we shared stories about our childhood? You really liked her... By the way, didn't you two go out after we broke up?"

"Maybe... And what about the time you brought that musician back to the house, the guy you met at the leadership conference? You kept laughing at your inside jokes right in front of me..."

"Yeah, I do remember that. I'm sorry."

"Yeah, I'm sorry, too."

We were both quiet as we remembered how much we had hurt each other. Then we looked into each other's eyes, realizing it was close to 10 years later.

Within months, Steve moved into my one-bedroom apartment. By then, my roommate, Darlene, had moved to Brooklyn. Though he had very few clothes and knick-knacks, Steve had heavy medical texts and a massive refrigerated wine cabinet he had built himself. The 180-bottle storage unit was so tall, it jammed half in and half out of the elevator, and Steve and his brother, Richard, had to saw off a bit of the top corner. I tried to look away when my neighbors emerged from the one working elevator, cursing at the new guy responsible for their delay. Once inside the apartment, Steve's homemade wine refrigerator was placed in a corner of the living room with its jagged top and scratched-off paint spots. I stared at the furniture-intruder for months until I insisted that Steve finish off the craggy top and paint the exterior.

Steve was a foodie and he loved to shop, cook, and sample foods and wine. That year alone, he introduced me to numerous binge foods I'd never had before: Zabar's chocolate croissants, Fairway's marinated goat cheese, H&H cheesecake (head and shoulders above Boston's Baby Watson), and then his own signature dishes: cold

Szechwan sesame noodles, black bean soup, Caesar salad, cheese fondue with sourdough baguettes, *isle flotante*, hazelnut dacquoise, tortellini de la nonna, and dishes from all over the world that he had experimented with and perfected. I added these foods to my usual fare of pizza, pasta, ice cream, and rainbow cookies.

Little by little, the pounds were mounting. The scale tipped at 175, a result of Steve's delicious meals and my old habit of snacking every time we had an argument. I was a stylish size 18-20, with brightly colored scarves, hand crafted jewelry, and expensive makeup. I booked my haircuts in chic French salons to make my face look thinner long past the time when my body could fit into their tiny monogrammed robes. Steve said I reminded him of the actress Raquel Welch, and I loved the compliment. She was exotic and beautiful with her voluptuous breasts and prominent cheekbones. One time he said I looked like the singer Linda Ronstadt, which I related to more because of her rounder face.

I was mad at myself because I had stopped going to the gym when my job grew more demanding. The only exercise I had was on weekends when Steve and I strolled around the city for hours, holding hands and meandering in and out of shops. I liked ticking off the miles after each 20-block stretch, but the pace was slow and not enough to keep my weight in check. Our sex life continued to thrive despite my weight gain and our busy schedules, but it didn't exactly constitute "exercise."

Food in the past was associated with family get-togethers and celebrations; it was a stand-in for love; a coping mechanism for loneliness, loss, and every other emotion. For the first time, under Steve's tutelage, I began to see food as something to be tasted, savored. With his worldly recipes and discerning palate, Steve taught me to identify individual spices in a recipe and to appreciate how the combinations of certain foods provided a synergy that far exceeded each food by itself.

I prepared an occasional meal but Steve's cooking was so superior to mine that I lost my motivation. We had dinner parties in our home and even my own parents would ask, "Who's cooking?" It was an accepted joke that although Steve bought me cookbooks and supported me through two different culinary classes at the Learning Annex, God did not put me on earth to cook. After living in the shadow of two great food sorcerers, Mom and Steve, I couldn't master the art of following a recipe. Nor could I cook by instinct, which at least would have fed into my creative side. It was inevitable that Steve became the master chef and I, his sous chef.

I was far better suited to the role of social director. This job was easy for me because I loved people and I loved to chat. Steve was not a talker and his typical responses to questions were one-word answers. Friends and relatives visited often and I carried on conversations while Steve cooked and selected wines. Steve's introversion reminded me of Dad, who was also very quiet and happy to leave the socializing to Mom. I remembered a comment Mom had made about their early years of marriage. In their generation, the title "Doctor" was a status symbol, and some doctors acted "superior" to other people. As Dad was painfully shy, he rarely spoke in social settings. People assumed that he was silent because he was a snob. Once people grew to know Dad, they realized that there was not an arrogant bone in his body. In fact, he was humble, modest—and shy.

I was aware that Steve's reserved style might also be misinterpreted. Though Steve was a VIP when he served food, I wondered what friends and colleagues thought of him when we weren't conversing about recipes or vintages. I rationalized that Steve's lack of communication might be due to sleep deprivation. Steve required more than eight hours of sleep to function well, and that was impossible given his medical school schedule. We learned to become immune to his missing half the conversation or falling asleep at the dinner table in a seated position.

Private exchanges between the two of us were difficult. Steve found most subjects stressful and any topic with a remote connection to feelings was out of the question. The exception to that was one conversation in early 1982 in which Steve was agitated and he talked for a long time. We were sitting on the sofa in our apartment. Steve was explaining to me about a mysterious ailment that was killing off many young men. The AIDS epidemic was still in its early stages but Steve had met many of these dying men at his city hospital in the Bronx. He was sharing with me how shaken he was by the ravages of this devastating disease and how helpless he and the other doctors felt when they couldn't do anything to help their patients. I listened without saying a word, watching his body racked with emotion. That was the longest I had ever heard Steve speak.

Despite our differences, our domestic situation fell into a comfortable rhythm. I began to imagine that I could settle down with this man and let go of any residual wild oats. In October, Steve and I vacationed in St. Thomas, our first trip together. We were drinking Cabernet on our hotel veranda and I asked him, "Where do you see our relationship going?" He was silent. I took that as a cue to continue: "We're both 27, and we love each other. We've known each other for a long time and we've been living together for over six months. I want to know what the next step is." (I should have stopped there but I didn't) "…because if you're not thinking of getting married, I need to know that. We're not getting any younger and I'll need to make some decisions. What do you think?" Steve kept his silence and never answered my question.

A few months later, on New Year's Eve, ten years and three months after we first met, Steve proposed to me in the most romantic way possible. He picked me up at the bank, took me to dinner at Nirvana, our favorite Indian restaurant, and then to see *Sophisticated Ladies* on Broadway. On a carriage ride through Central Park, he pulled out a bottle of champagne, two fluted glasses, and a ring, and popped the cork and the question. Of course I said yes, and in a dreamlike state, we went home, called both sets of parents (who couldn't have been more ecstatic), and then went out again to watch the annual New Year's Eve marathoners arrive at Tavern on the

Green. The fireworks that followed felt appropriate for the level of celebration we both experienced.

Our families embraced each other with open arms. My parents couldn't believe that I had come to my senses and was going to marry Steve Weinstein. His parents, Sonnie and Morty, and I bonded in no time. Sonnie and I were chronic talkers, and we floated with ease from conversation to conversation without worrying about whether we finished a topic or found the lost strand. Steve's family, like mine, was full of love and humor, and both sets of siblings were open and generous. The two families clicked and our parents became close from the first time they met. Steve and I were encircled by a loving and supportive extended family.

We were all blissful except for Steve. At the time, I attributed his anger and withdrawal to pressure to finish his Ph.D. thesis. Our new computer, an early model called Superbrain, had a way of losing data. Sometimes I would come home from work to find Steve tense and frustrated in his effort to recreate the lost data. I couldn't help him fix his problems and learned to leave him alone until he was ready to resurface.

Decades later, after I'd spent years trying to figure out why Steve seemed mad at me all the time, he revealed that his anger at me started on the veranda in St. Thomas when I asked him about our relationship. He wasn't ready at the time to plan his next step and I made it sound like an ultimatum. Though he had planned to propose at some point, Steve never liked feeling pushed. His timetable to think about the future, analyze events, and take action was much longer than mine. Instead of telling me why he was upset, Steve carried his anger below the surface and that's where it simmered well up to our silver anniversary.

CHAPTER TWENTY-FOUR

COUNTDOWN

Steve and I set our wedding date for June 12, 1983. That same day would be my parents' 45th wedding anniversary. At first I didn't want to share the date but there were a limited number of Sundays in June. As my parents had been happily married for a long time, I thought the fusion would add a special significance to our *simcha*. I called my rabbi and mentor, Avi Weiss, and asked if he would perform the ceremony. He agreed, provided we attended pre-marital spiritual counseling. Steve was willing and we met with Rabbi Weiss in Riverdale to discuss Jewish texts revolving around love and marriage. Steve took the meetings as seriously as I did even though he grew up in a much less observant home. As Rabbi Weiss illuminated the meaning behind some of the wedding rituals, Steve and I decided which ones we wanted to adopt and the three of us together created a unique and personalized wedding ceremony. With each tradition we studied, I was overwhelmed with awe at being a link in a long chain of Jewish brides.

My favorite tradition was the *bedeken*, the lifting of the veil, which traced back to Biblical times when Jacob was supposed to marry Rachel, for whom he had toiled seven years. Jacob's father-in-law, Laban, deceived him, and Jacob ended up marrying the veiled older sister, Leah, instead of his beloved Rachel. From that time on, Jewish men unveiled their brides before entering the canopy, to make sure they were marrying the right woman. Though Steve was not likely to make that mistake, nor was Dad the type to play a trick on anyone, we were touched by the idea that the groom, upon lifting the veil—a beautiful act of love in itself—sees his bride anew, as if for the first time. At the same time, she looks into the eyes of her *bashert,* her chosen, and sees him as though for the first time. I was even more excited about the preceding part when I would sit on a giant queen-like throne, flanked by my mother and mother-in-law as all the guests come to pay homage. Steve would be in an adjacent room with the men signing papers and drinking *schnapps.* Escorted into the women's hall by the intoxicated and frolicking men, Steve would ceremoniously stand in front of my grand, oversized white wicker peacock chair, and unveil me, to the tune of jubilant singing and merriment.

The other custom we were ambivalent about at first, but came to love, was my circling Steve seven times under the *chuppah,* the wedding canopy, accompanied by my mother and mother-in-law. Though there were many explanations for this, I liked the *kabbalistic* notion that with each rotation, a woman enters more deeply the seven spheres of her beloved's soul. Later Mom's friends asked me why I didn't smile but I took this mystical circling as a spiritual journey, sacred and profound.

Steve and I planned these customs amidst his complex doctoral thesis and my added responsibilities at work. We split the other wedding tasks: food and wine to Steve, and everything else to me. Even as a gourmet cook and wine connoisseur, Steve found the job challenging because all the food and wine had to be *glatt* kosher out of respect for my parents' friends and rabbis from my old neighborhood.

From the time we got engaged, December 31, 1982, until our wedding date June 12, 1983, I had five months and 12 days to lose weight. I operated well under tight deadlines, but I knew I didn't have a second to lose. During January, February, and March, I returned to an old stand-by: Weight Watcher's Quick-start meetings with weigh-ins. By April, I felt antsy that I wasn't losing fast enough and scouted around for something quicker. I discovered Dick Gregory's

Bahamian Diet, a 700-calorie powdered drink that tasted good and melted off the fat. Though the product officially launched in 1984, I found a supplier near work who was happy to keep me in cans. Weekly, I sashayed over on my lunch hour and admired my new figure in every reflective window en route.

Next to the elevator that transported me to my magic potion palace, I noticed a sign for vintage clothing on the third floor, and made that stop part of my weekly rounds. As I slimmed down, I was able to fit into a wider variety of clothes in the upscale retro boutique, and began to accumulate an eclectic and artistic trousseau. Zelda and Rini, the two shop owners, were young, fabulous women in their 30s who reveled with me at my shrinking body. I would stand in front of their art deco mirrors prancing about in a size 14, sometimes a 12, trying on every vintage outfit that would get past my bust line. Though my weight was dropping, I saw no sign of my breasts diminishing from their size 38-40 DD cup, and thanked my lucky stars that Steve was a chest man. I tried on dresses from the 1930s with bustier-style tops and pinched waists, and peplum jackets from the '40s that, as Mom would say, covered a "multitude of sins." Right before my wedding, the svelte owners handed me a beautifully wrapped sexy lace camisole they had been saving for me as I skated down the scale.

In addition to the weekly shop for shakes, I incorporated a new habit into my busy bride-to-be life. From the time I was a young child, I had been a hardcore nail and cuticle biter, compulsively picking at my nails and skin until they bled. At work, I covered my shame with assorted Band-Aids, but I knew that wouldn't suffice for displaying my diamond ring. Right after our engagement, I happened upon a nail salon featuring fake nails, a novelty in 1983. Ella, a young Russian, was a genius at making all ten of my nails look and feel authentic. The tips and silk wraps were expensive, but I was overjoyed that I no longer had to hide my damaged hands.

My other bastion of shame, asthma, was not as easy to fix. The disease still crippled me as I continued to wake up in the middle of the night with coughing spasms. When the hacking started, I would rush out of our bedroom and muffle the sounds in the couch pillow to avoid waking Steve. Nevertheless, my wheezing and coughing would wake him, and Steve would amble into the living room, and look at me with that same powerless expression I used to read on Dad's face. Steve, too, had no panacea, and to my great relief—no vaporizer. A trapezoidal-shaped pink pill had long replaced the foul-tasting liquid of my childhood, but that didn't thwart my asthma either.

One morning after a harrowing attack, Steve unfurled the tightly packed prescription insert to the pink pills and scrutinized every word of instruction, clinical trial data, warnings, and scientific formulas. After what seemed like an eternity, he turned to me with a grin and said, "I can't believe you're still taking this medication. I'm not a pulmonologist but even I know that this form of treatment is obsolete and it may actually be exacerbating your asthma."

That night at work, Steve consulted a specialist and returned home with two state-of-the-art inhalers, one of which had just been approved by the FDA. My first reaction was to freeze, too anxious to take the inhalers from his outstretched hand. "I don't think I should do this," I panicked. "These are loaded guns. You know I've had near-death experiences with inhalers." Steve convinced me that this combination was the new standard of care for asthma and it was worth a try. I trusted Steve and began the treatment. Within a few weeks, I was breathing better, sleeping better, and inhaling and exhaling with an appreciation I never had before. My lungs were finally working for me and not against me. I stayed on those medications for twenty-seven years, long past my lung cancer diagnosis, until 2010, when one of the inhalers was taken off the market because it was no longer profitable.

For the first time, I experienced the miracle of feeling healthy— physically, emotionally, and spiritually. Steve and I were in love and we were getting married. Mom and Dad were proud of me and were exhaling a sigh of relief. My body image was improving from my slimmer figure down to the fake tips of my fingernails. I still had less than five months to become the magazine beauty I had never been. Even if just for a day, I wanted to be a princess.

My future mother- and sister-in-law offered to take me wedding gown shopping, and I happily complied. Later I realized that I should have waited for Mom and Dad to come back from their annual cruise to include Mom, though I knew I'd never purchase a gown without Mom's approval. Mom had standards: nothing sexy or off the shoulder, nothing for the religious community to censure.

Steve's mom, Sonnie, and his sister Arleen, (we have in common sisters named Arleen), and I, *shlepped* to bridal stores so I could try on wedding gowns. "Try on" was actually a misnomer because all the wedding dresses came in sample size 10 and I could only guess at how a dress would really look on me. I was a little depressed because after dieting so hard and guzzling low-calorie shakes, I felt "thin" but was still plus-size to these bridal salons. Sonnie was reassuring and non-judgmental as I bemoaned that not one "modern bride" dress fit me; only "mother-of-the-bride" dresses made it around my torso.

Arleen was the first to spot a beautiful lacy, beaded, long-sleeved gown that covered the two key criteria: Miss Prissy (for Mom) and Gypsy (for me). I was very excited as I loved this dress and tried to imagine how it would look four or five sizes bigger. When Mom returned, she picked me up at my office in the Garment Center, and we walked a block to the bridal boutique where skilled fitters took my measurements and whispered among themselves how much extra fabric they would order. I held my head high and pretended not to notice that I was the biggest bride in the shop. I consoled myself that I also had the best hair.

With the dress under way, I turned to thoughts about a veil, jewelry, makeup, and hairstyle. As the countdown continued, I researched each with a vengeance. When I wasn't surging through nail salons, barreling through boutiques, purchasing diet powder, comparing cosmetics, sampling hairstyles, or getting fitted for my gown, I was calling florists, photographers, videographers, musicians, printers, and *tallis* and *yarmulke* makers. My sister Arleen, matron of honor, became my experienced consultant and confidante.

In May, one month before the wedding, I made an appointment with Steve, Dad, my father-in-law, and all of my brothers and brothers-in-law to visit the tuxedo rental store. Steve and all the men tried on black tuxes, my choice to complement the pinks and purples of the women in my wedding party. Steve looked handsome and sharp with the black hue against his dark features. For months, I had envisioned the wedding photo of the two of us together under the *chuppah*, with my shoulder-length black curly hair, long white veil and lacy, beaded dress, standing lovingly alongside my husband, his dark prominent features underscored by his elegant black suit and contrasting white shirt.

On June 9, 1983, I left our apartment on 72nd Street to return to my parents' house, honoring the tradition of not seeing my husband for three days before the wedding. On Sunday, June 12, I drove my car to the Nanuet Mall and Josie at the Lancôme counter made me up, as planned. She announced to every passer-by at Macy's that I was getting married and they all joined the chorus of well-wishers. Mom and Dad told me how beautiful I looked and then the four of us, along with my pouffed-out wedding gown, poured into the Chrysler to drive to the catering hall in Nyack, at the base of the Tappan Zee Bridge.

Helene, the elegant and attentive wedding planner, helped me wriggle into my wedding dress, commenting on how much weight I had lost. In truth, I had lost between 35 and 40 pounds but I had worked so hard on my tan, hair, makeup, nails, and constricting undergarments, that I felt a lot lighter than 148 pounds. Staring into the mirror on my wedding day, for the first time since I was a pre-teen, I felt truly beautiful. I didn't feel "less than" when I looked in all corners of the mirror and all angles.

When I stepped out to greet my guests, I caught a glimpse of Steve. My heart fluttered. *What was he wearing?!* I couldn't believe it! He wasn't wearing the dashing black tux we had picked out together, the same color that all the ushers were wearing. He had on a light-colored tux with shoes to match, a kind of silver/gray, that made his swarthy, handsome face look pale and washed out. I gulped—so different from what I had pictured! Yet, I was aware that it was my wedding day and it wouldn't pay to make a scene and ruin the ambiance. Our ceremony was set up outside, and it was a sunny, hot day; all the people we cared about were sauntering in, smiling broadly, filled with love. No, not the right time for a fight.

Later, Steve explained (or maybe it was his mom?) that when they went to pick up the tux, they realized that Steve would be hot in a black suit so they ordered him a lighter color. Just like that.

Despite the small setback, my husband, the groom, looked very handsome and the day was (otherwise) enchanting and perfect. Rabbi Weiss guided us through our sacred wedding service, and Steve and I basked in our love for each other and for our surrounding families and friends. At one point during dinner, Steve disappeared with his brother and his wine connoisseur medical school buddies to indulge in the special libations he had set aside for the occasion. These bottles were not kosher wines, and therefore not *halachically*-acceptable to serve at the reception, so the seven friends snuck into our bridal suite and finished off three Chardonnays: a 1979 Long Vineyard Napa Valley, a 1978 Chateau Montelena, a 1980 Acacia, plus a 1970 Chateau Ducru Beaucaillou, and a 1970 Chateau Lafon Rochet.

Upon his return, Richard, the best man, relaxed and red-faced from the wine-tasting party, offered a toast and we all drank kosher champagne. My siblings and I followed with a presentation to my parents on their 45th wedding anniversary, and Mom and Dad were very touched by our gift of three original lithographs by Michoel Muchnik, a talented Jewish artist from Brooklyn: The Ring and the Rose, *Kiddush*, and *Shabbos* Candles.

The reception flew so quickly that when the first guest came to say goodbye, I practically cried. I was far from done; I wanted more dancing, laughing, fawning, and more compliments. I loved the attention, and my wedding day was the best day of my life; I wasn't ready to close up shop. Mom called our affair "a storybook wedding" and even Dad, who rarely indulged in hyperbole, dubbed it, "The Wedding of the Century."

After everyone said goodbye, Steve and I retreated to our overnight room. On one side of the dresser were bobby pins, cosmetics, and hairspray cans strewn around from last-minute primping by the bridal party. On the other end of the bureau, stood five empty wine bottles, lined up as a badge of honor. I realized in that moment that I was starving. I hadn't eaten all night, too busy with all the other stimulating activities. We had no food with us except for the top of the wedding cake the caterer had given us to hold for our first anniversary. My new husband and I sat on the edge of our king-sized bed and ate the carrot cake, one year too soon.

CHAPTER TWENTY-FIVE

NEWLYWEDS

An early flight to Bermuda insured that we would get our full seven days' worth at the Southampton Princess. Part of the week it rained and the indoor activities for newlyweds were kitschy. On the sunny days, Steve wanted us to rent motorbikes and was disappointed that I wouldn't drive one myself. The summer before, I had signed up for a course through the Learning Annex: Bicycle Riding for Beginners—Adults only. The description boasted that at the end of four sessions, students would be riding a bike. Ever since age 6, when I fell off my red two-wheeler hand-me-down and was afraid to get back on, I had dreamed of riding a bike. Steve, an avid cyclist, was my incentive.

For weeks before that class, I visualized myself over and over balancing on a bike, riding a bike, turning, maneuvering, feeling safe on a bike. I rehearsed it so often in my head that in the middle of the first lesson, my dream came true and I was flying through Central Park on a two-wheeler. I had overcome a childhood phobia and was very proud of myself. One year later, when I took a long look at the motorbikes lined up at the kiosk in Bermuda, and I took another long look at the drivers on the "wrong side" of the road, I froze. I couldn't bring myself to rent a motorbike, moped, or any other kind of wheeled vehicle. I rode on the back of Steve's scooter but the glamour was gone.

When our honeymoon was over, Steve and I plunged headlong into our jobs. Steve was engrossed in completing his doctorate in physiology and biophysics before returning to complete medical school, followed by five years of residency and fellowship. I was a newly promoted Assistant Vice President and Regional Personnel Manager, responsible for human resources and organizational development for a large segment of the bank. I continued my Gestalt therapy studies with Laura Perls, wife of Fritz Perls and co-founder of Gestalt therapy. She was a disciplined teacher who continually corrected my posture and told me she didn't believe in applying Gestalt to organizations—which is exactly what I was doing—so we abided each other as I lumbered through a year of no-nonsense training. I also began a Ph.D. in managerial psychology at one of the first university programs "without walls."

Both Steve and I were hardworking achievers and we brought our best selves to our careers. That dynamic served us well as we were each successful in our fields and we developed a strong identification with our work. Psychologically, it seemed healthy to be autonomous and not have to depend on each other for self-worth. On the other hand, after long days and difficult demands, neither of us had much reserve in our fuel tanks to cater to the other person's emotional needs. I was in a better position to give Steve support than the other way around, but often he was exhausted and sat catatonic in front of the TV. Other nights, he fell asleep on the couch, eyeglasses pushed up on his head, wine glasses by his side, a wooden tray of crackers and goat cheese on his lap.

As a new wife, I had no clue how to comfort a dyed-in-the-wool introvert with an aversion to anything affective. A good deal of the time Steve was mad at me but he rarely told me why. When I retraced my actions, obsessed about everything I had done, I usually couldn't find a compelling enough reason to merit the silent treatment for days, sometimes weeks. After we'd made up, and Steve shared the reason (if he remembered it), I was often dumbfounded. The things he blamed me for seemed trivial. If someone held a gun to my head as I listed my faults, most of these items would never have crossed my mind. My transgressions included scratching the bottom of our new Teflon pans, not rushing off the phone when he walked in, or hosting a party where too many well-intended family members crowded the kitchen to help.

Because we had opposite personalities, I knew better than to treat Steve the way I wanted to be treated. I craved an imaginary Dr. Kildare, a loving and romantic soul mate who would kiss me longingly when I walked in the door and would ask about my day, allowing me to respond with interminable detail. As he listened to every word, this fairy-tale man would maintain soulful eye contact, acknowledge every emotion without judgment, and fondle my hair.

Then I would do the same for him, encouraging him to recount all the ups and downs of his day and his feelings as I massage his leg or rub his chest, intensifying as he reveals more of his inner life. After we each unburden and well up with closeness, we kiss slowly and sensually, then make love, reaffirming the intimacy that has deepened through this profound level of talking and touching.

I knew that Steve, a non-talker, wasn't going to be that man. Nor would I be that woman in Steve's daydreams, the one who greets her husband at the door with a glass of wine just right for the occasion. Stepping into their modest apartment, Steve sniffs the air, permeated by sybaritic smells emanating from the crowded oven in which exotic appetizer-to-dessert casseroles stew in complex juices. No one exchanges words; just sweet kisses on the lips, as husband and wife sit down at a table with well-appointed dishes and flatware, purchased on sale in bargain stores. The only expensive items on the table are an assortment of wine glasses tall enough to swirl, thin enough to ping, sturdy enough to last. Carefully selected wines are standing up for the pairing dinner, each a unique discovery mined from thousands of bottles in Scarsdale, a destination suburb to which the young couple had bicycled the previous weekend. Conversation at dinner is limited to which spices the wife skillfully combined to create a most delectable international meal and whether the bouquet on that last Cabernet had nuances more akin to black currants or blackberries? They agree to disagree.

After dinner, she, voluptuous but not fat, transports the crème brûlée dessert she whipped up, while he picks the appropriate Sauternes, and they meet in the bedroom. On the screen, she clicks on the videotape rented for $1.00 from the public library, his favorite, *It's a Wonderful Life*, which she enjoys watching over and over with him because he has memorized every line. Then they make love and he is delighted by all his favorite treats. He falls asleep quickly as his day was long. He is content and relaxed, unfettered by difficult questions or superfluous dialogue.

Because neither of us was able to live up to the other person's expectations, we both walked around in a chronic state of dissatisfaction. Without being able to talk about our problems, I sublimated my anger in food, Steve in Bordeaux and a brick wall. Perhaps his wall had been erected on a veranda in St. Thomas the night I pressured him into the topic of marriage. Or possibly it was built nine years before that, when I ended our college relationship.

More likely, Steve's barricade began in childhood, as he dodged the moods of his bipolar Dad pre-Lithium. As a child, Steve could be characterized as a low-keyed happy kid who loved puttering with his chemistry set. In between tinkering with test tubes, Steve was playing field hockey, shooting off model rockets, or practicing drums with his friends on the Grand Concourse in the Bronx. On any day, in a flash Steve's home environment could change as his Dad shifted from solitary depressive phases to animated manic ones, during which he'd buy out antique stores or fill his car with flea market paraphernalia.

Steve's mom, Sonnie, a peacemaker at all costs, did her best to keep a sunny disposition and shield her children from her husband's disorder. "*Sha, shtill,* everything is okay," was her mantra as her two boys tiptoed around intent on not upsetting Dad. Steve's reserved style intensified during this period as he learned to ignore his own needs in deference to his father's moods and his mother's unspoken plea for calm. Sonnie continually praised Steven and Richard for being very easy sons to raise; they never made demands, never made trouble, never raised their voices.

At 15, Steve slammed his fist into a door. While up at their country house, Steve and his sister, 8 at the time, were having a tiff in the living room. Arleen was teasing Steve, and he was taunting her. When the argument escalated, Arleen ran to her room and slammed the door. The lid blew off Steve's temper, and in a rage, he put his fist into his sister's door leaving a big hole that nearly penetrated through the other side. Sonnie came running over to see what happened. When she saw that her children were fine, she made Steve apologize and they all agreed not to tell Dad. Characteristic of Sonnie's ability to patch over the negative, she found a big sticker of a white daisy and placed it over the hole, where it remained for 30 years until the house was sold. Morty never found out.

This episode was a shameful admonition to Steve that unless he buried his rage beneath a cloak of calmness, his temper could lead him to lose control. He made an internal pledge that whenever he felt aggressive or angry, he would suppress that feeling and become passive instead, a less dangerous alternative. Hence my husband became the king of passive-aggressive. His medical school experiences didn't help, as there were no classes to help young doctors cope with the violent deaths, the young gunshot victims, and the ailing AIDS patients they treated all day long in his city hospital. Steve's way of coping was to shut down his emotions.

Despite Steve's masking defense, I could usually tell when he was angry. I observed the tiny vein in his temple throb ever so subtly before he clenched his teeth and commanded it to stop. I noticed the tension around his mouth when he decided to keep his mouth shut rather than say how he felt. His quelled anger was palpable to me as I likened it to Cecil B. DeMille's green goo from the movie, *Ten Commandments*, creeping up—silent and insidious—to capture its first-born prey.

There we were, newlyweds, dancing the dance of anger, neither one able to shake our method of managing emotions that had guaranteed survival in our respective family constellation. Both smart, both driven, both wearing a bubble over our heads that begged, "Please, please, love me despite my flaws. Please ignore my game-playing and my hurtful words (or non-words), and love me anyway."

At the rate our speeding trains were barreling down their tracks, neither of us stopped long enough to make the right connections and prevent our marriage from veering off-track.

CHAPTER TWENTY-SIX

DEATH ON
THE HOLLAND AMERICA

On the morning of January 22, 1985, 19 months after our wedding, Mom and Dad strolled the beaches of Cozumel. At lunch, they sat at the Captain's Table and were awarded a plaque for their 35th trip on Holland America cruise lines. In the afternoon, Dad went to take a nap in the cabin. Somewhere between Cozumel and Jamaica, he had a massive heart attack and died.

It seems that Dad wasn't feeling well after lunch, and Mom suggested they call the ship's doctor. Dad always had a phobia about doctors and he insisted that if he took a bath, he would feel better. When he didn't improve and started to look a little dazed, Mom called the ship's doctor. The doctor arrived to find my father unconscious—he performed CPR in an attempt to keep Dad's heart pumping.

When the doctor stopped pumping my father's heart, my mother turned to him and said, "I know you. I've met you before." This same doctor was also a rabbi. Years before, on a vacation to Alaska, my parents had attended local Friday night temple services, as they did wherever they traveled. The service in Anchorage was led by this man, the physician who had his hands on my father's chest. My mother remembered that back in Alaska, they had been invited to join the small crowd of synagogue-goers for their weekly *Shabbos* dinner at a nearby Denny's. The Alaskans shared their stories of local

Jewish customs, and my parents regaled them with stories of services they had attended around the world.

The contrast between that brightly lit restaurant and this small cabin was stark. Within a few hours of sightseeing in Mexico, Dad was pronounced dead in the cabin. No more dinners at Denny's, no more nights in faraway towns.

Mom tried to absorb the shock as the doctor-rabbi shuttled back and forth between their cabin and that of another man who was also dying.

Traumatized, Mom had to face a bigger challenge: how to get her husband's body home to New York. Because Dad was a traditional Jew, his body could not be embalmed or cremated and commercial airlines wouldn't allow un-embalmed bodies on their flights. The rabbi sat with my mother in her cabin and offered pragmatic and spiritual counsel as she calculated her next moves. Intercontinental laws and ship regulations required that my mother disembark with my father's body in Jamaica where she would wait at the American consulate. That moment came when the cruise sailed on and Mom was alone with Dad's body in a strange country. Mom was the consummate problem-solver; work out details now, cry later.

That night, January 22nd, I finished work at my new Water Street office overlooking the South Street Seaport, then left with a co-worker to have dinner and drinks in a Mexican restaurant. I had never been out with Emily before and didn't realize how much she liked to drink. Together, we downed two pitchers of Sangria though I was far more interested in the salsa and chips. As this was before cell phones (I would not own a cell phone for another ten years), I had no idea that anything traumatic had happened. Most nights, Steve and I both worked late and seldom expected to see each other before eight.

That night, I returned home at eight and Steve was already there. When I opened the door, I didn't immediately read that something tragic happened that would forever change my life. Steve was sitting in the overstuffed gold chair in the living room, looking contemplative and a shade sadder than usual. After I settled in, still giddy from my evening out, Steve said, "I think something bad happened to your father. Call Allan right away."

"Something bad? Like what?"

"I'm not sure. He may have died."

"What?!" I screamed and ran to the phone to call Allan. Allan told me that Dad had died and Mom was sitting with Dad's body in Jamaica, trying to get home. "But wait," I said, "Steve said he *may* have died. Maybe he didn't?"

"No, Marcia, he definitely died. He had a massive heart attack and died. Donna and I are packed to fly to Jamaica. Bobby and Margy are going to the house to tell Jay and stay with him. Arleen and Mel will be there tomorrow after they get someone to watch the kids."

"We'll leave right now. We'll drive Bob and Margy."

In a state of shock, I packed my bags with every black outfit I owned. Steve and I drove twelve blocks north to pick up Bob and his wife. On the way across the George Washington Bridge, we speculated about every possible incident. Among us, we filled in the empty spaces. Steve was silent as he drove the hour north to Spring Valley.

Once there, we gave Jay the news, terrified at how he might react. We had never seen Jay cry and didn't know what might happen to him physically or emotionally. When we told him, Jay said nothing and just nodded his head. Soon the phones started ringing and the Meislin grapevine was mobilized. My parents had two phone lines and both rang nonstop. First Arleen, then Allan, then Mom called though she could only talk for a minute on a borrowed phone. She was exhausted but well taken care of by the staff at the American consulate in Jamaica. The employees couldn't understand why she wouldn't embalm Dad's body so they could fly home. Mom told us she was working on some plans so we should hold still and await further instructions.

The next morning, we flew into full action. My brothers and I contacted private Medevac planes, known for medical evacuations. My sister called the local rabbi and burial society. Without cell phones, email, or texting, it was difficult to reach Mom as she sat in the Caribbean with Dad's corpse and waited. All morning, Mom's friends called and offered assistance, food, advice on religious issues, advice on everything. Finally we decided that we had to take them up on an offer; none of us had a big enough credit line to cover the entire cost of the private plane. I asked Shirley if she could lay out the money and Mom would pay her back when she returned. She was grateful to help.

The next night, in the blustery cold darkness, Mom's private charter plane landed in a small airport in Westchester County. I never saw Dad's body. My brothers took care of those arrangements to transport his body while I sat with Mom. She was drained and depressed, though grateful to be home. Steve had cooked vegetarian black bean soup, which distracted Mom for a few minutes. Then she told us bits and pieces of stories, but the main thrust of what she said was that Dad spent his last day doing what he loved—traveling, seeing new places, being with Mom, and not suffering. We all agreed that it's the way to go—for the departed, that is. For the survivors, the logistics and arrangements were a nightmare. The unfinished business was a nightmare. The shock was a nightmare. For Dad, he died happy and pain-free. That was consoling.

For the next week, there was never a problem getting ten men for a *minyan* to pray as we sat *shiva* in my parents' home. Back in the Orthodox neighborhood, women were not allowed to be counted, so my sister and I and all the women had to stand at the rear of the prayer area, which in this instance was our living room. This was a ritual for men. I relegated myself to the kitchen. In my progressive Jewish world, I would have been leading those services. At the very least, I would have counted. Not being counted only increased the intense pain I already felt.

Food beckoned more than ever. There were truckloads of food— mostly desserts. The neighborhood women cooked wonderful pasta dishes and traditional vegetarian Jewish foods. In the sea of food, I found my rainbow cookies. I was on high doses of prednisone at the time, a steroid that countered my asthma as it wreaked havoc with my moods, stimulated my appetite, and created swollen and puffy cheeks known as "moon face." Disoriented from the medication and the shock, I unraveled, and along with the rest of the family, made lame efforts to take care of Mom and one another. The flood of people for a week helped us get through those first seven days. Only when all the neighborhood women with their trays of food and the men with their prayer shawls had left, could we really cry.

I don't cry much in front of people. When I'm with people, I don't generally feel like crying, too busy soaking in the people. It's when the people leave, when I'm alone in the house, middle of the day, sun shining through my bedroom window exposing the dust on the Venetian blinds—that's when I am flooded with emotion. I feel so alone I'm convinced that if I start to cry, I'll never stop. I take that as a cue to go down to the kitchen for a salve that could stop me from feeling so bad. When I'm done with my first palliative, I feel empty again and forage for another snack to fill me until the tears dry up. After a massive sugar headache, I forget my despair and focus on my head.

It took several years to recover from Dad's death. The shock was paralyzing. Although Dad had been 77, he appeared healthy. Ten years earlier, he had had an aortic aneurysm and had flown to Texas for surgery by the world-famous heart surgeon Dr. Michael Debakey. After that operation, we believed that Dad was fine. Shortly before the cruise, when Dad was required to have a physical for his part-time retirement job, the doctor suggested that Dad see a cardiologist. With Dad's procrastination around doctors, he didn't see a heart specialist right away. He told Mom he'd make an appointment after the cruise. We'll never know if the suggestion to see a cardiologist was routine for a man in his late seventies or whether the doctor had seen something suspicious. Dad's sudden death, when he had looked the picture of health on vacation, left everyone traumatized and wondering why he had died.

I knew in my heart why Daddy died. It was my fault. Eight months before, when I was diagnosed with lung cancer and told to have my lung resected, I didn't confide in Mom and Dad. I didn't have the heart to tell them that at 29 years old, their youngest daughter, a nonsmoker, newly married, had lung cancer and was going to have a lung removed. I kept the secret.

Fortunately, I went for a second opinion and found out that the diagnosis was wrong albeit not before playing out my entire past and limited future during the 10-day waiting period. After two pneumonias and three bronchoscopies, I put my life into the hands of Dr. Steve Kamholz, who correctly diagnosed my allergic bronchopulmonary aspergillosis (ABPA), a condition rare in the United States but more common in Britain. He said I'd have to be on an inhaled steroid the rest of my life. Without his compassion, brilliance, and relentless pursuit of the correct diagnosis, I would have gone into surgery and potentially had a lung removed without reason. The misread pathology reports, CAT scan, and lab results by the previous "expert" in another hospital were so intriguing to the medical community that Dr. Kamholz presented my case that year at an international pulmonary conference.

I kept my parents out of the loop on all of this except for one or two of the pulmonary procedures. These procedures took place in a hospital, and because as a medical resident, my new husband couldn't always accompany me, I asked my parents. Even with their presence at some of the testing, I didn't reveal to them the full purpose of the tests, and the eventual lung cancer diagnosis. After the ordeal was over, right before their cruise, I told my parents what I thought was good news: I had ABPA, with mucoid impaction and a granuloma, which in my case was a small benign nodule. I didn't know the generic definition of granuloma, but Dad must have known: it could range from a harmless collection of cells to a malignant tumor. All I knew was that for me, the diagnosis was good because I didn't have lung cancer. When I told Dad, he looked sad. Then he and Mom left for vacation.

For a long time, I believed that I had killed my father with this news. Though my parents had survived a lot of upset in their lives, I became obsessed with the idea that maybe my diagnosis put Dad's heart over the edge. Maybe he thought I had cancer even though I never told him about the *cancer* (whisper) misdiagnosis.

In the end, Dad's death probably had nothing to do with me. Still, I was riddled with shame for withholding my secret, and riddled with guilt that Dad died soon after I divulged the truth (well, most of the truth). Dad would never learn that I was fine and healthy again. I also felt sad and guilty that I was never able to say "goodbye," or "I love you," or "thanks," and I turned my guilt inward, blaming myself for Dad's massive heart attack.

Food helped with the sadness. Or seemed to help. After Dad's sudden death, between the prednisone and the mourning I gained 60 pounds. In my better moments, I reflected on the high points of Dad's life. When my father was 75, he had a book published that he had been working on for years, *Rehabilitation Medicine and Psychiatry*. As editor and contributor, this large volume was a capstone of Dad's work as a dual diplomate in psychiatry and rehabilitation, and a pioneer in both fields. Although he was uncommonly modest, Dad was very proud of his book. Beaming, he said, "I've accomplished everything I ever set out to accomplish in life."

Shortly before his death, Dad and I reminisced about that comment and he retracted his words, "I never should have said that... a person should always feel that there's something more to learn, something more to accomplish in life."

CHAPTER TWENTY-SEVEN

ON BECOMING A MOM

Six months after Dad died, Steve and I moved to the suburbs. At 30, I was eager to start a family and convinced Steve we needed a bigger place. We scouted Westchester County, midway between his parents in Riverdale and my Mom in Rockland. After visiting several neighborhoods, we chose the one that felt most simpatico: excellent schools, modest and affordable houses, and enough Jewish liberal transplants from Manhattan. In an ironic twist, we found ourselves living less than two miles from my childhood home on Evergreen Road.

Life in Ardsley was an adjustment. I made one friend easily, the wife of Steve's colleague who moved from the Upper West Side to Ardsley a few weeks before we did. Maura had a 2-year-old and wasted no time choosing a synagogue, nursery school, and supermarket. By the time we unpacked our boxes, my new friend taught me the ropes to make a successful transition from urban to suburban life.

Meeting other DINKS (Double Income, No Kids) like us was a challenge because I was still mourning my father and recovering from a severe case of sciatica. The shooting leg pains immobilized me for a month. I worked from home and sucked Valium like candy. At the bank, I was promoted to Vice President but couldn't drag my body to corporate headquarters. One of the executives sent his driver on the Q-T to transport me to the festivities.

On weekends, Steve and I spent time together in between his on-call schedule and handyman responsibilities. Steve's dad, trained as an airplane mechanic, had taught Steve how to fix almost anything, and Steve became a skilled carpenter, electrician, plumber, painter, wallpaperer, roofer, and appliance repairman. Steve liked to do everything himself but on the occasions when I was allowed to hire an expert, he often questioned the competence of their work, convinced he could have done it better. I became Steve's assistant though I lacked the know-how, patience, and perfectionism to be a worthy apprentice. For years, our weekends were filled with fights, failures (mine), food, and our fair share of fun.

In October 1987, almost three years after Dad died, his namesake, Jonathan, was born. Three years later to the week, I gave birth to our second son, Adam. Despite having pressed Steve to have children, I found myself curiously unprepared. I had no idea what I was in for and assumed that my ability to achieve goals and master challenges would grant automatic success at rearing children.

As the youngest in my extended family, I didn't have exposure to smaller siblings or baby cousins to prepare me for children of my own. I had babysitting jobs but they were limited to a few hours at a time. Raising kids turned out to be much more difficult than work or school. I was still grieving my father when Jonathan was born and food was my only comfort. I was already frazzled, and being a mom compounded my eating and my guilt.

I divided my time between caring for Jon and Adam, maintaining a career, and bingeing out of control. I didn't mind the dual role of career woman and mom. In fact, I thrived on the "working mom" identity. I needed the self-esteem and satisfaction I gained from helping clients and earning money to boost my self-esteem in our marriage. But the bingeing meant that even when I was home, not working, I couldn't be fully present for my boys. Though physically present, I missed many key moments in their lives as I ate compulsively and obsessed about food.

In my first pregnancy, I began at a weight of 200 pounds. My doctor was concerned that at 5'3" (officially 5'2" and three quarters), I was at such a dangerous weight, that I should not gain more than

25, at most 30 pounds. Despite his admonitions, I used pregnancy as a legitimate excuse to eat. Toward the end of the seventh month, I had to weigh in every week. Before the nurse even put me on the scale, I offered up my best rationalizations for why I ate so much even though I knew it wasn't good for me. She was kind and sympathetic, and would wink at me and say, "We don't have to write down that extra pound," and she would round down on my chart. While I was gaining water weight and fat, my obstetrician never knew; it was the nurse's and my little secret.

In the middle of my eighth month, my blood pressure shot up and the doctor was very concerned. He became hands-on and weighed me himself, noting that I had gained a lot of weight in an unusually short period of time. Red light alert for pre-eclampsia. The old-fashioned name, toxemia, made me shudder because it sounded so scary and so... toxic. My physician set a major treatment plan into motion: bed rest, low salt, more-frequent visits. I was in a quandary: *Should I tell him the nurse fudged for me, or do I just do what he says?* Since pre-eclampsia was a confirmed diagnosis, and I was conscientious enough to know that my baby's life was at risk, I capitulated and spent my last month in bed following strict doctor's orders.

On Yom Kippur, October 3, 1987, I began to have contractions. My doctor and most of his colleagues were in temple, which left me in the hands of one of the few Gentile doctors in the practice. At 275 pounds, my contractions made me keel over in pain but my fat and my baby made it hard to feel comfort. This obstetrician confirmed what my own doctor had speculated: I would require a Caesarean section. My pubic bones were too close and the passage too narrow; my blood pressure was elevating, and my morbid obesity could lead to complications. I had prepared myself for a C-section and I was fine about it, but all my natural childbirth classes frowned on that surgery and a small piece of me still wanted to be "politically correct." Fat, uncomfortable, and vulnerable, I let go of my stab at correctness and asked the doctor to rush me into surgery.

Writhing in pain with every contraction, I was wheeled into the operating room. The room was freezing. A Chinese anesthesiologist explained to me in broken English that he was going to inject an epidural in my back and I had to sit (rather than lie down) on the table and bend forward. All I wanted to do was lie down and crawl into a fetal position but I did as I was told. With my legs dangling over the table, I hunched over and waited as the doctor punctured holes in my back. It seemed like he was taking a long time and I was getting increasingly uncomfortable. Under the harsh lights, in the cold room, bent over as best I could with a big basketball on my lap, I heard the doctors whispering and I knew something was amiss.

I asked what the problem was and no one answered. Finally Dr. Chu explained that the needle wasn't the right size; he had to get another one. I waited, painfully aware of my baby begging to be released. The doctor from my practice was very matter-of-fact, with few touchy-feely skills and I detected impatience in his voice. Luckily, the female OB who was brought in to assist from another practice was kind and nurturing. Dr. Bennet introduced herself to me, held my hand, and told me I'd be fine. I was so grateful to have a soft voice in that hard room.

Dr. Chu returned and told me not to worry; this needle would work. Then I felt the stabs a few more times in different parts of my back before I heard him speak again under his breath. I couldn't understand what he was saying but I knew it didn't sound good. The kind doctor explained in her soft voice, "Marcia, because of your weight, the standard needle won't go deep enough into your back so the anesthesiologist found a longer needle. This one doesn't work either. Dr. Chu has been trying to figure out a new solution but your contractions are more frequent and we're afraid your blood pressure will spike so we need to operate right away. We're going to have to put you to sleep."

I didn't like what the kind doctor said and though the disgrace washed over me more horrifically than the contractions, I knew I had no choice. My indiscretions caught up with me and my baby was in danger. I asked what my husband thought and they said he wanted to do whatever was right for me and our child. There was no dialogue— I signed the papers and allowed the doctor to put me to sleep so I could have my baby. In a faraway place in my head, I bemoaned that my son would be born into shame (my shame) but from that moment on, everything happened fast and I lost consciousness.

Despite my fears and guilt, I gave birth to a normal baby boy on Yom Kippur. According to Jewish lore, babies born on Yom Kippur have a special holiness. The C-section itself was uneventful but my blood pressure spiked and I had to be given a magnesium sulfate drip. I was so medicated between the pharmaceuticals for the delivery and the blood pressure drugs that I wasn't allowed to see Jonathan until the next day.

For years after, moms would talk about drug-free labor, natural deliveries, first bondings with their baby at their breasts. In order not to feel inferior, I'd keep silent. Every time I thought about being put to sleep in an era when twilight sleep was obsolete, I was flooded with feelings of inferiority and incompetence. I was mad at myself for being so fat, that I couldn't stop eating even when my child's life depended on it, and I was even more angered and ashamed that I had been exposed. Until now, I had determined that no one besides my doctors, my husband, and I would ever know the secret, which so shamed me, surrounding Jon's birth.

Once I detoxified from the medications and my IV's were removed, I kept my baby with me as often as I could, to make up for lost time. When I tried nursing, I wasn't successful and this sweet, patient baby of mine had more patience than I did. My breasts, engorged and huge to begin with, were way bigger than Jonathan's little head and I was nervous about smothering him, starving him, and not being good enough for him. Multiple times, the maternity nurse showed me how to adjust my oversized body so my son could nurse but it didn't work well and from the start, I had to supplement with formula.

For the first few years of Jon's life, I was filled with anxiety and stress. I had sworn after the epidural incident that I would stop bingeing and lose weight because no one could be more humiliated than I was. And yet, in my insecurity as a new mom, the only fallback position I knew was food. Nothing else comforted me, nothing else was as nonjudgmental and loyal a friend. I ate my food, then Jonathan's food (I even sampled his sweet baby fruits), and as he got older, I ate his soggy French fries and mushy toddler grilled cheese bits.

I always had a competitive streak. As the youngest, it was commonplace for me to compare myself to my siblings and their friends. As a new mother, I repeated this pattern and always came up short. While other moms in their pregnancy were playing Suzuki violin to their children in *vivo*, I was busy whooshing around in my high-powered career. While other moms ate healthy foods and fed their babies "Earth's Best" or their own organic homemade food blended in the baby-food processor, I wolfed down rainbow cookies and fed my baby commercial baby food. Like me, he favored the sugary fruit jars and rejected the healthy pureed green vegetables.

From minute #1 after my son's birth, I was convinced that I was inept as a mom. I hoped that enrolling in the right classes might get me on track. As soon as Jonathan could crawl, I called up Maura to point me in the right direction. She suggested Mommy and Me and later Gymboree, classes de rigueur for super moms to bond with other super moms and their babies. Both of these classes were mostly filled with stay-at-home moms or nannies. As I was a part-time working mom with a live-in nanny, I didn't quite fit in with either group, and I felt like an outsider at a time when I wanted so badly to feel included.

In our town, working moms often hired live-in nannies or au pairs from remote parts of the United States or from foreign countries. Most of these girls were 18-25 years old with a love of children but not a lot of professional experience. My situation was unique in that my au pair, Denise, a 30-year-old (obese) woman from Montana, was also a licensed practical nurse, an LPN. She knew a lot about babies and I always trusted that my children were safe and well nurtured under her care. Though I was two years older than Denise, I was intimidated by her knowledge, and that added to my own sense of inadequacy.

Every day, my physician husband and my nurse au pair discussed how many cc's of food the baby ingested and how many diapers he saturated within a certain period of time. I couldn't have commented on those details if you'd offered me a million dollars, but that became my definition of a good mother: someone so attentive that she would know the answers to all those questions. I took everything as a criticism and a sign of ineffectiveness: I'm feeding him too fast or too slow. He should be on his back, not his front. He should be on his front, not his back.

To handle my parenting anxiety, I worked even harder at my career. I left the bank to launch a part-time consulting business, and was able to divide my time between toilet training and leadership training; leadership training was infinitely more successful. I was at my best standing in front of a training class, addressing a large audience, or coaching an executive about her career.

One day, when Jonathan was a toddler, I had a particularly good day at work. I returned home relaxed. I didn't listen to the narrative about how many naps my son had taken (how many was he supposed to take?) or his reaction to a new food. I didn't analyze, *what would a good mom do?* Without thinking, I just picked him up, looked him straight in the eye, and laughed as I twirled him around higher and higher—as high as a bird. I was completely at ease; in that moment, it was just me with my adorable baby Jonathan. We connected, person to person and I was able to feel his heart and look into his delicious brown eyes. I wasn't second-guessing myself, or my abilities. I wasn't comparing him to anyone else or to the prescribed texts. We were two people joined in genuine pleasure and appreciation.

That was my first day of true bonding with my child, much later than the "natural labor" moms bonded with their babies. It came according to my timetable. In that moment, I learned how to be a "real mom."

By the time Adam arrived, I was more at ease. My pregnancy was relatively uneventful although I weighed about 250 pounds at his delivery. Throughout the nine months, my doctor had assured me that I wouldn't have the same physical problems as I had with Jonathan. Toxemia is more common in first pregnancies and as this was a planned C-section, I didn't have to go through labor. I was also 25 pounds less than my first delivery. I sighed with relief when the standard epidural needle glided into my skin, cut through the fat, and hit the first time. I was awake for Adam's birth and his first smile outside the womb.

I was able to appreciate Adam and his little body and tiny gestures without all the worries and neuroses I had as a first-time mom three years earlier. In the first week after Adam's birth, I reveled in the way his smile erupted into little dimples, and his face lit up every time his brother cooed. I noticed, even at that early age, that Adam had the same squeezable cheeks as me and the same feisty spirit, and I loved that genetic mirror.

Little did I know that one week after Adam's birth, my joy would be curtailed with horrific suddenness when my mother was rushed to the hospital. Within minutes, the emphasis in my life changed from being a new mother to being a daughter facing a terrible unknown.

CHAPTER TWENTY-EIGHT

NO REGRETS

There was never a family event without Mom at the center. The life of the party, Mom was also the hostess, gourmet cook, babysitter, storyteller, and crowd-pleaser. Yet, on October 3, 1990, Mom was nowhere to be found at Adam's *bris,* the circumcision ceremony held eight days after a male baby's birth. "Where's Mom?" I asked everyone. "We're not starting without her."

Mom was cloistered in our spare bedroom with her sister Elsie, and I had to tromp through the house to find her so that we could begin the ceremony. Annoyed, I walked back through the crowded living room accompanied by Mom and Elsie and announced to the *mohel* that he could start the blessings leading up to the circumcision.

Hours later, after the rituals, food, and desserts, half the crowd stayed for Jonathan's third birthday party, featuring Marsha the Musical Moose and her puppets. Mesmerized children were scattered about the floor, spellbound by the enchanting puppets. Jonathan was enjoying the spotlight after having been upstaged for the past week by the birth of his baby brother. Steve's parents were clapping and singing along with the moose, and I was laughing with the children until I realized that Mom wasn't in the room again. I excused myself for a moment and went looking for her. She and Elsie were in the office whispering again.

"Mom," I complained, "Where are you? It's Jonathan's party."

"Yes, honey, I'll be right there."

True to her word, Mom joined us soon after, though she barely participated in the festivities. Where was the vivacious, fun-loving, doting Grandma I knew Mom to be?

The next day was Thursday, and we were all exhausted. We had finally cleaned up from the two parties and the 50 people who had crowded into our living room. I nursed Adam a few times, and let Jonathan nap in our bed. At night we called Mom to say hi. She wasn't feeling well but said not to worry. Mom always said she was fine, not to worry, even through the last decade when she suffered from Polycythemia Vera, a rare blood disease in which she produced excess red blood cells due to an abnormality in her bone marrow. This blood condition was chronic and didn't affect Mom's quality of life except during flare-ups when the uncontrollable itching was intolerable. Then Dad would take Mom to the hematologist for a bloodletting; thankfully, not one that involved leeches. This time, Mom's symptoms weren't related to itching; she simply couldn't get enough oxygen and her chest strained from labored breathing.

On Friday, Steve and I bundled up the babies and drove over the Tappan Zee Bridge to check on Mom. Lively yellows and blues had long replaced the old institutional green. On that day, the house appeared gray. Mom was muted and pale—not lively and radiant as usual—and her breathing was heavy. Her regular doctor was away for the weekend, and Mom didn't feel comfortable contacting the covering physician, whom she didn't know. We wanted to take her to the emergency room but she refused. Steve took Mom's vital signs, which were stable. Mom insisted that we take the kids home as they were overly tired from the hectic week. It's hard to argue with Mom. We helped her upstairs to bed and elicited a promise that she would call if she felt worse, and she would rest over the weekend and see her doctor first thing Monday morning. Then we left.

Saturday afternoon, the phone rang. Miriam, one of Mom's friends, was on the line. Even before she finished "hello," we were troubled by the call: It was Saturday. Miriam was an observant Jew who never used the phone on the Sabbath except in a dire emergency. Jewish law states that if there is an emergency, you are obligated to make a call.

Miriam told us she had stopped by Mom's after temple and found her very sick. Mom had refused an ambulance but needed to go to the hospital.

Steve jumped into his car and drove to Mom's while I stayed home with the boys. Miriam's assessment was correct; Mom was very sick. Steve wrapped Mom in a warm coat and took her to the emergency room. All day, I alternated between holding vigil at the phone, tending to the children, and visiting the refrigerator. The leftover rugelach, sponge cake, birthday cupcakes, and pasta salad filled in the hours. There was no way to contact Steve; all I could do was wait. Steve called at one point from the emergency room to say they were waiting for a doctor, and then again late afternoon, "Your mom is being admitted to the hospital for more tests and she's resting now in a private room," he said. "I'll take care of a few more details and will be home soon." Not much information, but at least I wasn't completely alone fearing the worst.

Later that evening, when Steve came home, he could barely speak. He told me Mom would be hospitalized for at least a few days. Drained and exhausted, he fell into bed. I desperately wanted to pig-out—there were still so many cakes and cookies left—only first I had to mobilize enough energy to call the rest of the family and Mom's friends, giving them what little information I had. When I called Miriam, she was very abrupt: "You and Steve should never have left her alone yesterday. She was very ill, and she should have gone to the hospital."

I hung up the phone, stung by her words. Mom's condition that day seemed borderline, and we made a judgment call not to push Mom into doing something against her will. I was so used to my mother as the consummate problem solver and decision maker that I didn't realize that we could and should have overridden her decision. Months later, I felt some relief when her doctor reassured me that early on, Mom's condition was inconsistent; one day she could seem OK and the next day she could plummet. I made my round of phone calls and felt badly that Steve hadn't supplied me with details—then I could have addressed all my siblings' questions. The more I repeated what I knew, the more agitated I became. I called my in-laws and asked if they could babysit the grandchildren the next day while I visited Mom.

When the elevator opened on Mom's floor and I turned the corner to her ward, my stomach dropped. The sign above the swinging doors read Oncology. I was accustomed to Mom seeing a hematologist-oncologist for her blood condition, but I always focused on the hematology part, never the oncology. This was clearly an oncology ward. I did not voice the dreaded word but heard it replay in my mind in a whisper: *cancer.*

Typically a talker, Mom was quiet. She was undergoing procedures and tests, awaiting a diagnosis. Medications made her feel a little better, but she admitted she was uncomfortable. This wasn't like her. The rare occasions I'd heard Mom complain were after she'd cooked nonstop for weeks for the Passover Seder or taken care of one of her (now) seven grandsons for several days and was tired. Otherwise, no matter how she felt, Mom would put on her game face and take care of business. Not today. We chatted a bit about the *bris,* how wonderful it was to see all those relatives and old friends, and how my two little boys were so adorable. Then she dozed and I left, depressed in a way I had never been before—not even when Dad died. The thought of losing Mom, the fear of being an orphan, the sadness that my children would not know any of their Meislin grandparents—all left me feeling defenseless and defeated. On the way out, I stopped at the coffee shop and picked out a cheese Danish from under the glass dome.

I visited every few days. My siblings and I worked out a schedule so that every day one of us was at the hospital. My second visit was the worst. As I was entering, the doctor was exiting. His head was down in a chart on which he was writing. I went straight to Mom. The results of the tests were back, and she had her diagnosis: cancer—advanced lung cancer. Despite quitting cigarettes a quarter century earlier, Mom's tobacco habit came back to haunt her. Flashes of the Millman family tree flitted across my brain: Mom's father and two brothers, all heavy smokers, died of lung disease. Would Mom be next?

Without blinking an eye, I said, "OK, Mom, we'll figure this out."

As it was my visiting day, it was again my job to tell the family. I tightened the binder around my breasts to make sure my milk wasn't coming in and called the others. Despite—or because of—the seriousness of the message I had to deliver, I did what Meislins always do: I tried to keep my tone light, optimistic, as if there was still some chance that this wasn't true. If I had allowed myself to experience the true feelings roiling inside me—my life would have fallen apart right then and there on the linoleum floor of Good Samaritan Hospital.

In front of Mom, I put on my smiley face and proceeded to call the relatives, stifling any tears that might have otherwise escaped. The last times I'd cried in front of her had been six years before, first, at Dad's funeral and a year later, at the unveiling of his gravestone.

"Yes, Mom has cancer—lung cancer… Oh you know Mom, she can fight anything… No, we don't know yet. The doctor will be in later."

At one point, I left to find the doctor. He confirmed the diagnosis. I asked how long she might live with this condition.

"We can't really say. We don't know."

"But a range? Is there a range?"

I wouldn't let up. He averted his gaze for a moment then made eye contact and said, "Maybe six months. Maybe more. Maybe less."

Stunned, I stood like a stone. Despite the tight binding, my breasts were engorged with milk, and I was in pain. My head ached. My heart hurt. I turned off my feelings and turned on my brain. I would figure out a solution and make everything right. I told myself, She'll be fine. Everything's going to be all right. It's not like the old days when cancer was a death sentence. Mom will beat it. As I said this, I also told myself the truth. One look at her, and I knew I was lying. This ashen, fragile, bony creature—usually strong as hell—wasn't beating anything. Twenty-five years before, she had licked cigarettes, but the damage was done.

It was too late for chemo, too late for surgery. All that was left was radiation—and pain. Mom spent half the time in the hospital and half the time at home with an aide.

For the next three months, as Mom lay dying, I barely managed to pump my breasts, dress Jonathan for preschool, kiss Adam goodbye, and spend a long day in the hospital, the same hospital in which so many years before I had lain under the oxygen tent. I juggled the needs of a 3-year-old who now developed asthma, a baby who was semi-colicky, a mother who rarely complained, a husband who buried difficult feelings, a fledgling business that needed attention, and an au pair who was almost always irritated because the spare car we gave her needed repairs, the house was too hot, or the baby didn't nap.

In order to cope, I had to numb all my feelings: post-partum blues, shock, grief, anger, frustration, and overwhelming anxiety. I knew I could kill these feelings by feeding them to death. On the way to and from the hospital, I tanked up on snacks, while most of my meals-on-the-run consisted of pizza. I spent endless hours on the phone with family sharing updates and reaching consensus. The calls were made more tolerable by my automatic ingestion of one animal cracker after another... I nibbled rather than cried... my mouth in constant motion.

On Mom's birthday in early November, I went to Annie Sez and bought a new teal blue-and-gold dress with a jacket for Mom to wear to her best friend's granddaughter's wedding. For weeks, the dress stayed on its hanger in the closet. One day Mom said to me, "Marcia, that's a really pretty dress. But I don't think I'm going to the wedding. Why don't you take it back?"

"Mom, even if you don't get to the wedding, you've lost weight and your clothes are too big. Maybe I can get you something else to wear?" She said she'd think about it.

The teal blue-and-gold dress hung alone in the skinny hospital closet. One day Mom said, "I'll tell you what, Marcia. I'm going home soon, and it's very cold. I could use a winter coat."

I was thrilled. Finally I could do something concrete. A few minutes later, she changed her mind. "You know what?" She said. "Why don't we just wait?" I waited.

Shortly before Thanksgiving, Mom came home. It was my day at the hospital, and I was scared. I didn't know if I could support Mom by myself. I asked her friend Sarah if she would meet me at Mom's house to help us up the stairs. In the car, Mom seemed surprised that it was fall and the leaves had already changed colors.

"I don't like this time of year," she said.

"Why, Mom?"

"It's depressing. Even though it's pretty, you know that right around the corner is winter, and it will be cold and dreary."

I'd never heard Mom talk this way; she seemed so sad and wistful.

Sarah met us and carried Mom's teal dress on the hanger. I had Mom's suitcase in my hand, and we walked her into the house. The home health aide was waiting at the door. Allan and Bobby had been there the week before to help Jay set up the downstairs bedroom, and Arleen had filled the refrigerator with food. Mom went right in to lie down.

Mom insisted on cooking some of her Thanksgiving dishes. Alternating between sitting and standing, she made two of her signature recipes, eggplant parmesan and vegetarian chopped liver, and supervised the rest from her seat. Mom ate very little but watched in silence (when was Mom ever silent?) as platters of food were passed in front of her children and grandchildren in her sight for the last time. She was very moved when 3-year-old Jonathan turned to her and said, "Grandma, do you want something to drink?" She mentioned later that with all the commotion, little Jonathan seemed to be the one most sensitive to her needs. When I had time to reflect on those last weeks, I realized that the rest of us had been preoccupied with trying to collectively accomplish all that Mom had done solo for as long as we could remember.

The next month went quickly and slowly at the same time. My days revolved around visiting Mom and waiting for the phone to ring with the latest report. One day when I was with her, Mom pointed to the dress, now in her downstairs closet. "I want you to return that dress and buy something for yourself." I started to protest, but didn't. I think I knew what she meant.

In mid-December, I came down with a horrible cold and stopped visiting Mom for fear I'd infect her and make her sicker. As Hanukkah neared, it became clear that I needed to go see my mother. I discussed it with Steve, and we realized that my cold probably wouldn't matter to Mom at this point. Just in case, I wouldn't sit too close. I knew it would be tough emotionally, though less tough than if I stayed away completely.

At the end of December, Mom went back into the hospital. I started reading Elisabeth Kübler-Ross's *On Death and Dying,* which chronicled the stages of dying and grief. I was preparing for the difficult journey ahead. I knew my siblings and I were past the first stage, denial. I dealt with the second stage, anger, as I always did—by submerging it in food. Stage three: Each of us privately did our own bargaining with God, and with the doctors, angling to earn Mom just a little more time. That was not to be. The end of Mom's life was clearly upon us. We hovered somewhere in the fourth stage, depression. It would be a long time before we reached acceptance, the final stage. I returned the dress and took store credit.

Mom was gracious until the end. Steve hadn't seen her much in the last two months. As a doctor, Steve was used to seeing death up close, but when it came to his own family, he couldn't handle the feelings. Regardless of his fear, I convinced him to accompany me. On our way upstairs, Steve stopped at the hospital vending machine to buy two different chocolate bars. When he bent over her bed to kiss her hello, Mom pointed to the bars sticking out of Steve's pocket, "What's that?" she laughed.

"Want one?" He asked her.

"No, thanks." Mom was a chocolate lover.

When the oncologist suggested Mom start on morphine for her intense pain we all knew there was no choice. He explained that the level of morphine meant Mom would have no pain, and it also meant that her organs would shut down within a short time.

Mom looked regal in the black turban I had pulled out of our costume box. The morphine had relaxed her face and body, and she seemed pain-free. Hours before, my siblings and I had our final dialogue with Mom. My brother Bob, a social worker, asked, "Mom, are you scared?"

"No," she said. "I'm not afraid. I've had a wonderful life, and I have no regrets."

"We love you, Mom."

"I love you all, too."

She smiled at her children standing around her bed and closed her eyes.

It was time to say goodbye. I wanted so badly to stay in the hospital with Mom, but the doctor said he didn't know how long it might be— maybe hours, maybe days. My children were at Mom's house and I had been gone a long time. I read psalms at Mom's bedside then made the difficult decision to leave. The doctor called at five minutes past midnight as the year crossed over from 1990 to 1991 to tell us that Mom had died peacefully in her sleep. She hadn't awakened.

I left the kids with Steve and drove right back to the hospital to be with Mom's soul: Judaism teaches that the soul inhabits a person a full day after he or she has died, and I wanted to be there as long as the hospital would let me during this period. The nurse handed me her rings and allowed me to sit next to the bed and hold my mother's hand before they took away her body. Staring at Mom's tranquil face, her head swaddled in her turban, her body still and calm, I reflected on her last gift to us—as generous and loving as her life. Mom passed on to her children and grandchildren the legacy of her final words, "I'm not afraid. I've had a wonderful life, and I have no regrets."

It took me a long time to appreciate the miracle of that kind of death.

PART V

ADULTHOOD

"The path will wait while you take the stone from your shoe."

- Greeting card

CHAPTER TWENTY-NINE

DISEASE OF NEVER ENOUGH

Mom's death triggered a series of never-ending binges in a vain attempt to fill the empty hole inside. No matter how much I consumed, it wasn't enough to numb the pain. I had an illusion that if I ate just a little more, I would find relief. My preferences were for sugar and comfort foods because they reminded me of Mom and my childhood, a time when I had two living parents. For the first time, I felt remorse that I had wasted half my teenage years angry and rebellious, wishing that God had given me different parents. Neither the burnt corner piece of the macaroni and cheese casserole, nor the thick crusty heel of the fresh rye bread with seeds, provided the consolation I was craving. Both were Mom's favorites, too.

I never felt I had enough of anything: food, attention, love. The irony was that I was getting enough food; that was clear. I was getting enough attention; people had been very solicitous of me when Mom died. I was getting enough love. Jonathan and Adam were affectionate and cuddly and they seemed genuinely happy to see me whenever I walked through the door. That made me wonder if I had a rupture somewhere because even when I received enough, it never *felt like* enough. I honestly thought I was draining out of the bottom. I would pour food in my mouth, yet my stomach felt empty. I had friends who cared about me, yet I felt lonely and unloved. I knew there was a deficit in my marriage, but that was old news. I had already reconciled years before that our marriage would have its limitations and I didn't expect Steve to all of a sudden gush with love just because I lost my parents.

I was like a hamster on a treadmill—chasing more, more, more, forever chasing my own tail. I was sure that eventually I would find the right rainbow cookie to fill the pit. Or enough vanilla ice cream custard to cure the itch. Nonetheless, after a while, as with drug addicts, the usual fix was no longer sufficient. To get the same high, I needed to double my dose. The void would scream at me again, "Fill me! More! More! If I don't have more, I'll die." After a few minutes, I would counteract with a bigger, fatter dose to extinguish the fire in my belly. What I did by mistake was stoke the flame, rather than extinguish the sparks.

The binge often began with a pound of rainbow cookies from Saw Mill Bakery. I'd ask for a bag rather than the white cardboard box because the cookies were part of my covert operation. I headed half a mile down the road to Vinny's Pizza, an overt and legitimate operation because pizza constituted dinner. On the two miles to home, I consumed half the cookies by dipping my right hand into the bag as I navigated the tricky twists and turns of Snakehill Road with my left. Before I reached home, I made sure to hide the white smushed-up bag with chocolate stains in my pocketbook for later.

At dinner, I ate my two legitimate slices of pizza. As I cleaned the kitchen, I felt entitled to whatever sticky pieces of crust my young boys had left on their plastic Ninja Turtle plates. After the plates were washed and the table and high chair sponged off, everyone left the kitchen except for me. I claimed some last-minute cleanup, which turned out to be a grand slam cleanup of all the snacks and leftovers. Surreptitiously, I slinked into my large pocketbook and retrieved the rest of the tri-color cookies. Afraid that I might be found out, I popped three of the four cookies in my mouth in rapid succession, tasting almost nothing. I couldn't discern between the green, red, and yellow layer. I resolved that on the fourth and final pastry, I would take it apart, layer by layer and eat each color separately, saving the hard chocolate top for last.

Angry with myself that I crammed the first few cookies without luxuriating in them, I resolved to find something else that I could indulge in and savor. As I considered my options, I glimpsed the potato chips in the closet, and surmised I would have one or two in the interim while I decided which food would constitute my grand finale. Standing in the closet, one half-door open, the other one still shut, I pulled the Big Clip off the chip bag, determined to have just one. I folded the bag, and gingerly returned the clip to its rightful position. I shut the cabinet door.

Giving the chips a second thought, it occurred to me that my jaw might need some extra crunching. I returned to the chips, standing in the once again half-opened cupboard, bag in hand, with crumbs all over my face and shirt. I wasn't a big salt fan but I justified my choice with the adage, "Betcha can't eat just one." That was true; I had one and now I was on track to finish the whole bag. I felt disgusted and before the bag was empty, threw it away and walked out of the kitchen into the adjacent dining room. I was mad at myself, because I had obliterated the sugary taste of cookies in my mouth and was headed down a salty trajectory that didn't even interest me.

Since the sweet sensation had already been trounced, I thought better of the move and returned to the garbage to retrieve the last few chips, realizing that it almost didn't pay to throw them out with so few left in the bag. I demolished those, wetting my fingertips so I could consume every last morsel in the bottom of the bag. And still my mouth (aka my soul), wanted more. Back in the closet, there wasn't much of interest. I had already demolished the cookies, the pizza, and now the chips. Foraging through an almost-empty closet, I nabbed raisins, dried fruits, old peanuts, stale crackers. It didn't matter as long as it was more of something.

All that transpired in less than 30 minutes, sometimes just 15.

CHAPTER THIRTY

BINGEING ON SUCCESS

I had hoped that career success would offer immunity against bingeing, or at least occupy me so I wouldn't have time to binge. In fact, the opposite was true; success left me starving. And grabbing food, junk food, was a big part of my fast-paced life.

In October 1987, after Jonathan was born, I left my job at NatWest Bank to become an entrepreneur and split my time between training and tots. I negotiated with NatWest to spend two days per week teaching Customer Service to the branches. The other three days, I worked out of a spare-bedroom-turned-office (much to the chagrin of my live-in nanny, Denise, who was irritated that I didn't leave the house every morning) and began to build my management training and consulting business.

Though I lost an occasional prospect who was shocked that the person behind the buoyant telephone voice wasn't exactly buoyant, people who knew my capabilities hired me in spite of my weight, and I grew a vibrant and burgeoning business. I always put 150% into my training programs and made sure never to disappoint a client who took a chance on me. I worked much harder than most of my peers because I felt that as an obese woman, I had more to prove.

After Jonathan's birth, I lost about twenty pounds of baby weight and hovered around the 250 mark. I knew that obese women often came across slovenly and unkempt and I was determined to break the stereotype. I spent much of my profits on clothes, sporting only designer suits. I bought my accessories from MCM, a Madison

Avenue boutique whose handbags were imprinted with the same initials as mine. I had my hair colored and cut at the best salons, and was meticulous about manicures.

Every new client and new program generated a great deal of anxiety: Will I dazzle them? Will I be brilliant enough, aka, will I be so brilliant that they won't notice how fat I am? The biggest worry of all consumed me for weeks: What will I wear? Often the day before a speech—despite a closet full of expensive suits—I would rush into my favorite plus-size shop, and buy yet another new outfit determined that this one would camouflage my real size.

My typical workday started with two hours of primping to craft a confident, well-heeled (albeit corpulent) woman. By 7:30, I entered my corporate training room and began to move furniture. Despite my size, I bounced around the classroom to keep the sessions lively, and I needed clear passage through the aisles. Then I pulled up the Saran Wrap from the continental breakfast tray, sampled the muffins, and rearranged the rest to eliminate empty spaces. The morning was spent educating and enlivening my audience with the objective that the more entertained an audience is, the less they will focus on my fat. There is a reason for the stereotype "the jolly fat person."

I usually made it through the group lunch without eating excessively but the mid-afternoon break was a killer, especially when chocolate chip cookies were served. While my audience could only smell the freshly baked buttery-chocolaty aromas wafting from the back of the room, I had the privilege of both sight and smell which drove me mad as I was able to focus on little else. My mouth watered as I recalled the nightly ritual at Willard Straight Hall at Cornell, when fresh-baked chocolate chip cookies were released and all the students crawled out of the woodwork to stand on line.

At the end of class, clients would come by to de-brief the workshop and share superlative feedback they received from participants. They'd usually suggest I take home the leftover cookies for my children, which I did, knowing full well that my kids would never lay eyes on them. Yet, each time, I prayed that the excellent feedback and validation I received from the evaluations would be enough to sustain me; I wouldn't need added comfort. Yet, each time, I needed more. After consuming the cookies in the car, I'd continue the odyssey at Carvel and Vinny's Pizza, and arrive home in time for dinner with my husband. Steve would share news of his day, and I'd regale him with my stories, careful to omit mention of the binge.

At eight, I put the kids to bed, read them *Good Night Moon* (multiple times), listened as they recited their evening *Shema*, then headed up to watch TV. Around ten, I planted a seed in my head that perhaps the front door was unlocked and I better double-check. I stole downstairs and landed at the fridge, spoon in hand. With everyone asleep in the house, I dipped into the Edy's frozen yogurt, and relished the best eating of the day—what one of my diet programs dubbed, "This one's for me."

CHAPTER THIRTY-ONE

BODY IMAGE #3:
ASYLUM FOR ANGER

When the kids were older, I decided it was time to fulfill my dream of becoming a therapist; maybe then I could get at the root of my eating problem.

In my third year of training at the Gestalt Center of Long Island, my breakthrough came. I sat in the client chair, when Joyce, a skilled therapist-trainer, sat across from me and asked how I was feeling. Knowing me well, she suggested I let my body answer, not my head. I felt nothing in my body. My head swirled with a myriad of witty, sarcastic quips guaranteed to evoke chuckles from the six other students watching my work. After my second smart-aleck response, Joyce reminded me that my job was not to entertain an audience, but to stay in contact with feelings inside my body. Turning inside to listen for cues, all I could feel was the elastic waistband of my pants cutting into my stomach. I described this sensation to Joyce, editorializing with self-deprecating insults like "beached whale," "disgusting pig."

Mid-sentence, Joyce stopped me: "Do you always abuse yourself like this?" she asked.

"Yes, I always talk about my body like this," I answered, "I hate it."

Joyce invited me to try an experiment in which I would symbolically take off the outer layer of my body. I was riveted because in all my years of therapy, no one had ever suggested that I remove my fat to peek underneath. I metaphorically unzipped my skin down the front, as though removing a wetsuit, and shimmied out of my quivering body. I visualized lugging the huge bundle 3 feet away to a vacant chair.

Joyce asked me to describe my body now, without its shell. I had recently taken the kids to the Museum of Natural History, so it was easy to conjure up a skeletal image of myself that was all bone and muscle; just face, hair, and neck intact. Joyce proposed that I stand up and move in my new body. I jumped up in a flash, weightless and spry.

Less than three minutes after I inhabited my new agile form, I was startled by a familiar sensation of panic, anxiety, and adrenaline hosing through my bloodstream. In bright neon colors, these old allies sped around and around in a frenetic manner until they stopped short, crashing into each other. I pointed to where my big fleshy stomach used to be.

"I'm stuck, damn it. I can't push through this block and I feel like I'm going to burst." I identified the roadblock as anger.

Joyce asked me to make sounds, whatever sounds emerged. At the beginning I was embarrassed but she proposed that the group join me in noises of their own so I wouldn't be alone. Together, we pierced the air with jungle-like groans and screams for several minutes until my body erupted into a full-blown tantrum, raw and visceral. This explosion of rage had been lying dormant inside me for a long time. Exhausted, though energized, I collapsed into the couch.

The class proceeded to dissect my work. Despite Joyce's admonition to stay in my body, I wanted to jump back in my head and analyze the rage: *Was I mad as an infant because Mom was busy and she fed me on her timetable, not mine? Was I angry at Uncle Harry for dying? At God, for giving me asthma, or giving Jay his disabilities? Was I mad because of shame at being different?*

"Most of us will probably never know the exact reasons for our rage," Joyce taught, "but our cells, including fat cells, store these deep emotions and shield them with a protective armor. A catharsis like this can help release the feelings—and maybe even the fat."

Sooner or later, I knew I would have to get back under my skin, and I was ambivalent about re-entering my body. I loved being nimble, moving sprightly through space, having x-ray vision into my emotions. When Joyce announced it was time to get "dressed," I imagined zipping up my flesh.

When I reconnected with my skin, it wasn't as horrible as before. The anger was gone, the armor softer, more penetrable. Underneath, the sadness was still there—I felt the losses. I missed simple days when rainbow cookies cured everything. I missed my old body, the size 14 or 16 of my youth. Once the barrier of rage was lifted, the ache to be light and limber settled itself into my belly and wouldn't leave until I lost half my weight.

CHAPTER THIRTY-TWO

LAST HOUSE ON THE BLOCK

With anger out of the way, I had a clear line of sight to my grief. My therapist Liz and I tackled grief, sadness, and mourning, as I waited for the pounds to melt off. "Be gentle with yourself," she would say, "it's a process."

I had waited so long to be thin but only my patience was wearing thin, not my body. It seemed unfair that I had stripped off so much baggage and still couldn't unpack the weight. Liz asked me to write about all the diets and therapies I had tried, what I learned from each one, and why it didn't work in the long term.

I started with my mother's favorite, a "sensible" and nutritious diet program in which I received a lifetime of education about calories, portion size, food groups, and balanced meals. In addition, I learned a myriad of tricks and techniques for white knuckling my way through the day: chew lots of gum, fill up on diet drinks, eat free foods like sugar-free Jell-O as often as I want, and snack on their own brand of desserts.

The problem with this method—aside from having to weigh in— was that the main topics of conversation were low-calorie recipes, a moot point for someone who didn't cook. I also found myself eating a whole box of skinny desserts rather than the quota of one per day because my willpower didn't end after two bites of a lo-cal brownie. Regardless of the rapid accumulation of points, I couldn't stop after just one dessert.

The commercial diets that sold prepared foods offered very few vegetarian options. Nevertheless, I stocked up on frozen dinners, puddings, bars, and little packets of salad dressing. I enjoyed *schmoozing* with the saleswomen (aka counselors) in their offices, because the longer we talked, the more I could play with the gummy molds on her desk that represented "proper" serving sizes: teeny tiny white rubber pasta mounds, an orange cube of cheese the size of one die, and a 2-by-2 flat brown pancake. I walked out with a better understanding that I was a "volume" eater with a poor sense of perspective when it came to portions. These programs didn't last long for me because they were expensive and I didn't care for the taste of the food.

Expensive, but not as costly as the diet-pill docs to whom I wrote sizable checks for drug cocktails intended to melt off the weight in record time. With factory-like efficiency, I remember one doctor who handed me a panoply of multi-colored pills as he recited by rote his standard diet that began with 4 ounces of meat, chicken, or fish. Each time I interrupted to say, "Excuse me, doctor, but I don't eat meat, chicken, or fish," he acted as though I were invisible and continued on with the meat choices, eager to shoo me out of his office. Despite the affront, I returned for the quick results and the great boost of energy that kicked my life into higher gear than usual. I only stopped when the jittery side effects scared me more than my jiggly thighs.

Other than amphetamines, nothing worked faster than juice fasts and protein shakes. I could almost stand in front of the mirror and watch the weight peel off. With big breasts and ample hips, I nurtured a flutter of hope that even with curves like mine, I could actually have an hourglass figure. Before long, those hopes were dashed when I introduced "real" foods back into my diet and regained all of the weight I had lost—with a bonus.

All the holistic remedies I tried—acupuncture, acupressure, herbal supplements, seaweed wraps, colonics, metal balls behind my ears—made me feel virtuous because I was becoming healthy the natural way. For a brief period in college, I immersed myself in yoga and spent 10 days with a popular Swami at a retreat in the Bahamas. My spiritual practice consisted of a 4 a.m. wake-up, hour-long meditation, chanting, yoga, a light breakfast, then lectures, and more meditation. A "mellowed-out" Marcia returned to Ithaca and baked bread, saluted the sun, chanted in Sanskrit, and taught after-school yoga at the local middle school. I learned how to focus on my breath, care for my body, and reduce stress. I lost a few pounds, but mostly I just lost my momentum.

There were other failed attempts like low-carb diets, the one-type-of-food at a time diet, the eating-out-of-one-bowl diet, the color-card-deck diet. There were several forays into un-diets, in which there were no restricted foods but still plenty of rules that had to be followed: rules about listening to what your body craved so you could match the right foods to what was humming inside. Rules about eating alone so you could hear signals in your body that tell you you've had enough. I wanted to be that person who could listen to my body, eat intuitively, heed those internal hunger cues rather than the external ones that said, "You're passing a bakery—eat a pastry." Or, "It's six p.m.—do you know where your dinner is?" But after decades of overriding my natural mechanisms, this seemed nearly impossible. I couldn't stop eating certain foods once I started regardless of my stomach feeling full.

There were stabs at hypnosis, self-hypnosis, one-on-one therapy, group therapy, body image therapy, Gestalt therapy—individual, group, and training classes. Each new therapy, each new workshop, unearthed greater "aha" moments. Yet none of these were sufficient to break the deep-rooted habits of compulsive overeating, bingeing, and numbing my feelings with food.

The list of gyms and exercise programs where I had spent thousands of dollars was equally long. I couldn't imagine that there was anything left to try.

Liz listened to my litany of interventions and suggested it was time I join a program for food addicts. For two months, I obliged her, and found myself in church basements talking about food, God, and powerlessness. I had trouble accepting that I was powerless over food. Mom had convinced me all my life that if I just exerted more willpower, I could control my eating. Dad instilled the notion that as long as I ate in moderation, I'd be fine. Both tenets were challenged in this new model of my eating disorder as a disease, one that I was incapable of conquering by myself. I needed God, a mentor, and fellow addicts along the way who could help me.

I went to two meetings a week; the people were friendly and helpful. After two months in a recovery program, I didn't see any results on the scale and left. Leaving was made easier by a friend who said, "Marcia, of all people, you're someone who could accomplish anything you set your mind to. How could you all of a sudden throw up your hands, say you have no control over this problem, and give up? That doesn't sound like you."

Before I quit, I overheard several old-timers in the parking lot discussing their success at an inpatient rehab program, a kind of boot camp with rugged exercise, low-calorie food, and intensive therapy. I wanted to go. The boys were headed to camp and I was free for the summer. I applied for the expensive in-patient eating disorders program but my insurance only covered anorexics and bulimics, not morbidly obese compulsive overeaters.

At the suggestion of a world-renowned clinic, I underwent a psychiatric assessment for depression, a condition that might have deemed me eligible for coverage. As despondent as I was about weight and food, the doctor refused to certify me as depressed. He said I didn't qualify. In its stead, my insurance company allotted eight sessions with an eating disorders therapist on my plan.

Fresh off two months in recovery meetings, I walked into Mike's office and announced I was going to swear off snacks and walk the track. Each week, I reported my progress: snack/no snack, track/no track. Each account was accompanied by a corresponding positive or negative judgment about myself. Mike said nothing. I hadn't the faintest idea that I was mimicking Mom's self-proclaimed "good girl/bad girl" status dependent on that day's food intake or number on the scale. Finally, in week three, Mike stared at me and said, "I couldn't care less if you eat snacks or walk the track. You can lose weight or not lose weight; I don't care. I have no agenda for you."

I was shocked. "What do you mean you have 'no agenda' for me? Everyone has an agenda for me! Lose weight!" Mike wouldn't buy it. I left that session relieved and stunned. All my life, I pointed fingers at my mother, my husband, therapists, society, anyone—for my eating problems. It was *their* fault I was fat. Admittedly, I was the one who placed food in my mouth, but that was in reaction to *them*. The more *they* criticized me, the more I ate. I felt reassured having someone to blame.

But what if *they* didn't care about what I ate or how I looked? What if *they* were a "tabula rasa" and I had no opponent in a tug-of-war? What if I were the only person accountable for my eating and my weight? Mike had put a new chink in my armor. Only not quite enough to turn me around.

Almost a year after I left the churches and Mike, I found myself in a synagogue. It was the last day of Passover. I was 39 years old with two young children, at the end of my rope. I had crept up the scale to 250, 270, plateauing at 295, fairly sure that I had broken the 300 mark, but had stopped weighing myself. I worked harder than ever in therapy, "like a dog with a bone," Liz commented. I was tenacious about wanting to be thin and equally dogged about avoiding anything that smacked of deprivation. I stood in the large sanctuary staring at the brightly colored stained-glass windows listening to the cantor's doleful voice bellow out *El Maleh Rachamim,* honoring the dead. I broke down and cried for the past, the present, and the future. In that moment, I gave up the fight. I held out the white flag and beseeched God, "I give up. I can't do this. Help me!" I spent the rest of *Yizkor* having what Mom called "a good cry."

After services, I walked to the parking lot and noticed a thin congregant heading over to her sporty red Honda. I had no idea who she was though she looked vaguely familiar. She smiled and waved. I shrieked, "Nina, is that you?! I totally didn't recognize you!" With a huge smile, ear-to-ear, Nina sashayed over to my car in her trim black dress. She had lost 155 pounds and I couldn't stop screaming out my excitement and hugging her in congratulations.

"Oh, my God, how did you do it?" I begged.

Nina paused for a moment, then answered. " I go to a program for people addicted to food. We meet in a church off the highway."

Standing in front of me was living proof that my impossible goal could be possible. Over the years, when Nina and I ran into each other, we commiserated about our weight; we were both smart, competent, professional women who could accomplish pretty much any task placed before us. Except this. And now Nina had done it. She told me she was a size 8, sometimes a 6. We joked that even at birth, neither of us was a 6. I was spellbound, standing in the parking lot of the local synagogue. Maybe God could save me, after all.

That Tuesday night, Nina escorted me to her meeting. I spotted some faces from my daytime meetings the year before. Though skeptical, it was hard to deny the miracle of Nina, once morbidly obese like me, now thin as a board. This time I listened more closely and decided to take the plunge. I laughed when one of the speakers called her recovery program "the last house on the block." I had visited every house in the neighborhood, and I did believe this was the last house on the block.

For six years, I attended two meetings a week, and learned that you don't conquer your eating disorder overnight; each day you can start fresh and make sacrifices for one day that would be too daunting to give up "forever." What a relief not to have to wait until Monday every time I messed up with my food. I could change my behavior that day, that very minute.

I liked that we didn't discuss recipes and we didn't get weighed. In Mom's club, the first thing you did was get weighed. In this program, I was advised to stick my scale in a closet for now and that sent a flutter up my spine.

The approach here was three-pronged: physical, emotional, spiritual. My food situation was erratic; some days I mastered it, some days I didn't. Yet, I never left meetings feeling badly about myself.

Emotionally, I made huge strides forward in accepting my limitations and myself. Jealousy and competitiveness, longtime partners of mine, began to wane as I took on the affirmation: "I am enough, I have enough, I do enough."

Spiritually, I also made progress. Though Judaism was a substantial part of my life, I never focused much on my relationship with God. I never considered that God took an interest in what or how much I ate. Just as I resisted the notion of God as "mighty bean counter" in the sky, I also rebelled against God as "supreme calorie counter," documenting in a ledger whether I ate upside-down cake or beet soup.

Little by little, I began to connect the dots between God and my food.

I always had the impression that God had big plans for me; that I was meant to do something significant in the world to help other people. When I binged, I didn't care about other people. I only had enough wherewithal to care about my next snack. When I was stuffed to the gills after a huge feast, I wanted nothing to do with anyone else. Like an animal, I wanted to hibernate and sleep because my organs were busy digesting massive amounts of food; I had no energy for anything else.

I was able to see how my food addiction prevented me from being the person I was meant to be; how compulsive overeating caused me to withdraw, become self-centered, abdicate my role as responsible citizen. I had trouble zipping up my pants, let alone being a dutiful member of society.

Though I bolstered my emotional and spiritual dimensions, the physical was still tenuous. I assimilated the concept of "trigger foods"; those substances that once I started, I couldn't stop. Mine read like a list of ex-lovers: rainbow cookies, ice cream, pasta, pizza.

For four months out of that six-year period, I gave up entire trigger categories: sugar and flour. I monitored portion size, and weighed and measured most of my meals. I lost 44 pounds, and was ecstatic that I could shed pounds and control carbs. In February, my birthday approached. I pretended not to mind when Jon and Adam sang a jubilant "Happy birthday dear Mommy" and I lit into cantaloupe as they dove into Carvel cake.

After the initial three days of detox from sugar, I witnessed first-hand that my sugar cravings had disappeared and my weight was dropping. I thought, "This is it!! I got it!" By Day 100, my body still didn't miss sugar, but my mind began obsessing about desserts. I had a dream about warm apple cobbler and I white-knuckled my way through each subsequent meal, clinging to my motivation by a thread.

On the third night of Passover, having survived two consecutive Meislin *seders* with no flour or sugar, I said *Dayenu*, I had suffered enough. Like my ancestors, I wanted to be liberated from bondage. All I could think about was how to bust out of diet jail, become a free woman, and eat like everyone else. I quit the regimen and reinstated *matzah*, almond kisses, and kosher-for-Passover egg noodles. At first, I ate in moderation. By the end of the eight-day holiday, I was out in full force, acutely aware that I had relinquished a hard-earned prize.

I told my mentor, Katie, that I couldn't follow such an austere food plan anymore. "It's too hard," I complained. "If I weren't a vegetarian, maybe I could fill up on chicken or turkey, but I can't find enough things to eat with so many restrictions." Katie looked at me with furrowed brow. "You know we're very similar to alcoholics. Once we pick up the bottle, we can't put it down." I knew Katie was right. I wanted to change my destructive food patterns and finally had a glimpse into how, but as I grew closer to the solution, I ran scared. My defiance took the reins and I felt like I failed once again.

Nevertheless, I remained in the recovery program because I knew it was the last house on the block and at least I had hope. I studied the successful people in the program and realized they weren't all on the same food plan. Some people abstained completely from sugar and flour, others were able to eat those foods under certain circumstances and still keep off their weight. Some adhered to "three meals a day and nothing in between." I experimented with that approach and beat myself to a pulp every day at 4:00, when I ran into the kitchen for a nosh. Years later, my doctor said that the afternoon nibbles were more related to my blood sugar than a fatal flaw in my character.

Even so, I made wildly successful changes in my life. My binges became less frequent, and I learned to tune into my body for clues. In the past, no matter what the problem, I assumed the solution was food. I discovered that when I'm tired, I need rest, not food. When thirsty, I need to drink, not eat. When lonely, I need friends, not food.

Every day heralded new strategies to help me become a balanced, healthier person. I swept out skeletons in my closet that caused me to eat and let go of resentments that ate at me. I remembered to step back and reflect before opening my mouth and stinging someone with my words. I had a succession of "aha" moments that inspired me to behave more civilly toward everyone in my life including the customer service representative at the other end of the helpline who insisted on reading to me verbatim from a script. I was becoming a kinder, softer me.

I was growing in quantum leaps but unfortunately I wasn't growing thinner.

CHAPTER THIRTY-THREE

BEYOND THE LAST
HOUSE ON THE BLOCK

The day I spotted an article in the *Journal News* that Dr. Benjamin Hart was performing weight-loss surgeries, I knew I found my answer. Ten years earlier, Dr. Hart had repaired my umbilical hernia, and I liked his style and his expertise. After months of deliberating the legitimacy of weight-loss surgery, and discussing it with my husband, doctor, therapist, mentor, nutritionist, and a handful of friends, I decided to take the bold move and visit Dr. Hart. He asked me to tell my story and recount my résumé of diets, techniques, and treatments I had tried over the years. When I finished, Ben Hart looked straight at me with his big eyes and warm smile and said, "Sometimes it's hard to fight genetics." I cried.

The next few months were a whirlwind of doctor's visits, medical forms, and schedule re-jiggering, as I told my clients I would be out of commission for six weeks. I didn't waste a minute setting up the surgery. I was in a race against time. Jon's bar mitzvah was in October, and I had six months to take off a sizable chunk of weight.

Bariatric surgery was still in its early stages; I told only my inner circle and mustered the courage to share the secret with my home recovery group. Week after week, these same friends were spectators to my struggles, and they were supportive of my decision. One woman walked over to wish me good luck, index finger wagging in my face. "Whatever you do," she demanded, "don't ever leave this recovery program. You hear me?!" I nodded in submission.

I had explained to Jon and Adam, 12 and 9, that Mommy had an eating problem and she had tried everything she could to help her stay on a diet. They, of course, knew that, because they were first-hand witnesses to every diet and every shameful glance of bystanders at amusement parks and the town pool. They knew this was my Achilles heel. And they, as much as anyone, wanted a thin—or at least a normal—mommy. I told them I would be fine, that I will have stitches and it will hurt me to move and I won't be able to attend their Little League games for a little while, but not to worry because it would all be OK. I also explained that after I came home from the operation, I would be eating mushed up food at the beginning and only tiny portions. Steve contributed to the conversation that he would make sure everything was fine and that the boys could visit me a day or two later in the hospital. Grandma would stay with them in the meantime.

At the hospital, the metal bar on the scale leveled at 295. "I bet the plus-size robe weighs something!" I argued with Dr. Hart. "And last night's eating orgy shouldn't really count." The doctor gave in and we agreed on 290 as my starting weight. I actually liked that number. Three hundred meant you're desperate, a goner. Two ninety left room to be normal. I kissed Steve goodbye and lay down on the wide stretcher, custom-made for weight-loss surgery patients. "Magic bullet, take me away…"

The surgery was successful and I lost 145 pounds in the first two years. It wasn't that hard. I could eat anything, just in small quantities. I even figured out how many M&Ms could go down at once and how many minutes I'd have to wait before the next set so I didn't throw up. Throwing up was common with the type of bariatric surgery I'd had, vertical banded gastroplasty (VBG), or restrictive stomach stapling. I had trouble digesting foods that needed a lot of chewing, like broccoli, though cake and ice cream went down like a charm. Processed foods were much more digestible than fruits and vegetables, so I still ate my junk, but in moderate portions. At least I could eat the same foods as everyone else and feel normal.

When I ate too fast or too much, I threw up. Then I figured, well, now I have room in my stomach, so I can eat more. I'd eat again, and the same thing happened. Usually I'd stop then—or maybe after one more go-round.

The months passed, and the weight melted off. My clothing size shrunk from a 28 to a 10. Discarding my 28's, I filled my closet with size 26, then 24, (skipped 22 and 20 altogether), 18 (my mother's nemesis), back to the hated 16 and 14 of my childhood. Back then, 14 and 16 seemed huge. In this backward countdown, I was ecstatic to be in a size that teetered between the largest size in normal stores and the smallest size in plus stores. Only for minutes at a time had I ever gotten lower than that.

For someone who had never been thin for more than a few weeks, this was the thrill of a lifetime. I couldn't pass a mirror, a window, or a spoon without double-checking my reflection. I smiled at myself all the time and went shopping each month just to check my size. My dress for Jon's affair was custom-made. With each fitting, the outfit had to be taken in—another thrill. In October, for Jon's bar mitzvah, though still quite heavy, I knew I looked much better than I had before the VBG. On the dance floor I felt pretty and proud. Proud of Jon and proud of me.

I was delirious when I hit that 12—my ideal size. It didn't matter that women's magazines berated 12s for being heavy; plus-size models were often 12s and 14s, sometimes even 10s. For me, it was a dream come true. When I dropped to a 10 for two months, I dyed my hair blonde, drove to Woodbury Common Premium Outlets, and plunked down $1,000 at Jones New York for an entire wardrobe of business suits. Then I went next door to Jones Activewear and spent another $500 on shorts, tops, and pants.

Eight months later, the zippers no longer closed, and I donated the pantsuits to an old friend who had gained weight and needed new clothes. I rationalized in my mind that I was never meant to be that thin, and that it was OK to regain a few pounds back to a 12, especially since several people commented that I was too thin and my face was drawn.

Despite the number on my scale or the tag on my clothes, part of me felt like a fraud. Monday and Friday mornings, I attended recovery meetings, and was happy to finally share success in the physical arena, neglecting to mention my snacking and purging behaviors. On Tuesday nights, I attended the post-bariatric surgery support group where I was lauded for healthy eating and weight loss, but steered conversations away from food to psychological issues like: "Why do we look in the mirror and sometimes see an obese body even though we're thin?"

All that mattered was that I was looking good, flying high on my new body image. I was soaking up other people's reactions to me. Family, friends, bleacher moms, even the dry-cleaning clerk— everyone had something to say. Most people were excited for me, supportive, sincere. Occasionally, I would hear a comment, "You look so different; I didn't recognize you!" "You always had a pretty face, but now you look good," "Aren't you getting too thin? Pretty soon you'll waste away." Or "Where's your other half?"

I couldn't always figure out what those comments meant. Some of them felt like a dig, even an insult, and some felt like envy. Instead of driving myself crazy trying to figure out what every suspicious compliment meant, I made up my mind that people were genuinely happy for me, and besides, I refused to let anyone bring me down.

Little by little, the sneaky snacking caught up with me and I started to gain back the 145 pounds. It was slow at first, and I was able to live in denial for a while. When my monthly shopping sprees ended up as forays back into larger sizes, my jubilance shifted to fear compounded by failure. I refused to believe that I could outmaneuver a vertical banded gastroplasty.

Several members of my bariatric support group had already undergone a "revision" from the VBG to a Roux-en-Y (RNY), the gastric bypass surgery made famous by Carnie Wilson and Al Roker. I noticed that the new RNY-ers in our group were doing markedly better than those with the now-outmoded VBG. I refused to bend. Instead, I dug my heels deeper: I booked double therapy sessions, augmented my doctor's support group with an online VBG support group, upped my attendance at recovery meetings from two to three to five per week, switched to a no-nonsense mentor who would "whip" me into shape, read daily meditation books, and kept a journal. If I entered a supermarket for fruits and vegetables and moseyed over to the bakery counter, I phoned a friend who could offer safe passage until I exited the cash register line, produce (only) in hand.

I conceded that my eating behaviors were better and I wasn't bingeing as often as I used to, yet I couldn't stop tormenting myself. As a result, my eating increased and my self-esteem decreased. By the time Adam's bar mitzvah rolled around, three years after Jon's, I bought my dress at a fancy boutique in Great Neck, Long Island. This time at each fitting, the dress had to be let out to accommodate extra pounds. I was proud of Adam, not as proud of me. Food, once again, consumed me.

One day, after a grueling workshop standing on my feet all day, my suit was tight and my shoes were killing me. I'd had a class of managers who challenged every word, and I was drained. When class ended, my body ached and my brain was foggy with food. I needed to make the decision: to revise VBG to RNY or not.

The VBG was simply a restrictive surgery; it only decreased the size of the stomach. The RNY was a combination of restriction and malabsorption, in which some of the food bypassed a part of the small intestine, resulting in the body absorbing fewer calories. Due to this anatomical change, many RNY patients also experience "dumping," a flu-like reaction to sugar. Because of severe dumping symptoms, RNY-ers often eliminate sugar completely from their diets. Some dump for only a year, some longer, and some never dump at all. I had always prayed for a drastic move that would help me swear off sugar forever, as I couldn't seem to do it myself. Fear of dumping was that kind of incentive. I swore I would give up sugar permanently.

It was an agonizing decision. My choice to go under the knife again was fraught with emotional baggage: self-loathing, despair, fear (will this fail again?), resentment (at the time of my VBG, my surgeon refused to perform the bypass), and envy (of the RNY-ers). I concluded that even my best intentions and self-promises weren't enough; I needed another medical intervention.

This time I did more research. I investigated a world-renowned hospital where revisions were done routinely. Though I loved my surgeon, Dr. Hart performed only open vs. laparoscopic revisions, and I wanted to minimize healing time. I had expensive consultations with various professionals in this metropolitan hospital, which felt like a surgical weight-loss factory. When I returned home after the initial appointments, I had several questions and called their office. I left six messages in two weeks, and no one ever called back. Something didn't feel right about this, and I decided to stick with Dr. Hart in our small-town hospital. I traded off open vs. laparoscopic surgery and a longer recuperation to stay with a practice that answered all my questions quickly and treated me like family.

In 2005, the population of morbidly obese people who chose bariatric surgery was still small. An even smaller, more-marginal number underwent a second surgery because the first wasn't enough. I didn't want to be in this second category, which felt to me like a club of losers (well, gainers). Yet, desperation reigned, and above all, I wanted to live. My surgeon was very reassuring. Hart's record on revisions was good, and he believed I could make this one stick. Ten months after my 50th birthday, after five years of yo-yoing with big numbers, I went under the knife again.

Before Dr. Hart performed the revision, he opened my insides to examine how the previous surgery had affected me, how my body had adjusted. He inspected the mechanisms he'd put in place for the VBG, and checked to see that everything was where it was supposed to be.

Amazingly, neither the surgeon nor his assistant could locate the ring that was an integral part of the VBG; it was nowhere to be seen.

After searching a long time, Dr. Hart began to feel around for the ring. The object had embedded itself under my skin and scar tissue had grown over it, so even with deliberate prodding, it was barely discernible. Because of his meticulousness and the fact that the operation was open and not laparoscopic, my surgeon was able to free the ring and continue with the revision.

Dr. Hart and his colleagues were fascinated. This situation is very rare and is the fault of neither doctor nor patient; it's an anomaly that occurs in a tiny percentage of the population. Until my case, the experienced surgeons had only read about this complication in journals; they had never witnessed a live case. Once again, I was a confounding medical mystery.

As grateful as I was to have had the same surgeon operate and not a stranger, the timing of my decision was an even bigger miracle. Seven months after my operation, Dr. Hart died in a tragic car accident, while rushing back from vacation to tend to a patient.

The news was shocking. This man—my surgeon and my friend—was a significant weight-loss champion in my life. I was depressed for months, along with thousands of others whose lives he had transformed. My loss was mitigated only by the fact that Round 2 surgery was hugely successful. In those first few months of visits, Dr. Hart was elated at my rapid weight loss and I know it would have made him happy to see me reach an unprecedented 135 pounds on the scale.

To this day, I muse over lingering questions: Did the dislodging of the ring cause the first surgery to fail, or was it my fault for grazing, overeating, and vomiting? If this doctor hadn't performed the surgery, would I have had a metal ring embedded under my skin forever? Would it have harmed me? Why was I one of the few patients who had this complication? Over that five-year period, when did that happen? I had done so well in the first two years; was that despite the ring or in tandem with it? Why did this devoted doctor have to die? There are so many more obese people who needed his help.

I will never know the answers to these questions. My mentor suggested: If you have "Why?" questions that are impossible to answer, jot them down under the heading, "List of questions to ask God when we meet face-to-face."

I still have days when I castigate myself for being so pig-headed as to need not just *one*, but *two* bariatric surgeries. Invariably I come to that fork in the road: *should I be charitable to myself and presume that the first operation failed because a ring dislodged? Or, should I beat myself up because I am a hard-core addict who will botch up again if I'm not hyper-vigilant?* Occasionally, the answer is: "Yes, I need to kick myself in the pants or I will get lazy and complacent."

Then I recall the memorable words of the late Dr. Hart: "I only worked on your stomach, not your head. The rest is up to you."

CHAPTER THIRTY-FOUR

DOUBLE D

Halfway between Surgery #1 and Surgery #2, I fulfilled a life-long fantasy. After spending the majority of my life as a 5-foot-2 1/2-inch woman with a DD chest (DDD at my highest weight), I was finally eligible for the long-awaited, long-dreamt-of breast reduction.

Ever since I was a teenager, I'd looked for a cure for the pains in my back and the aching ridges in my shoulders. I'd yearned for the day when I no longer had to wear custom-fitted, old-lady bras that bound me like straitjackets. Even when I managed—for short intervals—to lose weight, I walked around feeling bulky and off-balance. No matter how thin I became, I remained top-heavy, forcing me to cover up with loose over-blouses and tunics, making me look even heavier. When it came to most sports, I sat on the sidelines because my chest size interfered with many of the movements.

Though a breast reduction was something I'd wanted for decades, I purposely delayed it until after I had children so nothing would interfere with natural breastfeeding. A few years after the children were weaned, I visited a well-known breast surgeon in a fancy office. Taking one look at me, the GQ doctor shook his head and with a look of disdain said, "Come back after you lose 100 pounds and you've kept it off more than a year." Not exactly the response I had awaited. As a souvenir, I took a glossy, multi-colored brochure with dramatic before-and-after pictures from his waiting room and promised myself that one day those images would be mine. But not with this man. I sought out another well-known plastic surgeon for a second opinion. With equal arrogance and contempt, he dismissed me in a similar fashion.

In 2002, in that window after I had lost and maintained over 100 pounds and hadn't yet regained half, I went back to my doctors and asked for a new referral. I requested someone who combined technical excellence with a modicum of sensitivity. Soon I was back on a gurney waiting to be wheeled into an operating room, only this time the gurney wasn't oversized and neither was I. As the anesthesiologist pumped sedatives into my veins, I was overcome with emotion. I was so thankful to be thin and so thankful that I'd soon be relieved of this medical deformity (my doctor's words) that I had literally been carrying around since I was a teen.

As excited as I was, I was also scared, both from surgery and the fear of disappointment. My physical "Double Ds" were nothing compared with the emotional Double Ds that formed the subtext of my story: my two archenemies, disappointment and deprivation. The time was right to downsize them all: Ds in my body, Ds in my soul.

The breast reduction surgery went well and that event became a huge turning point in my life. For the first time since puberty, I was able to walk, move, bend, exercise and dance unencumbered. My shoulders didn't ache, and my back didn't hurt. I buttoned my shirts and tucked them in at the waist, now a discernable part of my torso. I booked a normal appointment for a mammogram rather than the painful back-to-back double sessions needed to screen every inch of my breast tissue. I felt slim, trim, eager for the gym. Without having to lug pendulous breasts around, I was lithe and energetic, sexy and bouncy. My energy for lovemaking increased and Steve and I were able to experiment with new moves and new twists. Disappointment and deprivation (nearly) vanished from my vocabulary.

Not so for my husband. In deference to Steve, who had likened me to Raquel Welch, a voluptuous D, I asked the doctor to make me a C-cup, big enough for someone short and apple-shaped. I ended up a B, which the plastic surgeon maintained was the right proportion for my petite frame. I couldn't have been happier with the result. On the other hand, Steve's disappointment was palpable as he made snide remarks about "the slap-happy surgeon with his scalpel."

Wielding my new self-confidence, I was ready to annihilate old baggage and make peace with my past. I assigned myself an exercise in which I made a list of all the disappointments and deprivations I had ever experienced in my life, big and small. I included deaths, losses, illnesses, emergency rooms, fat genes, diets, more fat jeans, boy problems, girl problems, parent/kid/husband problems. I wrote pages and pages.

No stone was unturned in this digest of disappointments. I thought it would be cathartic to read the list to my therapist, burn it, and symbolically release a lifetime of resentment up in smoke. After reading the eight-page, single-spaced document, I didn't need to do anything more; writing and reading was cleansing enough. Fifty pounds lifted off me in an instant.

One week after I completed this exercise, I attended a fundraiser, and was startled to hear a name I hadn't heard in three decades. I meandered over and introduced myself to Rick, that very same college boy who had a romantic interlude with my best friend. We reminisced for a long time and Rick asked me to recollect everything I could about that period. I obliged, and included the incident with Shira.

After absorbing everything I said, Rick turned to me with a somber look in his eyes. "Did I hurt you?" he asked.

"Yes," I answered, a somber look in mine.

He blanched, then whispered sincerely, "I am sorry. I am *really* sorry."

It was a wondrous moment; after 32 years, I felt validated. I accepted Rick's apology and converted it in my mind to an apology from all men who ever hurt or disappointed me (with the exception of Steve, which was a lot more complicated). Another 50 pounds vaporized into thin air.

As I made peace and forgave the people who hurt me in my past, I realized how many people I had also hurt. When my eating was out of control, I was a rageaholic and launched into tirades when I was angry or things didn't go my way. Despite repenting every Yom Kippur (my nod to that ledger), I needed to do more, to make restitution to all those people whom I had deprived and disappointed.

The first people I made amends to were my parents at Beth Abraham Cemetery. I apologized to Mom and Dad that it took me so long to recognize how irascible and demanding I had been as a child. I begged them to forgive me. A year later, I returned to read Mom and Dad a long letter I had composed. I thanked them for their love and expressed the wish to turn back the clock and listen to their sage advice, especially now that I was raising two teenagers of my own. I apologized again for causing constant worry and drama.

From the jagged rocks sitting atop Jack and Mildred Meislin's monument, I heard Mom's distinctive throaty voice: "Enough, Marcia. We forgave you already. You don't have to ask anymore. You were a loving and wonderful daughter. Dad and I always loved you and we always will. We never expected you to be perfect, so stop being so hard on yourself. Now, get on with your life, and go spread around that sunshine of yours. And stop worrying so much!"

And with that, Mom, Dad, and I made peace. I was able to carry Mom and Dad inside me minus the guilt. Mom and I gave each other a pass for not being perfect; she did the best she could and so did I. I used to feel like the magician who extracted a series of colorful scarves from her throat, each one representing a deep inside wound. With every pull, there was a new scarf, a bottomless pit with no end in sight. It seemed I could never resolve an emotional problem in the present, because all the past hurts would lash out for attention. As I healed, I was able to deal with most problems as they surfaced in the moment, without all the back issues. Magically, I was able to feel gratitude and acceptance for my past and I no longer had to scarf down food to survive.

PART VI

RECOVERY

"If you can imagine it, you can achieve it."

\- William Arthur Ward

CHAPTER THIRTY-FIVE

LOOKING MY MOTHER IN THE EYE

Not all unfinished business from the past was finished. Tough holdovers, like marriage and intimacy issues, had yet to be untangled. Fear of rejection and abandonment still lurked, and one old wound reappeared often enough that I had to deal with the matter head-on.

I pulled out my bright Mexican blanket from a Barnes & Noble bag and wrapped it around myself. When Liz and I enacted scenes from my past to achieve closure, I needed to shut out the present. I took off my shoes, closed my eyes, covered myself up, and sat cross-legged on the couch—just as I had done as a child. I began my internal regression back to the early incident that occurred when I was 5. For a few minutes I sat steeped in memory, silently reliving that awful period. Neither of us spoke. In the previous session, I had provided Liz with the background details:

It was just over a year after we'd moved from the little white Cape Cod on a dead-end street where kids rode their bikes up and down and moms in their halter dresses sat on the stoops. The new house was a cavernous colonial in a labyrinthine neighborhood where men in black skullcaps walked to and from shul. Everything inside the new house was drab green, the darling shade of the 1950s. My parents themselves were still shades of gray, recuperating from their losses. Downstairs where Grandpa lived was black and white with men in prayer shawls, hats, and suits; dark rooms without much light. My colorful siblings were at Jewish day school from eight to five.

Then, without explanation, Mom vanished—gone. I don't remember anyone having a conversation with me or giving me warning. Aunt Anne was supposed to stay with us, but as Uncle Harry had died not too long before, I don't think she did. Into this scene came the new neighbors, who took turns checking on us.

To this day, I'm not sure where Mom went. Columbia Presbyterian Hospital comes to mind because Dad took Mom there for her annual eye exams. What I discovered only after Mom's death when we cleaned out her papers was that Mom had melanoma of the eye. She left abruptly because she needed surgery to remove her cancerous eye and replace it with a glass one. I don't know how long she was gone. I do know that I was never able to look at Mom in the same way again—literally. Several times each day, Mom put eye drops in only one eye for glaucoma, and it was only later that I realized the other eye was false.

When Mom was diagnosed with lung cancer, the hospital chaplain, a rabbi who knew my family well, said to me, "This isn't your Mom's first battle with cancer."

"Yes, it is," I countered, confident in my conviction. I'd heard the C word whispered about Uncle Harry, but never, ever about Mom.

When I was fully immersed in being 5 years old, I was ready to begin the psychodrama. In that little-girl voice, I asked the question that was foremost on my mind, "Mommy, when you came home with a patch on your eye, where did you get it from?"

Liz/Mom paused, took a deep breath, and said, "Honey, I was sick. I had a sickness in my eye, and I had to go to the eye hospital to get it fixed."

"But why didn't you tell me? You just... left."

"I'm so sorry, Marcia. When the doctors told me—it was such an emergency. There was really no time. I had to go, and I had a lot of things to do to get ready. That's not a very good reason for not telling you, but I wasn't really sure what was going to happen. I didn't want to talk about it with anyone. But I should have. I'm really sorry. I should have told you that I was going away to have my eye fixed."

"Did they fix it?"

"Well, sort of. They couldn't really fix it, so they took out the eye that was sick and gave me a new one."

I gasped. "You can do that?"

"Yes, Marcia, the doctors know how to do that. They can give someone a fake eye that looks real."

"Can you see with it?"

"No, but I can still see from my other eye, my real eye. So I am fine. I can see you. I can see the pretty red dress you're wearing. I can see the way your little curls have some brown in them, some yellow, and even a little red."

"You really should have told me."

She paused, and a few moments later with incredible compassion and knowing, replied, "Yes, you're right, I really should have. But honestly, Honey, I was afraid. I didn't know what it was going to be like, and I was afraid to talk about it. I know that's not fair. It's my job to come to you with these talks, not the other way around—but I couldn't. I didn't know how. I wish I had come to you sooner. I'm sorry."

Well, fair enough. I really kind of got that, even at 5. Mom always told me to talk about things that scared me, but there were lots of times when I didn't, when I kept scary things to myself. So I understood Mom when she said she didn't know how to talk about it, even a long time after.

Liz asked me to open my eyes so I could look into hers. Straight into her eyes. She asked me to stare at the real one and the fake one. I looked long and hard. Though my therapist's eyes were green, I honestly saw two blues, one darker than the other.

"But, Mom, they don't really match. This one is darker than that one," I pointed.

"Well, Marcia, you love pretty colors, so why don't we pretend that you have a giant Crayola box? What colors would you call the two different blues? You can even make up names."

I thought and thought, mentally going through the 64 colors in my box.

"I got it: 'hug-me-blue.' One is the dark hug-me-blue and one is the light hug-me-blue."

I really liked the color I made up and it felt good to be able to talk about Mommy's eye together. And I liked that now I knew how to look at her: I could look at one eye (the real one), or I could look at the other eye (the fake one), or I could try to look at both of them at the same time. Now her eyes even had a name. And most important—Mom wasn't sick anymore and she could still see me.

The 50-minute appointment flew that day. Mom and I chatted the whole time. When you're 5, and you come from a big family, any alone time you can get with your parent is special. That day, I received the closure I had needed for a long time.

Before I left, Liz said something that I'm pretty sure Mom would have said had she been able to have this conversation: "Marcia, you are very brave." I knew that was true. I was brave to ask questions, talk about my fears, and look my problems straight in the eye... all my problems.

CHAPTER THIRTY-SIX

SLOW FUSE

With my svelte body and healing scars, almost everything in my life was getting better. Everything, that is, except my marriage. Steve and I, now comfortably ensconced in our suburban lifestyle, managed to live independent lives, intersecting at key moments to take care of finances, host family parties, or cheer at our sons' ballgames. Every Sunday, Steve marinated a NY strip and he and the boys grilled steak (and fake hot dogs for me) while I tossed Steve's special Caesar dressing into the romaine in the precise manner he taught me.

On the surface, our life looked normal. Underneath, our marriage was emotionally black and blue. Over an eight-year period, Steve and I discussed separating on three different occasions. This possibility of separation was first proposed in 1998, 15 years into our marriage. We had just returned from a horrific combo business trip/family vacation to France that amounted to a perfect storm.

Steve's medical meetings in Paris lasted longer than anticipated which left me alone with Adam and Jon, ages 8 and 11. The first morning, it rained and I slipped and sprained my ankle climbing onto a bus for the Eiffel Tower. The boys had to help all 250 pounds of me stand up and limp back to the hotel for ice so we could venture out again. At Musée de l'Orangerie in Paris, Adam insisted on moving too close to the paintings, and triggered the alarm more than once, nearly getting us kicked out of the museum. Neither son had a sophisticated palette and when we ordered plateau de fromage, they refused to sample the smelly local cheeses. I asked for cheddar cheese, and the indignant waiter looked down his nose at me and huffed, "Madame, we do not serve wood in our country."

For a change of pace, we spent a few days outside of Paris in the Loire Valley and I imagined the boys would get a kick out of staying in the turret of a castle. After 30 seconds of "Wow, this is cool!" they asked for the pool and game room. Instead, we took them to a giant corn maze at Chateau de Thoiry and stupidly allowed them to go through the second maze on their own, equipped only with a map. An hour later, we were still panicked when we couldn't find our children anywhere and nobody understood us as we begged the officials to go inside and find our boys. Eventually, Jon and Adam emerged out of the tall stalks, and all I could do was hold them and sob. Neither Steve nor I found any of our European escapades amusing and we blamed each other for the misguided trip.

Shortly after our return, we repacked and set out for the annual Meislin Rosh Hashanah get-together in Woodstock. We usually slept at Allan and Donna's house but because they were renovating, we stayed in a cheap motel. Steve and I shared one full-size bed and the boys shared the other. Steve's chronic back problems forced him to sleep on his back. Between his snoring and my girth, I couldn't sleep or lie comfortably so in the middle of the night, I moved to the floor. The next morning, I was tired and cranky. Even the religious services under the big white tent—the spiritual highpoint of my year—were supplanted by rehearsed conversations over and over in my mind in which I was telling Steve that we needed to separate.

At that moment, the wizard Rabbi Jonathan suggested a new Rosh Hashanah activity: "Turn to the person next to you and ask them what blessing they hope for in the New Year. And then offer them that blessing by saying, 'May it be so.'" As the chair on my right was empty, I turned to Steve on my left, and asked him what blessing he desired for the upcoming year. He deliberated, then replied, "I pray that you and I will spend more time together next year..." He continued talking as I drifted off, thinking to myself, *"that won't be so."* Instead of offering a blessing, the words that spilled out of my mouth were, "I don't think so. I think we need to spend some time apart."

Both of us were shocked by these words, as tears dripped onto the pages of my *mahzor*, the Rosh Hashanah prayer book that sat open in my lap.

Steve responded, "Let's talk about this tonight after the kids are asleep."

All day long, through an extended Meislin luncheon, a long drive home in the car, dinner, showers, and bedtime rituals, Steve and I thought about our pending conversation. At 9:30 that night, we tentatively made our way to our king-size bed. I opened by saying that I felt we had been living a charade for a long time and that I still loved him but couldn't live with this kind of strain anymore. I knew he was always angry with me, and I reacted by being angry in return, and we needed a break from all that tension. I was concerned about disrupting the kids' lives but once we sat down and figured out how to make it work, we would have an honest conversation with our children. I suspected they might not be surprised. Our boys had seen us fighting and they were used to my loud yelling and Steve's silence. Maybe they wouldn't be freaked out; some of their friends' parents were already divorced. I ended by saying that I thought we were both "first-class people living in a second-class marriage."

Steve and I began to talk. We discussed everything—marriage, family, careers, love, sex. Three years earlier, Steve's dad had died and this was the first time Steve uncorked the bottled-up sadness and allowed himself to cry. He shared his trepidation around inheriting his father's heart disease, Parkinson's, and bipolar disorder, and the fear of passing them down to our boys. Then the subject veered to my health, and Steve worried that I was at high risk for diabetes or stroke, and that I could leave our children motherless.

My tears were uncontrollable as I expressed remorse for what I had done to him, to our family, to myself. I apologized for jeopardizing my health and destroying my looks. I apologized for my turn-around from the lascivious sex partner Steve had married to a woman beaten down by food, fat, and fatigue. Despite all the early years I compensated for my weight by being an overachiever—even sexually—now I was underperforming, a result of fear and shame. Many nights, yearning for connection, I would lie on my half of our 80-inch mattress, aching to reach over a mere 20 inches to touch Steve's shoulder or graze his cheek. Scaling the Great Wall of China might have felt easier than stretching my leaden arm across the invisible divide separating his side from mine. I'd obsess about making a move, test it over and over in my mind, but our mutual fear was so deep, that we both lay back-to-back, neither of us ready to make the first move, lest we get rejected. Sooner or later, one of us would take the risk—the risk of intimacy—and initiate a kiss, a caress, a bold embrace. That would lead us back into more regular lovemaking until the next speed bump, when we would again detach in wordless combat.

That morning, as Steve and I lay bare the truth about our sex life, intimacy issues, and disappointments, neither of us wanted to continue the hurtful patterns we had established. We both took responsibility for how our relationship evolved, and we agreed to continue the dialogue that night. As the second night of conversation progressed, we felt closer and more tender toward each other. At 2 a.m., Steve asked if he could kiss me. We kissed longer and harder than we ever kissed before and this time, Steve was the one crying. We hugged and fell into an exhausted sleep, having worked tirelessly to mend our delicate relationship.

For several weeks, we kept talking and relating on a deep level, and the exchange became lighter and more relaxed. One night, I said, "Steve, I feel like we have already come a long way. Maybe we don't need to spend time apart in order to reconnect, maybe we've already done that?"

Steve agreed and we aborted all talk of separation. We had restarted our relationship without having to split up. Our marriage was now characterized by open lines of communication, honest sharing of feelings, and neither person taking the other for granted. I was happy and relieved. The boys seemed to thrive under our new partnership.

Five years later, our efforts fizzled, and we had to revisit the conversation. Intervening years were marked by a series of sessions with therapists who specialized in marital problems. One time, we went upon the advice of a guidance counselor who speculated that our son's acting-out behavior indicated trouble at home. Shortly after the sessions began, Steve stopped showing up. At that point, he was commuting 90 minutes to work each way and that became his excuse for not making the meetings. The therapist kept haranguing me, and I defended myself saying, "Stop yelling at me! I'm here! You're preaching to the choir!"

Several years later, we tried a different approach, which didn't work for us either. The therapist was too touchy-feely even for me, asking us to gaze into each other's eyes for several minutes, and describe how we felt. We both agreed that these exercises were not our style.

I searched for a more intellectual approach that Steve might embrace, and found a third professional whom we stayed with for over a year. In the first six months, Steve made major strides forward and then clammed up. His commitment dwindled and the two men began to share recipes and wine picks.

All three therapists had come to the same conclusion: Steve needed to face his own childhood issues—separate and apart from couples' therapy. I wasn't off the hook; my obesity and eating disorder were certainly cause for greater exploration but I was already in therapy and had been for years. If we wanted long-term results in our marriage, it was Steve's turn to ante up. All three times Steve made excuses and each therapist shrugged their shoulders, told us to save our money, and invited us to return if and when Steve took that step.

For decades, I assumed that Steve was mad at me because of my weight. But 18 years into our marriage, I lost 150 pounds and Steve was still mad at me. I had no idea why I was so terrible or what I had done that was so unforgivable. The chasm between the kudos I received outside my home and the censure I received inside was widening. Whenever I complained to Steve, "A lot of people out there think I'm great!" he'd smirk, "They don't have to live with you." I knew I was temperamental so I sought out a psychiatrist to prescribe anti-anxiety medication. She recommended, instead, a mood stabilizer. I took the drug for a year and it took the edge off as we slogged through one of our worst years of teenage maelstrom. As mellow as I had become, even chemicals didn't alter the dynamics within our marriage.

By the time Steve and I were in our mid-50s and had reached our 22nd anniversary, I had under my belt 25 years of individual therapy, five years of Gestalt therapy training, three rounds of marriage counseling, 11 years of recovery, two weight-loss surgeries, and one year on a mood stabilizer. I continued moving forward despite my marriage. Steve and I were fighting a lot—mostly under our breaths as I gave up shouting as a way to shake my unflappable husband. I asked Steve again to get some help. He hemmed and hawed so I set a two-month time limit.

"By July."

"By August," he countered.

"Fine. August is fine."

I watched Steve that summer. As far as I knew, he hadn't made a single phone call to find a therapist. I signed up for a meditation weekend at Omega, a spiritual retreat center, to get away for a weekend and reflect on my next move. When I arrived in Rhinebeck, I took off my wedding ring just to see how that felt. Though I knew the demographic was mostly women, I wanted to see if I could do it, if I had the guts to be single.

During one of the meditations, I conjured up an old image of myself as an uninhibited, free-spirited, out-of-the-box artsy type, undeterred by what other people thought of me. I dubbed that old '60s part of me who loved to hang out with hippies and unconventional people "Woodstock Woman" (aka WW). The notion came to me that if WW represented my happiest times, I needed to be that woman whether married or single, whether I lived in a big house with window treatments, or a bachelorette pad with beaded macramé curtains. As mom, wife, or divorcée, I needed to channel WW and free my soul.

That weekend, it also came to me how much I loved Steve. If our marriage were going to work, I needed to accept Steve as he was and not wish to change him. I couldn't keep waiting for him to go into therapy and have a Damocles sword hanging over our heads forever. I either needed to love him warts and all, therapy or no therapy, or change my current situation.

As I drove the 90 minutes home, I placed my ring back on my ring finger where it belonged. When I pulled into the driveway, Steve came out to greet me and carry my suitcase. I shared my insights and he was skeptical, though pleased I would drop the therapy ultimatum. Secretly, I harbored the hope that he would make the appointment anyway, realizing it was the right thing to do for our family.

Several months went by. The summer deadline came and went. We packed Jon up and dropped him at his freshman dorm at college. Steve set up Jon's electronics and I organized his clothes. I tried to keep my anxiety to a modicum of "normal" and we managed to blend in with all the other anxious first-time families.

While all this turmoil was going on, I had begun to confide in a colleague at one of my training sites whom I had known for years. Jeff was trustworthy and honest and we had become close friends, akin to brother and sister. When we worked together, we ran amazing and creative programs and in between, we were sounding boards for each other. Over the years, we chatted about everything, no holds barred. I could always count on Jeff to listen objectively, support me when warranted, and kick me in the pants when I was self-centered or unreasonable.

After trying for so long to engage Steve in personal conversations only to be rebuffed, it was a relief to have a place to run away from the sadness, anger, and despair that marred my marriage. I liked shifting my focus from a man who was emotionally absent to one who was emotionally present. Because Steve was turned off by dramatic outbursts, I had learned to censor myself. If I wanted to have a conversation with Steve, I had to suck in my emotions so I could talk with him in a calm, composed, rational manner. Otherwise, I would trigger Steve's annoyance and he would withdraw. In contrast, with Jeff, I didn't need to disown parts of myself because he was actually sparked by my passion and emotionality.

I was conscious of what I was doing. I knew that discussing my marriage outside made it harder to discuss it inside. After Jeff and I interacted, we went home. After Steve and I interacted, we were home.

The more Jeff and I shared, the closer we became. Our friendship had inklings of an "emotional affair," intimacy without the sex. There was nothing illegitimate about our relationship and yet something was nagging at me and I began to question whether having this "other" man in my life was somehow disloyal. I turned to my recovery friends for advice. Half said, "We all have a fantasy of the 'perfect man' we run to when we're needy. As long as you don't get physically involved, you're fine." The other half said, "An emotional affair can be more damaging than a physical one. Get out now so you can fix your marriage."

I toggled back and forth between the two views, and continued my own therapy, still hoping Steve would start his. Deep down, I knew there was mutual love beneath the anger. Both of us had parents who role-modeled a loving marriage and a traditional family set-up: mom, dad, and kids, all living under the same roof. I had hoped we could demonstrate to our boys that marriage is a long-term commitment; if two people love each other enough, and persevere through the hurdles, they have a chance of preserving the marriage.

Gradually, I began to let go of my intense friendship with Jeff. I quit jumping at opportunities to co-train. I stopped dialing his number the minute I needed a friend. I told him the truth—that our relationship began to feel too close for comfort. We agreed we would work together but we would be "all business" and refrain from chatting about personal topics.

One day, while driving a long distance with Steve, I mustered the courage and asked him to pull over to a rest stop so we could talk. Taking a risk, I opened the conversation: "Steve, we've been married for 22 years. I love you, and I believe that you love me. But I think we've both been frustrated for a very long time. I feel that I'm doing all the work on our relationship myself. You've been promising to work on your own issues, but you keep putting it off. While I was waiting all these months, I began to open my heart to someone else. I didn't plan it. We never had an affair or did anything illicit. We're just close and our relationship has kind of grown into a very deep friendship. I wanted to come clean with you and be honest. I want to be with *you*, I'm not interested in anyone else. I got tired of waiting for you to change, and I began to look for that emotional intimacy elsewhere. I am really sorry. I am totally committed to our marriage, and that's why I'm telling you now. I made the decision that even if you never change, I want to be with you and stay with you. I'm working on accepting you exactly as you are and not waiting for you to be different. I love you, and I hope you love me and want to stay with me, too."

That is the toughest tête-a-tête I've ever had with my husband. It was bold. It was honest. It was real. And we both knew that the stakes were high. Steve thanked me for opening up to him and being direct even though he didn't like what I said. Then he went off to think about my words.

That week, Steve had a fight with Adam and lost his temper. Two days later, he went for counseling. After the first session, Steve came home and sat me down. He took my hands, looked me straight in the eyes, and said, "Marcia, I've been a jerk all these years. You've been so loving and giving, but I put up a huge brick wall. The brick wall is coming down right now. I love you and never want to lose you. I'm sorry it took me this long."

On that night of November 28, 2005, 22 years, five months, and 16 days after our "storybook" wedding, while swiveling on tall wooden stools in our renovated kitchen, Steve and I renewed our vows. This time around, "I do" had new meaning. It meant airing differences rather than holding them in or seeking solace elsewhere. It meant that we would trust each other, let down our guard, knock down the walls. Over the next year, Steve learned to diffuse anger by acknowledging grudges and letting them go, resentments he had carried for decades toward me, his family, his career.

We both had to relearn things about each other. I had become hypersensitive to Steve's body language. The minute his temple started pulsating, I was on the warpath. "What happened? Why are you mad?" That was enough to escalate the situation. The "new me" had to remember to be quiet and not react, to give Steve his space. Whatever he was upset about would usually resolve itself within minutes or after a glass of good wine and an old movie. If the anger didn't dissipate, Steve knew he needed to tell me why he was mad and not leave me guessing. Half the time, his anger had nothing to do with me.

As a way to release aggression, we revived rituals from our early dating period, silly games like "got you last" with the dishtowel, or "pinchy-picky-pully." As much as Steve and I were inching our way toward a merger, we still had very different personalities. If we didn't laugh about the tension, we knew it would fragment us, and neither of us wanted to go back to the way we were. Our drug of choice became laughter. For years, I had put down Steve's sense of humor. I consciously did an about-face and incorporated his brand of joking into our interactions, especially when he was about to blame me for something. It was fun to watch Steve's snicker turn to a smile as I enacted a clever rendition of a Steve Martin skit or a Monty Python routine.

I also learned to pick and choose my battles. Steve had zero interest in sartorial matters and refused to spend time shopping for clothes even if I handpicked them. He preferred to purchase his clothes from Sam's Club during an early-morning run to buy toilet paper and paper towels.

When it came to shoes, Steve was more finicky because his feet were a constant source of pain and perspiration. Instead of donning loafers, as I suggested, Steve discovered "Crocs," clunky plastic shoes with rubber soles and holes on top for ventilation. Steve filled his closet with multiple pairs in titanium, pewter, and gray, which he wore everywhere—to work, weddings, even funerals.

In the first year of Steve's rubber shoe obsession, I protested every time we stepped out of the house, until I realized that Steve was immune to my arguments or taunts from family and friends. I learned to hold my tongue though underneath I was still embarrassed when we entered a formal family function with my husband wearing a black suit and beach shoes.

One day, I asked myself honestly why this issue irked me so much: "Steve is such a great guy, why do you even give a croc?" No sooner did I ask the question, when a picture of Mom popped into my consciousness. From a deep old script emerged Mom's warning: "Your husband is a reflection of you; the way he acts, the way he dresses..." I resolved to trade in Mom's old script for an even older one, a page from the rabbinic tradition that better suited my needs. "Shalom bayit" is a Jewish concept that refers to "peace in the house," domestic tranquility, family harmony. I translated that to mean not sweating small stuff, like clothes or shoes.

For the sake of shalom bayit, Steve and I have both become more discerning. I don't comment on how he looks; he doesn't comment on how I cook. When we run into hiccups, we address them directly, or give ourselves a few days to think; not the weeks, months, or years we used to allow a problem to fester. In the interim, instead of distancing ourselves emotionally, we continue to act intimately toward each other—we hold hands, we interact, we make love.

There are times in our marriage when boredom sets in or tempers flare. At those moments, I'm tempted to flee in my mind to that "secret garden" where the white knight awaits, eager to wave his magic wand and fulfill all my dreams. Then I remember that running away is like eating a rainbow cookie: alluring, seductive, beautiful— and evanescent. The mystique lasts only a few moments and then I'm faced with bigger troubles. If I've succumbed to the fantasy and consumed a crock of cookies, my problem (and my weight) multiplies. Likewise, when Steve and I are in a difficult spot, I remind myself to stick out the discomfort and not run away, dissociate, numb the pain, or go back to food. If we stay in the moment, no matter how painful, we're able to work out our issues faster without defeating our purpose.

For decades, I never dared to dream that Steve and I, two smart and stubborn contrarians, would come together and form the healthy union we have today.

CHAPTER THIRTY-SEVEN

BODY IMAGE #4: RAPTURE

Two years after my gastric bypass, I weighed 135 pounds and had never been so happy or thin in my life. I was convinced that at a size 10 petite, sometimes an 8, on occasion a 6, I had "arrived," and I would never be unhappy again. While all my friends were bemoaning menopause and middle age, I was touting my 50s as the best time of life, a life that just gets better and better. Friends who were former prom queens and cheerleaders mourned their faded beauty, while I walked around like Aphrodite, feeling more fabulous than I ever felt in my youth.

My lifestyle, too, had changed. I was so strict after the gastric bypass that when I accidentally landed in bed with dumping syndrome from multi-grain cereal and 1% milk, I was dumbfounded. I spent 10 hours recuperating from symptoms mirroring the worst flu imaginable, and I vowed never to go through that again. I dumped one more time, again by accident, from a low-fat, raspberry vinaigrette salad dressing. Apparently, it was low fat but not low sugar. After this second episode, I read labels religiously and turned into one of those persnickety people I used to scorn. With few exceptions, I didn't eat sugar, white flour, or artificial sweeteners.

As a family, we continued to visit our usual restaurants where I would order appetizer portions and still have plenty of food left on my plate. Kind waiters and waitresses would pop by to make sure the food was OK because I ate like a bird. One of the kids would lament, "Mom, I feel bad for the waiter because they think you don't like the food." I laughed and replied, "What's my alternative? Should I eat everything on my plate and make the waiter happy or bring most of it home and stay thin?"

The boys reneged right away, because Jon at 20, and Adam at 17, were in love with their "hot" Mom with her petite stylish clothes and blonde hair. When we came across old photos, Jon and Adam would gawk at my before-and-after pictures, awestruck that their mom now looked normal and could fit through tight turnstiles.

As vocal as the boys were, that's how silent Steve was about my weight even after the brick wall came down. While Steve worked hard to make me gourmet, pureed food after my surgeries (I'm convinced he made the best-tasting mashed food on the planet), he rarely said a word about how I looked or about my metamorphosis. When pressed, he would say I looked good, but the rest of the time, he was mum. I could hardly complain; my weight was a taboo subject all those years when I was obese. Why would he all of a sudden be allowed to comment on my body?

On the other hand, everywhere I went, I was showered with compliments. When we went out socially, and our friends raved about how great I looked, it wasn't unusual for someone to ask, "Hey, Steve, you feel like you're married to a different woman?" or, "What's it like having a mistress?" He didn't answer and the rest of us would laugh off the comment.

At my lowest weight of 135, which lasted about six months, Steve did volunteer that he thought I was too thin, that I looked gaunt and my cheeks and throat were too taut. At dinner one night, Steve took my hands in his, pushed his glasses on top of his head, and examined my fingers. He diagnosed "interosseous wasting," a lack of muscle between the bones in the upper part of my hand. Steve started me on protein shakes, so I frequented a local juice bar where the owners became like family. One of my doctors and two friends also felt I was getting too thin, but I paid no attention. What could "too thin" mean to a person like me? There was no such thing.

At that time, I was also exercising every other day. I had always aspired to play tennis. Other than a complimentary lesson here or there at a resort, I had never played because I was too fat to run around the court. The summer I was at my thinnest, I signed up for tennis lessons and played with a vengeance under the tutelage of a young Wimbledon hopeful. I worked out even on the hottest days, determined to become a player. That summer and the next, I progressed at a rapid rate, alternating tennis lessons with personal training sessions. I was in great physical shape and loved nothing more than running around in my short tennis outfits, flaunting the Nike swoosh that became my new mantra, "Just do it!"

I couldn't wait to call my brother Bob, a tennis junkie, and tell him about my game.

Marcia: Bob! I can play tennis now! You should see me!
Bob: Sounds like you're having a ball!
Marcia: I am! It's love!
Bob: Point well taken.
Marcia: Well, you've been playing for years. You definitely have the advantage.
Bob: Marcia, you're not even in my league.
Marcia: ... I know, Bob, but net, net, you gotta admit. I'm way funnier than you!
Bob: I could take you to court over that.
Marcia: That would serve you right.
Marcia: OK, Bob, I'm done. Gotta go to my lesson now. (Marcia, wanting to end on top)
Bob: Have a good one. Don't raise a racket. (Match goes to Bob).

When I wasn't playing tennis with my instructor, I tried rustling up games with anyone who would play with me. My neighbor invited me to join what she called her "geriatric" game Saturday mornings but I couldn't hold a candle to the 80-year-olds who made up her quartet. I played once with another beginner, but never managed to return the ball inside the lines. My inability to ace the game killed any pleasure I had in the sport and I retired my racquet along with hopes of being a geriatric tennis player myself.

Though I quit tennis after two seasons, I kept up my workout sessions with Rebecca, a personal trainer and professional nutritionist whom I adored. Rebecca had a gym in her basement, and every week she had me strengthen abs and crank out crunches. Amidst lifts and lunges, she offered helpful tips regarding my food plan and eating behaviors. Weights in hand, I would gaze at myself in the mirror, in utter shock that the image staring back at me actually looked like an athlete. Aside from her dimpled thighs and extruded midriff, this trim healthy-looking middle-aged woman with curls tumbling out of her scrunchie, was sweating and puffing as she created "definition" in her shoulder blades.

Some days, my body image was abysmal despite all my efforts. I would stare at my reflection and replay old scripts of self-hatred, directed at the permanent rolls on my back and midsection, and the jiggling batwings under my arms. Immune to spot training, these areas defied my workout, and made a mockery of me in the mirror. In those moments, the only body parts I could appreciate were my small breasts.

When I was in those moods, Rebecca's constant encouragement kept me plugging away. Sometimes I didn't stop grimacing until she made me finish my exercises with my back to the mirror. Her patient and understanding tone helped me see that my body was normal for someone my age yet I still wanted my newfound body to make up for lost time. I was angry that I was no longer a young woman with elastic skin that bounced back after the fat was gone.

My "muffin top" (Mom labeled hers "midriff bulge") was particularly pesky and didn't even respond to liposuction or nips and tucks by a plastic surgeon. I scheduled a session with a body image therapist who could help me accept all parts of myself. As Anna guided me through a visualization exercise, she asked me to touch my soul. I pointed to my abdomen. "This is where my soul lives," I said, first with pride, then with a whimper when I felt the unrelenting hump in my belly. In a gentle reframe, Anna whispered, "Marcia, you have such a huge soul. Your stomach needs to be big enough to hold your big soul!"

I liked that and decided to ease up on criticizing my body and be more compassionate. That affirmation was a big step forward in my ongoing struggle to love all of me. I began to stare in Rebecca's mirror and instead of seeing a midriff bulge with legs, I saw an average-sized woman with a glowing smile and lively disposition. I liked feeling "average," a word I had previously banned from my vocabulary.

Having reached a state of self-acceptance, I felt alive in everything I did. Whether hiking up the steepest hills in town, addressing a large audience on a big stage, or prancing about in the latest fashions, all of it was sheer joy and rapture. I truly felt that God had listened to my prayers. I stopped wanting to trade places with anybody else's body, or swap to any other moment in history because the present was so precious. I had what my mentor called "a spiritual awakening." I happily gave up sugar, flour, fat, anger, and grief, and felt like I was living in nirvana.

My state of mind and body was almost too good to be true. A nagging inner voice kept muttering, "This won't last!" trying to convince me that the good stuff would end, that I would be a fat slob again, and this was the high before the fall. I refused to listen. I was the duck that paddled, paddled, paddled for so long, now all I wanted to do was glide. As a triumphant princess, I wanted my happily-ever-after.

During those years of grace, I had no way of knowing that soon I would face a medical complication that would once again turn my world topsy-turvy.

CHAPTER THIRTY-EIGHT

BITTERSWEET

May 17, 2009: Steve and I were riding high. Jon had just graduated college, a math major with a bright future. The three of us celebrated at Jon's favorite Indian restaurant. After a succulent dinner of shared vegetable samosas and half an entrée of rice and *Shahi Bhindi,* okra in cream sauce with vegetables and almonds, I indulged in three spoonfuls of Steve's pistachio ice cream. Since December 26, 2005, the date of my gastric bypass, I had given up sugar except on rare occasions when I would have a small snack or a taste of Steve's dessert. This day was one of those occasions.

After dinner, we dropped Jon at his house in Binghamton where he was staying for the summer, then headed eastbound on Route 17. Per our custom, I was the driver. Because Steve liked to drink wine or beer with dinner, we had a standing agreement that Steve drives to the destination and I drive home. Slightly tired and headachy from the events of the day, I adjusted the mirrors for the return trip. Inside I felt happy and proud.

After about an hour in the car, I suddenly felt warm and couldn't twist out of my jacket fast enough. Nearing the Florida/Goshen exit, I heard Steve's voice yelling at me, "Get off at the next exit!" I flew past the exit sign as I couldn't quite process why I was supposed to get off. He said it again. As we neared the next exit, it hit me that Steve was yelling and that was unusual. At the last second, I veered off onto the exit, the odometer clocking 80. The car flew around the circular ramp until it registered in my head that I was supposed to slow down on an exit ramp, especially when making a sharp turn. I decelerated quickly, and pulled into the first parking lot I spotted which, fortunately, was empty.

My heart was beating very fast as I stopped the car and turned to my husband, who seemed to be mad at me though I had no idea why. He shook his head and I felt a ripple of fear through my body. I felt like a little girl who knew she messed up but wasn't sure what she'd done or why. I suggested Steve drive and though he drank one beer at dinner, it was hours before and he was able to take over the wheel.

As soon as I buckled myself into the passenger seat, I wanted to eat. It's not that I was hungry, having eaten an ample meal two hours earlier. Nevertheless, I was driven to stick my hand into the brown bag from the farmers' market and eat a banana. I ate in silence and we drove home in silence. A part of me was still mulling over what had happened but I wasn't prepared to talk about my driving mishap. Instead, I took a nap, as my eyes felt heavy.

When we arrived home, I was still shaken by the incident and I apologized to Steve: "I don't know what happened but I'm really sorry I wasn't driving well and that you had to take over."

He said, "I understand, Marcia, but next time when I tell you three times to get off at the next exit, you should listen to me!" I stared at him in disbelief. Sheepishly, I asked, "You said it three times? I don't think I heard you." We both knew I suffer from a slight hearing loss but apparently Steve had been talking to me in a loud voice, not his usual soft-spoken manner. We were both puzzled and over the next week the lapse continued to bother me. Gradually, I forgot about it and chalked it up to fatigue.

On Friday, June 12th, Steve and I celebrated our 26th wedding anniversary. On Saturday, we searched the Internet for same-day Broadway matinee tickets for "God of Carnage" starring James Gandolfini, Marcia Gay Harden, Jeff Daniels, and Hope Davis. On the ride down, I prayed that the several hundred dollars we shelled out on the premium site weren't part of a scam. Given our rush to make the show, Steve and I skipped lunch and I hoped that breakfast was enough to sustain me.

The show was outstanding. Steve and I loved the plot, characters, and third-row seats that allowed us to catch subtle facial expressions of "Tony Soprano" and the ensemble cast. With three hours to spare before our dinner reservation, we exited the theater beaming. I told Steve I needed a healthy snack. We found a frozen yogurt shop, and I ordered a small yogurt cup with fresh mangoes and strawberries on top, congratulating myself for finding a healthy, low-calorie meal substitute.

On our way back to Westchester, we stopped in the Bronx to visit Steve's mom, who was thrilled to partake in our anniversary celebration. As usual, Sonnie offered us food, which we declined, unwilling to spoil our appetites. She asked several more times and finally Steve popped a Mr. Goodbar in his mouth and I chose a small clementine.

Our dinner reservation was for 7:30 at an Indian restaurant. The gracious owner visited our table to describe his specials in detail. Steve and he discussed Indian spices and the man was impressed that Steve knew so much. When I mentioned it was our anniversary, his face lit up, and he regaled us with stories about his blissful 40-year marriage.

Steve and I shared an appetizer of vegetable samosas and pakoras, and I ordered *Aloo Gobi*, a cauliflower-potato dish. I cut my entrée in half and packed up the rest for take-out, placing it at the far end of the table. After dinner, it was no surprise when the owner came over singing Happy Anniversary, with ice cream and fruit "on the house." That night, for the second time in a month, I decided it was OK to have several spoonfuls of dessert for our special occasion.

At home, we placed our doggy bag in the fridge, and sat on the sofa to unwind. As we flipped through the channels, we stumbled upon a movie Adam had recommended, "Forgetting Sarah Marshall." The movie was set in Maui and the splendid ocean views, majestic mountains, and lush flora brought back memories of Steve's and my "second honeymoon" to Hawaii seven years earlier. Feeling warm all over, I dozed off on the couch.

The ringtone was a blur though I remember Steve handing me the phone saying, "It's Jon. He wants to wish you a happy anniversary." I mumbled a few words and handed the phone back to Steve. The next thing I remember was Steve talking on the phone in a firm voice, "If you can't come right away, don't worry. I'll take Marcia to the hospital." I had a vague sense that something was wrong but didn't have the energy to raise my head.

"What?" I asked from some near sub-conscious level.

In an authoritative voice, Steve asked: "Where are we?"

I thought for a split second. "Maui," I answered, having just experienced the vivid blue skies and verdant landscape.

Steve disappeared for a minute, then came back with a cup. "Drink this!"

"What is it?"

"Drink it—now!"

I obeyed because it was clear there was no wiggle room. It took me a moment to identify the familiar taste. As I sipped the orange juice, I rose in slow motion to a full sitting position and noticed my surroundings. I gathered that I wasn't in Hawaii. I was confused again when the doorbell rang and in walked our neighbors, Gary and Carol. Gary handed Steve an object and they whispered in a conspiratorial way. Steve gently took my hand, turned it palm up, and explained that he was inserting a pinprick into my finger but it wouldn't hurt. A few seconds later, he announced, "38."

"Keep drinking," he commanded.

Still baffled by the circumstances around me, I slowly became more lucid. Then I remembered Steve's words, which had woken me from my slumber. I asked if we were going to the hospital.

"It depends," he said, "I'm going to take your glucose level again."

Steve waited a few minutes and this time the number was 78 and I visibly saw him exhale. He and Gary did a modest high-five and there seemed to be a muted jubilance in the air. Steve told me to wait a few minutes, and then eat a piece of cheese and everyone sounded happy. Except for me. I had no idea what was happening.

With the color restored to Steve's face (and apparently to mine), my husband sat down next to me. With love and patience, he explained that I had a hypoglycemic reaction, and my blood sugar had dropped so low that I passed out, into a trance-like state. Though my eyes were open, I couldn't decipher what was going on, as though my brain had disengaged. Steve said that I would need to see an endocrinologist but in the meantime, I could use Gary's extra glucose monitor and check my blood every few hours. Starting that night, I would chart the time, blood sugar, food, quantity, and any other symptoms worth noting as I woke up, and before and after every meal.

I was scared to death and a million questions popped into my mind: *How did this happen? How discombobulated was I and for how long? Did I do permanent damage? What if I was alone; would I have come out of it by myself?* Then a horrible thought crossed my mind: *Did I blank out like this the night of Jon's graduation? Was I driving on autopilot with my eyes open and my brain dissociated? Did I almost kill my husband and myself from a hypoglycemic reaction?*

At that moment, I was awestruck by the miracle in both of these events: on the two nights when I was in extreme danger, I was with Steve. My very own Doctor Kildare saved my life—again.

Steve showed me how to use the glucometer, needles, test strips, and control liquid. Then he headed to his computer to look up the latest studies and I headed to mine. On Google, I searched low blood sugar, clicked on reactive and postprandial hypoglycemia linked to post-gastric bypass surgery early-stage dumping, then scrolled to late-stage dumping. I pounded my keyboard, frantic to understand the connection between hypoglycemia and late-stage dumping, a term I never heard before. For the first time, I learned that there are two forms of dumping and the one I had, which can occur two-to-three hours after consuming sugar, is characterized by lightheadedness, dizziness, difficulty concentrating, and decreased consciousness.

I went over with a fine-tooth comb what I had eaten that day. Other than my usual wholesome breakfast, the rest of the day was atypical. In comparison to previous celebrations, my menu for that day looked almost sparse. Yet, at closer glance, I had to admit that I ingested a disproportionate number of carbs. Several days later, I analyzed the meals with Rebecca, and learned that in addition to high carbs, fried foods like samosas and pakoras could also contribute to hypoglycemia. Add to the mix that there wasn't enough protein to slow the digestion of the starches. *Voila:* an excess of carbs that sent me into a nearly fatal comatose state. Over the next few weeks, I overreacted, and checked my blood sugar every half hour. Steve told me that was overkill but I was living in terror that it would happen again.

Throughout that summer, I leaned heavily on Rebecca, who spent countless hours re-teaching me how to eat, when to eat, what foods to combine, how to recognize an oncoming attack. I went from a liberated food plan that kept me minimally focused on food to one in which I was afraid to eat, afraid to *not* eat, and afraid to go to sleep lest my blood sugar drop while I was asleep and I wouldn't wake up. According to Rebecca, I did what many people do when first diagnosed: they over-treat their disease. I was so nervous about blacking out that I ate mini-meals every two to three hours. I hated what I had become: a person obsessed with food and with this extra food, I became obsessed with gaining weight. I tracked my food on an online diary that analyzed my daily intake of each nutrient, and I tied a virtual umbilical cord to the computer to keep the figures up-to-date.

After the initial hysteria, I calmed down and realized I had gone months without another attack. I was eating correctly for my condition, and had learned the warning signals to prevent a problem from escalating. And I hadn't yet died in my sleep.

Eight months later, after resuming a sense of normalcy, I began to gain weight. I found it impossible to keep up the level of scrutiny I had that first summer, when I micromanaged my blood sugar and my weight. The recommended six mini-meals daily evolved into three "squares" plus three snacks, too many calories to maintain my body weight. Snacks, which used to consist of a single piece of fruit, now had to be combined with a protein: apple *and* cheese, berries *and* yogurt, cantaloupe *and* cottage cheese. I was no longer lean and mean but I did manage to stave off future attacks through listening to my body and over-managing my hypoglycemia. It seemed like a fair trade.

CHAPTER THIRTY-NINE

RUNNING ON FULL

Ever since June 12, 2009, and that fateful anniversary four years ago, I haven't had a hypoglycemic attack. Along with monitoring my blood sugar, I learned how to regulate my emotions. Last week, I spent all day with a new client who continually referred to me as "calm," an adjective I was amazed and delighted to fold into my narrative. I have traveled a long journey from the Sarah Bernhardt of my childhood; this Drama Queen has softened her edges.

Over these past five years, I watched as my size 10 petite pants slowly crept up to a 12, leveling off at 14. At the beginning, I refused to buy new slacks. When I couldn't hold out any longer, and my waistbands pinched and zippers snagged, I bought one pair in 12 and one in 14. As usual, I made promises to myself I wasn't able to keep. I simply couldn't get back my mojo. Despite all this work I did on myself, I was back to that 14 cusp: largest size in a regular store, smallest size in a plus store.

Only this time, I didn't stare in the mirror and grimace. Instead, I smiled and the radiant image beamed back a huge, toothy grin. She and I agreed that yes, I could afford to lose 15 pounds, and no, I wouldn't twist myself into a pretzel for not being perfect. Damaging self-talk was no longer an option. My self-worth was greater than the number on the scale or the size of my pants.

For five years, as I wrote my story, I shone a spotlight on the ugliest parts of my life. On occasion, recounting those moments, the disease was so powerful that it threatened the very success story I was trying to tell. As I dredged up humiliating details around intimacy, sex, and self-esteem, my anxiety reached insufferable levels, and I found myself back at the kitchen cupboard, sometimes browsing, sometimes reaching into a bag of almonds before I even realized what transpired.

Only a short time ago, before this last Passover, I was editing my chapter on marriage. I detailed how I felt ashamed and unlovable, even while I had a husband who loved me. I expounded on the private moments of loneliness, when I needed so badly to be held yet was terrified to reach out for fear of being rejected. No sooner had I typed the words, deleted them, typed new words, deleted those, than the pain became so palpable, I had to jump out of my seat. I kept bolting to the kitchen, where my stash of kosher-for-Passover goodies awaited the massive *Seder* I was hosting at my house. High atop the pile of prepared foods was the carton of rainbow cookies that I planned to serve. Each time I ogled the box, my heart palpitated, pheromones oozed out of my pores, and my adrenals released extra adrenaline to prepare for conquest.

When I couldn't contain myself any longer, I slashed the plastic with a knife and seized a bold red-yellow-green square of potato starch. The angst had peaked and I forgot— in my fragile state—that I don't act this way anymore. I stared at the rainbow cookie. I brought it up to my lips and picked up its scent, dizzy with unwholesome desire, addiction points in my brain signaling my mouth. *Chocolate topping, raspberry jam, spongy cake with neon-colored red, yellow, green food dye... I actually brought the cookie to my open mouth...* Within seconds, the executive reasoning in my brain took control and I tossed the cookie and the whole box into the trash and left the room.

Throughout that weekend, as I probed the painful isolation of my past, I felt a deep magnetic draw to the garbage can to retrieve just one of those rainbow things.

I lasted until midnight Sunday, then tiptoed like the thief I was (but stealing from myself) to the dark kitchen, and lifted the lid to the garbage can. What a Pandora's Box that can was—as if by some supernatural force field, the rainbow cookie had risen from a bottom layer to within my bleared sight. I bent over and dove into my own trash, reaching down with my hand to retrieve the mangled—though still irresistible—cookie. I was shocked at my behavior. I had no idea I could drop so low after all those years of recovery and insight.

Then, some other instinct rose. Instead of taking the fatal bite, I mentally lashed out at the phosphorescent object, "Get out of my life! You are toxic and I am done with you! I have been obsessed with you for more than 50 years and now I don't care how pretty and seductive you are—you are still heroin to me—and I refuse to give in to this infatuation. You and I are getting divorced. From now on, I will think of you as meat and I'm the vegetarian; I will not and cannot go near you. We are done! Done! Goodbye, cookie… goodbye!"

I doused the enemy with dishwashing detergent.

That *Seder*, as we unveiled my homemade *Haggadah*, with hand-picked family photos dating back seven decades, I experienced my own exodus from Egypt. I was free from bondage; no longer slave to a starch. I listened to the familiar off-key singing of *Dayenu* and felt immense gratitude sweep over me. My life is full. I no longer need to chase rainbows to feel fine about myself.

I am enough.

I have enough.

I do enough.

It would be enough.

Dayenu.

PART VII
SELF-HELP BONUS

HOW TO APPLY
THE GOODBYE COOKIE
TO YOUR LIFE

From L-R: Dr. Jody Popple, Marcia Meislin

by

Dr. Jody Popple, Clinical Psychologist
and
Marcia Meislin, Gestalt Therapist
& Certified Coach

CHAPTER FORTY

INSIGHTS INTO FOOD ADDICTION, BINGE EATING, AND RELATIONSHIPS

What is it about food that makes it a dysfunctional relationship for some of us?
What causes someone to develop Binge-Eating Disorder?
Emotional eating is ruining my life—how can I recover?

The answers to these questions may have been what drew you to Marcia's book in the first place. In this section, we'll answer these common questions and more, while exploring how they relate to *The Goodbye Cookie*—and how you can apply them to your own life as well.

We may have come to the end of the book—but the discussion lives on! Be sure to visit our website, www.thegoodbyecookie.com, for blogs, vlogs (videos), photos, self-help tips, and more!

1. How do we begin to understand our relationship with food?

Food is a source of many things: it's primal (a basic need to survive), nurturing (through preparing and sharing meals), and cultural (a way of passing one's heritage down to the next generation). People often subconsciously associate food with love, such as Marcia did in her relationship with Uncle Harry and his Sunday treat of rainbow cookies. In some instances, food can become a sort of bargaining tool—a way to gain a sense of power or control, which we see everywhere from a child refusing to eat to political protests and hunger strikes.

Some of us wonder if we are born with a genetic predisposition towards body size, weight, or food addiction. Research shows that genes do play a role in these matters; however, genes alone are not our destiny. There are a multitude of other factors that interconnect to form our body size and relationship with food: culture, family history, early childhood dynamics, personality, brain chemistry, metabolism, health issues, medication, lifestyle, dieting history, amount of exercise, and many others.

In *The Goodbye Cookie*

For a culturally and religiously Jewish family like the Meislins, food was a significant symbol in their beliefs. The Talmud, an ancient Jewish text, teaches that since the destruction of the Temple, the table in a Jewish home is considered an altar, a sacred place, exalted through the abundance of food. Weekly Sabbath meals and holiday celebrations brought the Meislin family together around the festive dinner table.

At the same time, excessive eating and weight gain became a metaphorical rope in a tug of war between Marcia and her mother. In addition to overeating to soothe or tamp down old wounds, Marcia used food as a rebellion against the values of her mother's generation, which demanded that women be defined by their looks. In her quest to differentiate herself from her mother and forge an identity of her own, food may have seemed like Marcia's route to empowerment, but inadvertently caused the opposite result: a sense of powerlessness.

While it is possible that Marcia was born with a genetic predisposition to obesity (as she mentions that her family was comprised of mostly big people and big eaters) she was also born with a strong drive and insatiable desire for "more, more, more." This hunger manifested itself in her lifestyle, career, and especially in her relationship with food.

2. What are the symptoms of Binge-Eating Disorder (BED) and why do people binge?

The diagnostic criteria for Binge-Eating Disorder is excerpted here verbatim from the DSM-5 (Diagnostic and Statistical Manual of Mental Disorders Version Five), published in May 2013. [1]

A. Recurrent episodes of binge eating. An episode of binge eating is characterized by both of the following:
   1. Eating, in a discrete period of time (e.g., within any 2-hour period), an amount of food that is definitely larger than what most people would eat in a similar period of time under similar circumstances.
   2. A sense of lack of control over eating during the episode (e.g., a feeling that one cannot stop eating or control what or how much one is eating).
B. The binge-eating episodes are associated with three (or more) of the following:
   1. Eating much more rapidly than normal.
   2. Eating until feeling uncomfortably full.
   3. Eating large amounts of food when not feeling physically hungry.
   4. Eating alone because of feeling embarrassed by how much one is eating.
   5. Feeling disgusted with oneself, depressed, or very guilty afterward.
C. Marked distress regarding binge eating is present.
D. The binge eating occurs, on average, at least once a week for 3 months.
E. The binge eating is not associated with the recurrent use of inappropriate compensatory behavior as in bulimia nervosa and does not occur exclusively during the course of bulimia nervosa or anorexia nervosa.

---

[1] *Reprinted with permission from the Diagnostic and Statistical Manual of Mental Disorders, Fifth Edition, (Copyright ©2013). American Psychiatric Association. All Rights Reserved.*

For some, food has a calming effect to manage emotions, anxiety, and fear. When used as a "co-regulator," (a way of balancing oneself), bingeing on food does not bring about equilibrium, though it may be perceived as a numbing or distracting factor in the moment. Because bingeing and excessive overeating are often followed by feelings of guilt and shame, the negative emotions are actually intensified—not regulated.

In *The Goodbye Cookie*

For Marcia, gorging on food was a way to stuff (and stifle) negative emotions and bury them. As Marcia describes the anatomy of a binge in Chapter 29, "Disease of Never Enough," even the large amounts of food didn't seem sufficient because her hunger was emotional—not physical. All the food in the world wouldn't have satisfied the emotional and spiritual craving. As she later reflected in her poem, "Ode To Rainbow Cookies":

Then one day I learned
That food wasn't a feeling
It was the wrong place for healing
(See www.thegoodbyecookie.com for the complete poem.)

3. Does bingeing go beyond food? Is it possible to binge on life?

In Gestalt therapy, founder Dr. Fritz Perls suggests that any behavior can be seen as a microcosm for how we live in the world, including how we eat. In this form of therapy, there is a concept known as the "needs cycle," or "contact cycle," which, in simple terms, looks like this:

1. Identify need or sensation (I feel hungry.)
2. Take action to meet that need (I look for food.)
3. Fill the need (I eat the food.)
4. When we've had enough, the need subsides (I feel satisfied.)

5. Become aware of a new need (I'm no longer hungry. What new need is emerging in me right now?)

For people who suffer from Binge-Eating Disorder or compulsive eating, food is almost always seen as the need—though the sensation may not always be one of hunger. Therefore, there may never be a feeling of satiation because the solution didn't address the need. Or, the satiation point was overridden by the desire to eat more, regardless of what the body is signaling. In keeping with Perls' concept, this type of behavior can apply to other parts of a person's life as well. Often these same people make themselves so busy bingeing on "busy-ness" that they don't notice when their bodies have had enough until they get sick and are forced to slow down.

In *The Goodbye Cookie*

Marcia, a binge eater, lived her life trying to take in as much of the world as she could. With her big personality, big dreams—and big body—she sucked in, like a vacuum, world experiences: relationships, adventures, stimulation. She lived her life "large," and was as promiscuous with these experiences and people as she was with food.

4. What role does asthma (or similar childhood illnesses) play in an eating disorder?

When the brain's resources are preoccupied with asthma and breathing (or other ailments), it doesn't have as much capacity to multitask and manage impulsive behavior. Brain activity tends to shift from parts that foster judgment and decision-making to the emotional centers. When this happens, you're less likely to make good decisions and your emotions are heightened (for emotional eaters, this is a trigger), and your impulses to eat are less controlled.

Some researchers have discovered a link between childhood asthma and symptoms of depression and anxiety. Children may turn to food to help alleviate those uncomfortable feelings. Also, when an individual suffers from a disease like asthma, she can feel out of control of her own body—and may attempt to regain this control by developing an unhealthy relationship with food.

In *The Goodbye Cookie*

Because Marcia's asthma was so severe, she couldn't exercise or participate in physical activities with her classmates, which contributed to her weight gain. Sitting on the sidelines, especially to someone who liked to be in the middle of things, caused Marcia to feel socially isolated. During those times, food became a surrogate friend. Eating also gave her the illusion that she had power over her body, even as she felt powerless over her breathing.

5. How do eating disorders affect marriages?

When an individual is suffering from an eating disorder, she has an intimate relationship with food—a relationship that becomes threatened with the introduction of another intimate relationship: marriage. If emotional needs aren't being met in a marriage, often the partners look elsewhere for support—sometimes, in third-party relationships known as "emotional triangles." A person can "triangulate" with any kind of vehicle that provides comfort— whether it is food, work, or another individual. This makes it easier to avoid working on the issues that surface in the marriage.

The person with an eating disorder can feel guilty, inadequate, not worthy, anxious or depressed—all of which can add to poor communication and a lack of intimacy and openness. When one of the partners also has a poor body image or feels uncomfortable about her weight, it can add tension, shame, or embarrassment to the sexual relationship.

In *The Goodbye Cookie*

Both Marcia and Steve had emotional needs that were not being met in their marriage, and they both looked elsewhere for emotional comfort: Steve in wine and work; Marcia, in food and work. Until she dealt with her food addiction, Marcia was unable to communicate directly with Steve about these issues because food was always a safety valve, as was his preoccupation with work. Marcia's weight also affected her body image and self-esteem and this too intruded into her intimate relationship with her husband.

6. Why might successful people sabotage themselves through self-destructive eating behaviors?

Some overweight people become overachievers to prove to the world (and themselves) that they can be successful despite the stigma often associated with their size. This overcompensation may make them more successful, hardworking, and valuable employees. Ironically, some of these same high achievers may suffer from "imposter syndrome," a phenomenon in which a person feels that she doesn't really belong or measure up, and sees herself as a fraud. For people with eating disorders who have a secret life with food, this feeling is intensified and can become all-consuming, causing them to sabotage themselves even more.

In addition, there are people who suffer from a fear of success: as they flourish, they might find themselves engaging in more self-destructive behaviors. This fear can also manifest itself emotionally. If someone who is used to feeling badly about herself begins to feel better, she might find these emotions unsettling and revert back to negativity, which is more comfortable and familiar. For example, when a woman who has been struggling to lose weight all of her life finally succeeds, she may have an internal battle between her old self-image and her new one. This may also cause her to have difficulty accepting others' compliments. If these underlying issues are not addressed, she might resort to her old eating habits, which could result in "yo-yo-ing" up and down the scale.

In the book *Willpower,* Baumiester and Tierney claim that when people have to make important decisions all day long, it depletes the energy available to their rational minds, therefore increasing the number of impulsive and irrational choices they may make.[2] This is why people can make good choices at work, and then poor choices about food when they get home. When coupled with a workaholic personality (another form of addiction), a person may neglect self-care and speed through life relying upon fast-food drive-thrus and sweet "pick-me-ups."

> ### In *The Goodbye Cookie*
> Marcia became so focused on her career as a way of overcompensating for her weight. During this time, one of her favorite posters read, "Success means biting off more than you can chew, and chewing it"—a mantra of how she lived her life. Before her recovery and despite her successes, Marcia felt like a fraud in some aspects of her life. Growing up in an Orthodox community, she felt like an imposter attending Orthodox schools and not being observant herself. Later on, she felt insecure as a mom and a wife because she felt like everyone around her knew what they were doing, while she did not. And even at work, despite a stellar career, she ended her days bingeing, wondering if she was good enough.

7. What are the key turning points that can aid in recovery from an eating disorder?

One of the most radical changes that a person suffering from an eating disorder can make is the way she thinks about the disease. When an individual believes that it is in her power to change her habits by using her knowledge or skills ("if I just use more willpower then I can lose weight; if I eat in moderation, I wouldn't have a weight problem"), this is known as a "First Order Change." While this can temporarily cut back on destructive habits, often an individual has to go through a "Second Order Change" to truly have a grasp on the disorder. A "Second Order Change," as defined by

---

[2] Baumeister, R. F., & Tierney, J. (2011). *Willpower*. New York, New York: Penguin Press.

Watzlawick, Wekland, and Fisch in *Change*, is a shift in the way of thinking about the eating disorder—instead of trying to change the behavior in the system, you have to instead change the principles that support the structure of the problem.[3]

In *The Goodbye Cookie*

First Order Change: Marcia's many attempts to recover from her eating disorder (fad diets, exercise programs, weight-loss surgeries) were unsuccessful for her because they were all forms of "First Order Change," which helped to reduce the bingeing and weight sporadically—but did not deconstruct the true structure of the eating disorder.

Second Order Change, or Key Turning Points (what Marcia calls "aha moments!"):

✓ **A friend helping with an asthma attack.** When Marcia allowed her friend to comfort her during an asthma attack, she saw that her illness wasn't a punishment or something to be ashamed of: she could be vulnerable and imperfect and still be a good person.

✓ **Steve reframing food as something to be enjoyed.** In the past, Marcia saw food as synonymous with family celebrations, love, and a cure for loneliness, loss, and other difficult emotions. But with Steve's worldly palate, Marcia "began to see food as something to be tasted, savored." Eating turned into an enjoyable experience—not a shameful one.

✓ **Becoming a "real mom".** Throughout the first year of her first-born son's life, Marcia questioned if she was a good mother—and only until she let go of her own self-doubt did she truly bond with her child and feel like a "real mom."

---

[3] Watzlawick P, Wekland J, & Fisch, R. (1974). *Change: Principles of Problem Formation and Problem Resolution.* New York, New York: W&W Norton and Company.

✓ **Letting go of criticisms and judgments.** Though it may have been subconscious, Marcia felt that it was others' criticisms of her that drove her to eat. During her recovery, Marcia stopped blaming others for her eating disorder. She also began to understand herself and her body differently by accepting herself for who she is—limitations and all.

✓ **Deepening her faith:** In recognizing her own powerlessness to confront her food addiction, Marcia turned to God and a supportive community for help. She incorporated a spiritual orientation in which she developed a closer relationship with God, strengthened her connection to Judaism, and learned to step outside of herself to be of greater service to others.

✓ **Reconstruction of relationships:** Marcia recreated the relationships in her life as she developed a deeper awareness of her needs and behaviors. She was willing to address her own distortions, and create a healthier way of interacting with others. As a result, she learned to accept others for who they are, just as she learned to accept herself.

It is why, today, Marcia chooses to pick up her pen first—instead of the fork.

For more questions and answers, check out our website: http://www.thegoodbyecookie.com
We will continue to explore such topics as:

How do you curb emotional eating?

What about metabolism?

What is the difference between obesity and Binge-Eating Disorder?

How do you help your child who is overweight?

How do you talk to a friend with an eating disorder?

What is "intuitive eating" and does it work for everyone?

CHAPTER FORTY-ONE

PRACTICAL TIPS ON
HOW TO OVERCOME OVEREATING

While the previous section answers the most common questions regarding Binge-Eating Disorder, food addiction, and compulsive eating and overeating, you may be asking yourself the most important question of all: *What can I do to cope beyond food?*

What follows is a "smorgasbord" of opportunity—tools and tips to help you navigate the challenging forks in the road. You may end up having to try many different tools before you find the right ones for you.

As Thomas Edison once said, "When you have exhausted all possibilities, remember this—you haven't."

1. Honor Food

✓ **Find food-free traditions.** Create new family or holiday rituals that don't revolve around food.

✓ **Plant a garden and eat what you grow.** Connecting with food from seedling to finished product will help you appreciate food, treat it with respect, and be more mindful of what you're putting into your mouth.

✓ **Decorate your table with flowers and candles.** Use nice plates and pretty table settings as a way of honoring the act of eating. Feel the difference between that approach vs. eating standing up while reading emails and mindlessly putting food in your mouth.

✓ **When you eat, just eat.** Focus on the food and the flavor, rather than distracting yourself with the T.V., computer, cell phone, etc. *Side note:* Researchers have found that overeating often occurs when in front of a T.V.

✓ **Eat an occasional meal in silence, or with relaxing music.** Use this opportunity to pay attention to the food as it enters your mouth, is chewed by your teeth, goes down your throat, and into your stomach. Sit back in amazement at all the activity your body engages in just to bring you sustenance and keep you alive!

✓ **Chew slowly.** Challenge yourself to chew 25 to 30 times for each mouthful.

✓ **When a meal is over, stop eating.** After a meal, declare out loud that you are finished. Consider calling a friend to say that you are done eating and don't need to eat any more until your next meal. Or consider brushing your teeth after every meal to signify that you are finished.

2. **Beware of Triggers**

✓ **Identify your "trigger foods".** Know which foods trigger you physically or emotionally and cause you to keep eating more and more of that substance, finding it hard to stop. Experiment with alternative foods or behaviors: instead of ice cream, try Greek yogurt. In place of birthday cake, use colorful fruit with a candle. Ask a waiter to hold the breadbasket instead of bringing it to the table.

✓ **Identify people, places, or situations that trigger you to want to eat.** When in those circumstances, see if you can separate out the event or the person from the desire to eat. For example, if going to a movie theater sets off a yearning for popcorn, notice this behavior.

✓ **Avoid "impulse shopping".** It can be extremely difficult to avoid "trigger foods". If you're in a grocery store and don't want to be tempted by candy at the check-out aisle, phone a friend. Ask her to talk with you until you're safely out of the store without extra impulse purchases.

✓ **Don't shop when you're hungry.** Go grocery shopping after a meal, when you are less likely hungry and less tempted to buy additional (unnecessary) items.

✓ **Brush your teeth after every meal to signify that you are finished.**

3. **Love Your Body**

    ✓ **Get physical.** Find a physical activity that stirs your passion (e.g., dance, basketball, golf). Keep experimenting until you find something you like, and build the time into your calendar. And remember: exercise doesn't mean you have to go to the gym and lift heavy weights. Think about an activity you enjoy doing and see if you can incorporate movement into it. If you love to talk with your friends, turn the conversation into a "walk and talk." If you enjoy nature, make gardening part of your routine.

    ✓ **Get smart.** Some smartphones have apps in which you can track what you eat during the day or how much exercise you do. These tools can be helpful in learning what your body needs.

    ✓ **Love what you wear.** Wear clothes that make you happy! Buy clothes in your favorite colors; don't limit yourself to just wearing black just because somebody may have told you that black is slimming..

✓ **Thank your thighs.** Or if your thighs are not your least favorite body part, pick whatever body part that you tend to criticize most. Thank that body part for all the benefits you gain from it. For example, if you do "hate" your thighs, thank them for attaching your legs to the rest of you so you can get from place to place; if you curse your behind, thank it for enabling you to sit down because you'd get awfully tired standing all day. You could also make commitments to those specific body parts to make them healthier. Have fun with this exercise as you make friends with your body.

✓ **Love yourself.** Remember: You are not your body. You HAVE a body that carries your true self through life. Even if you're dissatisfied with your body in the moment, don't walk around hating yourself. Losing weight or taking care of yourself needs to come from a place of self-love, not self-hate.

4. Listen To Your Heart

✓ **Don't eat your emotions.** The most reported emotion before a binge is anger. Being able to identify the source of your anger is a key step to preventing the binge (e.g., if you're angry with people, don't obsess about them and let them take up "rent-free space" in your head).

✓ **Just say no.** Learn to say "no" if you're the type of person who takes on everything all the time. Put yourself first on the "to-do" list so you can refuel before you start taking care of everyone else and burning out.

✓ **Learn from mistakes.** It's easy to close off your heart if you've been hurt in the past. Instead of turning to food to ease your loneliness, learn from previous mistakes and open your heart to giving and receiving healthy love. This will nourish you in ways that go well beyond food.

- ✓ **Nurture a support network.** Find friends and foster relationships with those who appreciate and support you, and don't waste your time on those who don't. When you do cultivate "real" friends, allow them to be honest with you and to offer you tough love when needed.

5. **Pick Up a Pen Instead of a Fork**

- ✓ **Keep a food journal.** Insight is important for change. Keep a food journal to increase your awareness. Write down what, when, and how much you eat, and how you're feeling as you eat. You may notice a pattern between your moods and when you overeat or binge.

- ✓ **Know your history.** For greater awareness of your history with food, ask yourself these questions: As a child, what role did food have in my family? At what age did I first notice my eating pattern to be a problem? What is the first feeling I had when I became aware eating was a problem? When did I tend to binge? What else was going on at these times? What foods did I indulge with the most? What foods do I think about or crave the most? Is there an emotional history with those foods? When was my first attempt to stop bingeing? When was my first "diet"?

- ✓ **Label your emotions.** If you have different reasons why you overeat, label them. Identify which one is going on in the moment (e.g., "Exhausted Eating," or "Bites of Boredom") to help you find alternative behaviors that meet your true needs.

- ✓ **Express Your Inner Self.** Write letters that you will never send, just to get out all your feelings so they're not bottled up.

Writing, drawing, or other expressions of creativity can lower stress and be therapeutic. In addition to tapping into your soul, they might reduce cravings and other food thoughts.

6. Attitude of Gratitude

✓ **Keep an Attitude of Gratitude.** Cultivate a spiritual orientation to life: focus on the blessings rather than the negatives.

✓ **Focus on forgiveness.** Look at the big picture and ask yourself what's really important and what isn't. Let go of the small stuff and open yourself up to the possibility of forgiving the big stuff.

✓ **Learn to experience the moment.** Don't let regret over the past or anxiety over the future cloud your ability to be in the present, which could be full of wonder and awe.

✓ **Offer help.** Reach out and help others, while keeping balance in your own life.

✓ **Embrace the Great Outdoors.** Spend time in nature and breathe in the sights and smells of the outdoors.

✓ **Find your soul's purpose.** Go after your dreams; the more meaning you find in your life, the less you need to rely on food and other substances.

✓ **Have faith.** If you have faith in God or a Higher Power, you can use prayer to ask for help with your food and underlying struggles. Some of us think God may be too busy to deal with our food or body issues, but merely asking for help can be a big step towards healing.

7. **Learn Chemistry![4]**

✓ **Be aware that the chemicals in your brain can affect your eating behaviors.** Once you understand more about brain chemistry, you can take actions to change some of the levels in your brain that impact your eating. <u>The best way to do this is to consult your doctor or other professionals for an individualized plan.</u>

✓ **Balance your brain.** Oftentimes, people with eating disorders lack sufficient amounts of the chemicals acetylcholine and serotonin. Their dopamine levels may also be off-balance. Acetylcholine is responsible for focusing and paying attention. Some foods rich in choline include eggs, broccoli, wheat germ, as well as some types of fish and meat. Serotonin produces a sense of well-being, calm, and satisfaction. Exercise, massages, remembering happy events, and foods rich in tryptophan are some examples that may help increase your serotonin levels. Dopamine is a neurotransmitter that helps control the brain's reward and pleasure centers. It plays a part in many drug, food, and sex addictions. Certain foods can help in regulating dopamine levels, such as red beets, strawberries, blueberries, bananas, kale, apples, eggs, and others. Playing sports or doing aerobics causes the brain to produce dopamine.

✓ **Retrain your brain.** The good news about the brain is that it has neuroplasticity, a natural ability to change its structure in response to new situations, behaviors, or stimuli. Even if you've been bingeing or compulsively overeating for many

---

[4] *Some of this information was adapted from "Eating Disorder Treatment: Teach Your Mind To Cure Your Brain," by Dr. Irina Webster, MD.*

years, you can still create new pathways in your brain by regularly and repeatedly performing new healthy eating habits.

8.   NEVER GIVE UP!

✓ **There is no such thing as failing at recovery.** "Failure" is a crucial part of success. Finding all the ways that don't work is critical in figuring out what does. Each attempt will provide you with more skills and building blocks to put the pieces in place when your efforts finally click.

✓ **Think of every moment as a teachable moment.** Ask yourself what you gathered from each experience.

✓ **Ask for help.** There is no shame in asking for help—in fact, it is an act of courage. Many people seek out therapists, psychiatrists, nutritionists, addiction specialists, 12-step groups, rehab centers, endocrinologists, health coaches, or other professionals/programs that specialize in eating and body issues. Our complex relationship with food is not something to tackle alone.

✓ **Treat yourself kindly** and make healthy choices because you want to be healthy in body, mind, and spirit. Change is best sustained when it comes from a place of "want to" not "have to."

✓ **Stick with it.** Your day will come!

ACKNOWLEDGMENTS

The proverb "it takes a village..." is as true for writing and publishing a book as it is for raising a child. My village is vast and vigorous, operating 24/7/365.

- Thank you, Casey Fallon, my dedicated assistant and right arm, who for the last 10 years never let me waiver from my dream. Even as you slipped inspirational quotes and made-up fortune cookies into my attaché case, you were racing toward your own Iron Man dream, teaching me never to give up.
- Michelle McGahan, my book assistant: you came to me as an entertainment writer and expanded into a self-publishing expert. You lived, breathed, and devoured *The Goodbye Cookie* as I did, lifting me up when I was discouraged, always keeping me focused on the bigger vision.
Thank you both for your love and loyalty.
- Dr. Jody Popple, Clinical Psychologist: before we ever met, I asked you to read my memoir and explain my eating disorder in a way that could be helpful to others. Your brilliant words and insights, coupled with in-depth research, greatly contributed to the self-help segment of the book in which all readers can gain insights and learn helpful tips while drawing hope and optimism about their futures.

Thank you to the professionals whose diligence and expertise transformed a manuscript into a book and then a brand:

- Sarah Clarehart, jacket designer: your beautiful design and masterful integration of artistic and technical skills turned my vision of *The Goodbye Cookie* into a stunning reality.

- Abbe Aronson, publicist: you weren't kidding when you said, "Abbe-cadabra!" From the minute I trusted you with my project, you took it over, waved your magic wand, and allowed me to sleep at night.
- Jason O'Malley, graphic artist, and Nan Tepper, website creator: I tasked you with making a website that wasn't "cookie cutter." I'm more than proud of my unique site and original illustrations.
- Carter Smith, interior layout designer and production coordinator: thank you for your infinite patience and hard work with layouts, fonts, photos, and multiple revisions.
- Danielle Radeljic, for teaching me more than I ever wanted to know about intellectual property.
- Eric Duchin and Wilson Kowaleski, my social media team: you forced me to Tweet, Tumble, Instagram, and hashtag; your tenacity may actually succeed in bringing me into the 21st century.
- Jonathan Pillot, film producer and director, with lightning speed, you "got me" and crafted my story in film and photography. Thank you for your circle of creative geniuses: Ben Shaul, Chris Vernale, Kala Mandrake, Denise DeBaun, Julie Doynow.
- Bart Erbach, copywriter and "word whisperer": thank you for finding the simplest phrases, whispering them gently into my soul, and "Never Giving Up."
- To my editor as well as the wonderful writers I met at the Woodstock Memoir Festival, especially Executive Director Martha Frankel and fellow author, Mary Lou Edwards: you all helped me find my voice and forced me to go deeper within to excavate the rawest of feelings. Now that I have found that voice, it will never go back into hiding. For that, I am indebted.
- Thank you to early readers and devoted friends, Merri Rosenberg, Carol Booth and Erica Leon (also my gifted nutritionist and trainer) for your valuable feedback, powerful insights, and unflagging support.

Love and gratitude to those who helped me on my healing journey:

- Shout-out to my alma mater, the Gestalt Center of Long Island, where I grew into a therapist and a woman capable of feeling my feelings, asking for help, and making genuine contact with others. Special thanks to Robin Kupietz and Joyce Magid.

- To my fellow coaches in our Coaching for Transformation Community: you coaxed me into my first book reading, rewarded me with a standing ovation, then handed me a parachute to take the plunge.
- Thank you to three special rabbis who helped me find my place as a Jew through their own wisdom, compassion, and humanitarianism: Rabbi Avi Weiss (The Bayit), Rabbi Jonathan Kligler (Woodstock), and Rabbi David Ingber (Romemu).
- In sixth grade, I sat alone at the lunch table and couldn't even imagine a day when I'd be surrounded by an abundance of friends. I am enormously grateful to all who have shared this journey with me and taught me how to be a friend, and how to love and be loved.
- Special kudos to my Book Club friends who insisted I read chapters from my fledgling book and cheered me on while serving up rigorous literary critiques of the world's most accomplished writers.
- To my circle of faithful clients and colleagues: thank you for trusting me with your stories, your problems, and your triumphs. Whether we shared class together, a team-building retreat, a coaching relationship, or an inspiring (or difficult) conversation, you fueled my passion to carry on my mission to promote change and hope.
- Day to day, there is one big fellowship that keeps me alive and thriving on a physical, emotional, and spiritual plane—I am indebted to each of you and to that "still small voice within." I thank God and all you angels for the miracles that enabled me to turn a life of pain and shame into a blessing and a gift.

There aren't enough words to express how grateful I am to my family for this phenomenal life of wonder and joy.

Every Passover, at our Seders, my extraordinary parents invoked the ancient Jewish ritual, "And you shall tell it to your children." Their beloved stories filled our souls as I pray my story will fill the souls of my children and theirs. Mom and Dad, you instilled in all the Meislins such a strong sense of family and loyalty that the whole is truly greater than the sum of its parts. You graced each of us with the gifts of love, laughter, courage, and resilience. And I can't get over my luck at having siblings who are so colorful, caring, generous, and hysterically funny.

Speaking of humor, anyone who has ever cracked a negative mother-in-law joke has never met Sonia Weinstein. She is the quintessential loving, generous, and nonjudgmental mother and grandmother. She and the late Morty Weinstein devoted their lives to their children and grandchildren and built a legacy that continues, especially at Thanksgiving time as the family comes together to laugh, love—and eat.

Thank you, dear families, to each of you as individuals, and to all of you as our collective safety net in an uncertain life: Jack and Millie Meislin, Jay, Allan, Donna, Arleen, Mel, Elliot, Lisa, Chris, Eric, Kristine, Evi, Jared, Maria, Bob, Margy, YM, CM, NM, MM, Maddy, Steve, Jon, Adam, and Sonnie and Morty Weinstein, Richard, Dani, Arleen, Shaine, Elijah.

Truly, the happiest days of my life are those spent with family.

Saving the best for last. How blessed was I to fall in love (then fall in love again) with a man who would stand by me through thick and thin, love me despite my faults, and give me license to explore all my dreams, especially this one. Steve, how generous of you to permit me to share our marriage with the world; to tell our story that relationships can be tough, and are sometimes filled with rage, quiet disappointments, and lonely, unmet needs. And then our story continues that if two people love each other enough and they don't give up—love can find its way back, problems can be managed, and new ways of coping can be found. Honey, that is our magic; a marriage that keeps evolving, revealing itself and getting better, like a fine red Bordeaux that improves with age.

Out of this amazing union emerged the best gifts of all: our two sons, Jonathan and Adam. From their comfy spot in the crook of my elbow arose two young men who now tower over their mom (though that's not hard), and are kind, loving, successful, smart, and funny. I made a lot of mistakes along the way, and I never quite perfected the toggle between hovering and letting them do their own thing. But for all the bumps along the road, as I watch my two sons pioneering their own path, my heart overflows with love and pride beyond my wildest dreams.

35968882R00173

Made in the USA
Lexington, KY
01 October 2014